SAGE was founded in 1965 by Sara Miller McCune to support the dissemination of usable knowledge by publishing innovative and high-quality research and teaching content. Today, we publish over 900 journals, including those of more than 400 learned societies, more than 800 new books per year, and a growing range of library products including archives, data, case studies, reports, and video. SAGE remains majority-owned by our founder, and after Sara's lifetime will become owned by a charitable trust that secures our continued independence.

Los Angeles | London | New Delhi | Singapore | Washington DC | Melbourne

ADVANCE PRAISE

This inspiring book challenges mainstream ideas about development, held in both the global South and the global North, arguing that we must learn from the lives of low income women to reconstruct ideas about how economies function and what economic policies should be adopted at local, national and international levels. It should be read by everyone concerned to reduce inequality and end poverty.

— **Diane Elson**
Emeritus Professor, University of Essex

Decades ago Devaki Jain highlighted the significance of unpaid and unrecognised women's work—which is now being recognised the world over as critical for economic analysis. This valuable collection of some of her important contributions shows how much she has innovated to expand analytical and empirical approaches in many other areas, in ways that will continue to be useful far into the future.

— **Jayati Ghosh**
Professor of Economics, Centre for Economic Studies and Planning, School of Social Sciences, Jawaharlal Nehru University

I am a long-standing admirer of the work and life of Devaki Jain, one of the most respected and influential Southern voices in promoting the advancement of women and gender equality. The unique combination of Devaki's political nous, economic brilliance and grassroots activism, has made her the voice of the unheard and disadvantaged women in developing countries. Through her work as an active member of the global women's movement, as co-founder of many institutions such as Development Alternatives with Women for a New Era (DAWN) and as a member of the erstwhile South Commission, she has fought tirelessly for Southern women's rights and brought visibility to their economic and social marginalisation. I am thrilled that Devaki's important contributions are now to be collated and published in two volumes by Yoda Press. Part one, *Journey of a Southern Feminist*, will give the reader an insight into how Devaki brought into the public spotlight the conditions and contributions of women at the lower end of the global economy, and how and why she attached such importance to designing programmes generated from the characteristics of the Southern hemisphere. A must read for any feminist, development economist and activist.

— **Winnie Byanyima**
Executive Director,
Oxfam International

The Journey of a Southern Feminist

Thank you for choosing a SAGE product!
If you have any comment, observation or feedback,
I would like to personally hear from you.

Please write to me at **contactceo@sagepub.in**

Vivek Mehra, Managing Director and CEO, SAGE India.

Bulk Sales

SAGE India offers special discounts
for purchase of books in bulk.
We also make available special imprints
and excerpts from our books on demand.

For orders and enquiries, write to us at

Marketing Department
SAGE Publications India Pvt Ltd
B1/I-1, Mohan Cooperative Industrial Area
Mathura Road, Post Bag 7
New Delhi 110044, India

E-mail us at **marketing@sagepub.in**

Get to know more about SAGE

Be invited to SAGE events, get on our mailing list.
Write today to **marketing@sagepub.in**

This book is also available as an e-book.

The Journey of a Southern Feminist

Devaki Jain

Los Angeles | London | New Delhi
Singapore | Washington DC | Melbourne

First published in 2018 by

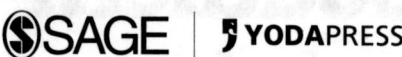

SAGE Publications India Pvt Ltd
B1/I-1 Mohan Cooperative Industrial Area
Mathura Road, New Delhi 110 044, India
www.sagepub.in

SAGE Publications Inc
2455 Teller Road
Thousand Oaks, California 91320, USA

SAGE Publications Ltd
1 Oliver's Yard, 55 City Road
London EC1Y 1SP, United Kingdom

SAGE Publications Asia-Pacific Pte Ltd
3 Church Street
#10-04 Samsung Hub
Singapore 049483

YODA Press
79 Gulmohar Enclave
New Delhi 110049
www.yodapress.co.in

Published by Vivek Mehra for SAGE Publications India Pvt Ltd, typeset in 10.5/13 pt Berkeley by Zaza Eunice, Hosur, Tamil Nadu, India and printed at Chaman Enterprises, New Delhi.

Library of Congress Cataloging-in-Publication Data

Names: Jain, Devaki, 1933- author.
Title: The journey of a southern feminist/Devaki Jain.
Description: Thousand Oaks: SAGE Publications India Pvt Ltd, [2018] |
 Includes bibliographical references and index.
Identifiers: LCCN 2018004300| ISBN 9789352806218 (print (pb): alk. paper) |
 ISBN 9789352806225 (e pub 2.0) | ISBN 9789352806232 (e book)
Subjects: LCSH: Feminism–India. | Women in development–India. |
 Feminists–India–Social networks.
Classification: LCC HQ1742 .J343 2018 | DDC 305.420954–dc23 LC record available at https://lccn.
loc.gov/2018004300

ISBN: 978-93-528-0621-8 (HB)

SAGE Yoda Team: Aruna Ramachandran, Arpita Das, Amrita Dutta and Guneet Kaur Gulati

CONTENTS

LIST OF ABBREVIATIONS

AAWORD	Association of African Women for Research and Development
BRICS	Brazil, Russia, India, China and South Africa
DAC	Development Assistance Committee
DANIDA	Danish International Development Agency
DAWN	Development Alternatives with Women for a New Era
GDP	gross domestic product
IAWS	Indian Association for Women's Studies
ICSSR	Indian Council of Social Science Research
ILO	International Labour Organization
IMF	International Monetary Fund
ISST	Institute of Social Studies Trust
LDCs	less developed countries
MDG	Millennium Development Goals
MNC	multinational corporation
NAM	Non-Aligned Movement
NBA	Narmada Bachao Andolan
NGO	non-governmental organisation
NCEUS	National Commission for Enterprises in the Unorganised Sector
NIAS	National Institute of Advanced Studies
OECD	Organisation for Economic Co-operation and Development
PRI	panchayati raj institution
SAP	structural adjustment programme

SAREC   Swedish Agency for Research Cooperation with
           Developing Countries
SEWA   Self-Employed Women's Association (Ahmedabad)
SIDA   Swedish International Development Cooperation
           Agency
SME   small and medium enterprises
UN   United Nations
UNDP   United Nations Development Programme
UNESCO   United Nations Educational, Scientific and Cultural
           Organization
UNICEF   United Nations Children's Fund
UNIDO   United Nations Industrial Development Organization
WIEGO   Women in Informal Employment: Globalizing and
           Organizing
WFPR   workforce participation rate
WTO   World Trade Organization

ACKNOWLEDGEMENTS

Chapter 1, 'Development as if Women Mattered: Can Women Build a New Paradigm?', Lecture delivered at the pre-Nairobi consultation of the OECD Development Assistant Committee (DAC) group, Paris, 1983.

Chapter 2, 'Advances in Feminist Theory: An Indian Perspective', paper presented at 'Social Change: Problems and Perspectives', 11th ISA World Congress of Sociology, New Delhi, 1986.

Chapter 3, 'The Leadership Gap: A Challenge to Feminists', Presidential address at the Sixth National Conference of the Indian Association for Women's Studies, Mysore, 31 May–3 June 1993.

Chapter 4, 'Minds, Not Bodies: Expanding the Notion of Gender in Development', speech delivered at the Inaugural Plenary of the Fourth UN World Conference on Women, Beijing, 1995.

Chapter 5, 'Indigenising Feminism', first published as 'Feminism and Feminist Expression: A Dialogue', in Kamala Ganesh and Usha Thakkar (eds), *Culture and the Making of Identity in Contemporary India* (New Delhi: SAGE, 2005), pp. 184–201.

Chapter 7, 'Globalism and Localism: Negotiating Feminist Space', paper presented at the seminar 'Rethinking Gender, Democracy and Development: Is Decentralisation a Tool for Local Effective Political

Voice?', Ferrara University and Modena University, Italy, 20–22 May 2002.

Chapter 8, 'Women's Participation in the History of Ideas and the Reconstruction of Knowledge', Lecture delivered at the National Institute for Advanced Studies, Bangalore, 2004.

Chapter 9, 'Feminist Networks, People's Movements, and Alliances: Learning from the Ground', first published in Luciana Ricciutelli, Angela Miles and Margaret H. McFadden (eds), *Feminist Politics, Activism and Vision: Local and Global Challenges* (Chicago: University of Chicago Press, 2004).

Chapter 10, 'To Be or Not to Be: Problems in Locating Women in Public Policy', paper presented at the conference on 'Challenges of Governance, Equity and Empowerment', Institute of Social and Economic Change, Bangalore, June 2005. Published in Gopal K. Kadekodi, S. M. Ravi Kanbur, Vijayendra Rao, *Development in Karnataka: Challenges of Governance, Equity and Empowerment* (New Delhi: Academic Foundation, 2008), pp. 107–24.

Chapter 11, 'What Is Wrong with Economics? Can the *Aam Aurat* Redefine Economic Reasoning?', Durgabai Deshmukh Memorial Lecture, India International Centre, New Delhi, 15 July 2011.

Chapter 12, 'The First Challengers: The Feminists of the South', *Making It Magazine* (UNIDO), 5 February 2013.

Chapter 13, 'The Evolution of Ideas: A Feminist's Reflections on the Partnership with the UN System', first published in Ellen Chesler and Terry McGovern (eds), *Women and Girls Rising: Progress and Resistance around the World* (London: Routledge, 2016), pp. 89–101. (Published here with permission from Taylor & Francis.)

Chapter 14, 'Looking Back at the South Commission', Lecture delivered at Ambedkar University, New Delhi, 11 February 2015, first published in *Economic and Political Weekly*, vol. 51, no. 9 (27 February 2016).

INTRODUCTION

The Birthing of a Feminist and Her Journey

Perceiving the world, its people, its ideas and its adventures through a gender lens shakes one up, as it distorts if not challenges whatever reality we may have known before we peered into the world through this lens. Coming as I did from a university setting—not only in my academic background but also experience, as I had by then taught economics at Miranda House College of Delhi University for six years[1]—jumping into the field of women's studies and thereby the women's movement was a transforming experience. Most of the knowledge I had inherited needed to be upturned if not abandoned. From being a neutral observer of the world and its phenomena, I became political. The characteristics of every sphere, mental or physical, as I had known them earlier changed as a result of looking at the world through this gendered lens and with the feminist mind.

WHO I WAS

However, this transformative experience was not a smooth one. The economics department at Miranda House was full of women with onerous family duties—demanding husbands and small children—and they were always divided between these two parts of their lives. The college offered them some brief respite from their household duties, but they were inevitably called back to some domestic duty or other. I can see the extent of their difficulties now, having later experienced some of what they did myself, but at the time, I must confess I was much less understanding. I was unmarried and had come back from Oxford University with a sense of being liberated.

I greatly enjoyed being the only, or one of the few, women in a room of authoritative, intellectual men, holding my own in conversation with them. Young and single, I was rather turned off by the sight of my departmental colleagues sitting in the staff room knitting and talking about babies. How much more exciting it was to walk down to the coffee shop at the Delhi School of Economics nearby, and sit with Amartya Sen or Sukhamoy Chakravarty, with their students (largely male) gathered around them, talking about Pareto optimality and welfare economics! I enjoyed those settings and conversations much more than what confronted me in my own staff room. I am not proud of the way in which I drew this distinction, and the fact that I saw things this way. It shows just how far off I still was from being any kind of feminist.

THE PARADIGM SHIFT MOMENT

Sometime in the late 1960s, Raj and Romesh Thapar began to plan a special issue of their intellectual magazine, *Seminar*, on the subject of 'the Indian woman'. The historian Romila Thapar, an active member of that world, who was then making waves as a historian of ancient India, persuaded me to contribute to that issue. I spent a while thinking about what I wanted to say, and then an old memory from childhood came back to me. My mother, I remembered, used to say some words of blessing whenever she gave her daughters an oil bath. She would invoke the so-called *panchakanyas* (five young women of mythology), Ahalya, Tara, Sita, Draupadi and Mandodari—paradigms of female virtue—and call for us to emulate them. All these women were good wives and daughters who either obeyed or (as in Draupadi's case) were forced to submit to the authority of the men in their lives, their fathers and husbands. I saw them as women subdued by patriarchy, and I could no longer in good conscience accept them as models worthy of my emulation. In my article for *Seminar*,[2] I called for a new panchakanya, for the celebration of the more rebellious women in the tradition, women who stood up for themselves such as Ambapali, Gargi, Avvaiyar, Savitri, Sita, and others who did not define themselves in relation to men.

The editor at the Publications Division of the Government of India thought I was dissident enough to write a book replacing an earlier one called *Women of India*, written by Tara Ali Baig in 1950, with a more modern outlook. She wanted the book in time for International Women's Year in 1975. It would be home-based work and therefore manageable in what was then a crisis of my own creation.[3] But I knew almost nothing of the subject.

It seemed too vast a domain to handle in a year. So I decided to make it an edited volume. I cast a net over some of my academic friends at the University of Delhi, great scholars like André Béteille, Veena Das, Ashok Rudra, Romila Thapar, Ashish Bose and some journalists, drawing them out of their disciplines to consider the status of Indian women. I was also able to bring in friends from abroad such as Ester Boserup, whose work on women in agriculture in Africa had been one of the first to highlight gender roles.

The opening essay in the book, called 'The Demographic Profile',[4] was written by Ashish Bose, a demographer who was then a fellow at Delhi University. He presented a table tracing the sex ratio in India over a span of 70 years, 1901 to 1971, using the official decennial census. This presentation of the data revealed the extraordinary decline in the number of females in relation to males in the population of India, from 972 females per 1,000 males in 1901, to 930 in 1971. Later, as the mortality rate of newborns was published, the horrific phenomenon of sex-selective abortion apart from the post-birth killing of female babies came into the public consciousness. This phenomenon which still haunts India, has been given great publicity and attention by Amartya Sen, who calls it the phenomenon of India's 'missing women'.[5]

Other essays revealed the strength of women who had found ways of strengthening themselves in a patriarchal rural environment, such xiv The Journey of a Southern Feminist

as the essay by G. Morris Carstairs and Olivia Stokes. The economist Ashok Rudra took on one of India's paradoxes, the tradition of worship of female gods while women were eliminated on earth. The great writer Qurratulain Hyder portrayed Muslim women. So many other 'kinds' of women were profiled—nuns, nurses, students, matriarchs.

It was the journey of compiling this volume of essays that led me to both respect for women and a concern for the inequality between men and women, and even more the huge gap in knowledge about that inequality. The volume was released by the president of India in 1975, commemorating the International Women's Year announced by the United Nations (UN), and was taken to Mexico as India's official submission.

JUMPING INTO THE WHIRLPOOL

Doing fieldwork to gather data on my new interest, however, required funds and an institution. I was fortunate in that some of my earlier professional associations had enabled me to meet people such as the late Professor Raj Krishna and the late L. C. Jain. These persons put together an institution—a registered society to facilitate field research on programmes that were meant to provide employment as well as alleviate poverty. This was the Institute of Social Studies Trust (ISST). With the support of the Indian Council of Social Science Research (ICSSR), and using this registered society, I plunged into data collection on these inequalities, expanding into the collection of information on women's economic roles as well as their capacity to work together, to co-operate in strengthening their economic spaces. The studies led to reports and books, each revealing not only the extraordinary capabilities of women, but the depth and width of their role in the Indian economy.

Simultaneously, other centres in other parts of India and in Delhi were also uncovering women's capability apart from revealing the neglect and discrimination to which they were subjected. This led to an initiative supported by the then chairperson of the University Grants Commission, Madhuri Shah, namely, registration of the Indian

Association for Women's Studies (IAWS). I was one of the founding members of the association.

The uncovering of gender, especially within poverty, became the special feature of work at the ISST, and this in turn provided the reason for my being invited to many conferences and consultations that took place as part of the momentum of the decade and the World Conferences on Women.

RESEARCH FOR POLICY AND ACTION

Field visits not just to one region but the whole of India, often as part of a project to evaluate the impact of some government scheme or the other, and often funded by the government itself, led to my 'discovery' of how many innovative, self-strengthening organisations and initiatives women themselves had created. Women could form institutions or even informal collectives to strengthen themselves, increase their income, or to resist unwanted intrusions. As a group, we then wrote books and articles on the extraordinary intelligence and ability of women to come together for a common objective, whether the objective was 'resisting' an enemy or 'strengthening' themselves through economic benefits. This power of women to work together across the various strong boundaries in society and the economy—the boundaries of caste, language, religion and location—revealed the potential for transforming the approach to economic development, and the reasoning driving it, from that of giving 'handouts' to supporting women's own organisational strength and goals.

The conventional perception of women as 'beneficiaries', requiring support of the kind usually clubbed together in the 'health and welfare' department, concealed this extraordinary capacity and strength. Thus, I pleaded for reorienting the focus of not only the government, donors and economic policy makers, but of women themselves, the women's movement, away from issues related to women's bodies towards emphasising their extraordinary minds, their collective efforts, and recognition of their survival strategies. Women's skills in self-organisation and their ideas needed to be seen as characteristic of their minds.

My constant argument with my sisters in the feminist movement was to say, 'Let us not only lament that we are excluded, that theories and propositions do not include "us". Let us move to offering well-designed and well-constructed theories which include the knowledge that we have gained through women's studies and working with women.' Amartya Sen's exhortation comes to mind:

> Women should be seen not as patients whose interests have to be looked after, but as agents who can do effective things—both individually and jointly. We also have to go beyond their role specifically as 'consumers' or as 'people with needs', and consider, more broadly, their general role as agents of change who can—given the opportunity—think, assess, evaluate, resolve, inspire, agitate, and through these means, reshape the world.[6]

GETTING GLOBALISED

The UN World Conferences on Women that began in 1975 in Mexico City, followed by two more—Nairobi in 1985 and Beijing in 1995—and the conferences that followed nationally and regionally, provided a large ocean of knowledge and plenty of bonding space, stimulating thought and action. I was fortunate to have attended all the four conferences—in Mexico, Copenhagen, Nairobi and Beijing—as well as the pre-conference meetings both at the national and at the regional levels, that is, at the Economic and Social Commission for Asia and the Pacific, the UN's regional structure located in Bangkok. I was often included in special workshops and expert groups' consultations in the field of data collection and poverty removal strategies prior to the conferences. I was also included on the committee set up by the Government of India to prepare the country reports for these World Conferences. This volume of my writings tries to capture that lived experience, the knowledge that I gained, and the stimulus it provided me for plunging into the women's movement and engaging in feminist thought.

LEARNING FROM THE GROUND

Thus, I began to work in the area of women's studies and undertook field-based research to challenge the numbers associated with women's economic contribution. I then moved on to looking at the design and content of transfers of funds from donors of the North who wished to enable women's progress in the South. In the process, I was able to see their inbuilt ignorance about our ground-level conditions. I found myself wanting to build a platform of women from Southern continents who would be able to articulate and design development frameworks in such a way as to be responsive to the conditions of women in the South. Such analysis, as well as proposals based on it, I thought would help both sides—those providing financial support for women's advancement in the South, and women themselves, the so-called 'beneficiaries'.

In the perception of the donors, we appeared to be poor and illiterate, trapped in convention and in archaic cultures, needing to be drawn into more modern systems. Southern women objected to the incompleteness and inappropriateness of this analysis and its implied claim of cultural and political superiority. There was also a certain inequality in such descriptions, since Northern women seemed to be economically marginalised and socially trivialised in their own milieus.

CHALLENGING THE NORTH

I got a chance to examine in some depth the contents of development transfers, thanks to an invitation from the Women in Development wing of the Development Assistance Committee (DAC), Organisation for Economic Co-operation and Development (OECD), Paris, to give a lecture at the group's pre-Nairobi planning meeting. I analysed almost 145 project evaluation reports of North–South transfers of funds for what were called 'women in development' projects. The review revealed that almost all had a negative impact on poor women because their roles had not been correctly identified, and thus they lost out.

I circulated my lecture, which I titled 'Development as if Women Mattered: Can Women Build a New Paradigm?',[7] to a selection of women from the South continents whom I had met in my travels. Each of them felt that this reality that I described was their experience too. So when I invited them, one from each continent, to a seminar in Bangalore in 1984 to thrash out our alternative, they came willingly. We identified the macro situations within which poor women's experience of development needed to be contextualised—the food crisis in Sub-Saharan Africa, the cultural crisis in North Africa and the Middle East, the debt crisis in Latin America, and poverty and militarism in the Asia-Pacific region. And there in Bangalore, in my parents' home, was born the Third World women's network, Development Alternatives with Women for a New Era, or DAWN.

Over the course of the next year, the group met two more times to design a framework for locating women in the development arena, and to organise some panels for presentation at the UN World Conference on Women in Nairobi in 1985. The framework was to be such that it linked poor women's situation, both negative and positive, to the macro-economic and political framework of their region. The DAWN network suggested that only if the struggles and contributions of poor women in these regions were seen against this larger background could there be an understanding not only of the 'what' of development, but an indication of the 'how'. The levers to bring about a transformation would be revealed by such contextual analysis linked to macro political and economic features.

The discussions in Bangalore were followed by other seminars of the same group, leading to a publication titled *Development, Crises and Alternative Visions*. The final text was written by Gita Sen and Caren Grown, and it was widely circulated and used. DAWN also has a lively website.[8] This intervention by DAWN into the discourse on women and development not only transformed the intellectual underpinnings of that discourse, but also shifted the creativity, the intellectual leadership, from 'patrons' in the North to 'clients' in the South.

The combination of a focus on neglected statistics and the experience gathered through fieldwork about women showed that while they might be suffering from discrimination and from every other form of underclass experience, women had the mind and the skills to design their own emancipation.

LANDING IN FEMINISM

In earlier decades, that is, 1975–95, for those of us from the Southern continents, the economic and social space of women and thereby of development funding and human rights were priority topics. But by 1995, the strong intermingling that had taken place between women across various countries, classes and preoccupations had brought in the idea of feminism. While it may have been a term that had been much used in the West earlier, and much more around the 1970s, its spread and adoption as a term to define ourselves, in my view, caught up with us in India only in the 1990s. However, because of my friendship with one of the early proponents of the term, Gloria Steinem, a founder of *Ms.* magazine, and my own attraction to its ideas, I slipped into the use of the word 'feminist' to describe myself in the 1970s.

I began to write papers on themes such as 'Can Feminism Be a Global Ideology?' (1977) and 'Advances in Feminist Theory: An Indian Perspective' (1986).[9] Others were also challenging the notion that feminism originated in the West, and were interested in exploring the expression of feminism as it emerged in our own countries—what was called 'indigenous feminism'.

CHALLENGING INHERITED KNOWLEDGE

Feminists from all over the world were challenging given theories in psychology, political theory, even theology. In other words, they were upturning inherited knowledge. This trend fascinated me, and I tried to bring this phenomenon to the attention of people in the spaces to which I was invited, be they scientific institutions or UN organisations.

But there was also the question in my mind whether the huge effort that was being made at that time to get women included in public policy, programmes and projects was in fact enabling. I argued that inclusion did not necessarily mean leadership; in other words, it did not give women agency.

At every point, in the fields of knowledge, programme and policy, I felt compelled to ask the question, what is wrong with the theories that we had inherited, especially economic theories? This was also true of the perception of poverty, which often did not recognise the very strong differences between men and women in their locations and the different barriers they faced within poverty. I found myself constantly arguing or proposing that feminists from Southern continents were the real challengers of given theory and practice, especially with regard to development.

INTO THE DEEP SOUTH

The political context that I had chosen, namely, championing developing countries, led me smoothly to the work that Julius Nyerere, former president of Tanzania, was doing to build the economic South. What left me extremely demoralised, what dealt a crushing blow to all the efforts and idealism that had led me so far, was the failure of the outcome of the South Commission's work. The commission could not break the grip of Northern intellectual frameworks, and therefore could not generate a political upheaval in the South. Thus, this one last endeavour to overthrow colonialism also seemed to have failed, leaving me as I am now—demoralised!

LOOKING BACK TO THINK FORWARD

Over the decades, especially since 2000, not only internationally but very especially in India, there has been almost an explosion of women and girls laying claim to feminism. Online networks seem to be multiplying, not only selecting special domains of knowledge, but also just giving space to articulation and debate across disciplinary domains. At this time, I cannot claim to have done sufficient research into these online networks, but the general impression I get is that their focus is on sexuality and of course on violence against women. Feminist networks engaged in economics or politics do exist, but in smaller pockets in India. However, at the international level, the International Association of Feminist Economists flourishes, and my perception is that many more academics in the North explore and present ideas and questions in relation to the social sciences. They go beyond seeking equality and affirming rights to interrogating and reconstructing knowledge. In fact, not only is this a well that needs to be drawn from by, let us say, feminists in India, but there is also need to construct our own well and our wealth through reconstructing knowledge from our roots.

Again, this statement could be disputed as there are many intellectuals and scholars in India who are interrogating historical, political and other narratives of the past, scrutinising them with a feminist lens. But it is my view that this interrogation and reconstruction have not actually emerged as a platform in the public space. The 'big voice' is still related to the female 'body', not the 'mind', though we have made inroads into the sphere of political, economic and legal injustices.

Having worked basically in the field of development, and often in some kind of dialogue or partnership with the state, whether at the national or the international level, despite so much vitality, interaction and networking energy in the feminist movement in India, we have not been able to bring down the walls—theoretical, policy, legal walls. But perhaps this is only a lament by someone who is now far removed from the field and thereby ignorant? I hope so.

NOTES

1 I had joined the department as a lecturer in July 1963.
2 Devaki Jain, 'The Social Image', *Seminar*, no. 53 (December 1963), pp. 20–23.
3 Having had children in close succession, and unable to accept someone else taking care of them, I had chosen to resign from my lectureship, albeit not without a deep sense of denial of a career, of recognition, of work. Thus, a crisis of my own creation.
4 Ashish Bose, 'A Demographic Profile', in Devaki Jain (ed.), *Indian Women* (New Delhi: Publications Division, Ministry of Information and Broadcasting, Government of India, 1975).

5 Amartya Sen, 'More Than 100 Million Women Are Missing', *New York Review of Books*, 20 December 1990, http://www.nybooks.com/articles/1990/12/20/more-than-100-million-women-are-missing/ (accessed 2 September 2017).

6 Amartya Sen, 'The Ends and Means of Sustainability', Keynote Address, International Conference on 'Transition to Sustainability in the 21st Century', Inter Academy Panel on International Issues Tokyo, May 2000.

7 Reproduced as Chapter 1 in this volume.

8 Gita Sen and Caren Grown, *Development, Crises and Alternative Visions: Third World Women's Perspectives* (London: Earthscan, 1988). For Dawn's website, see www.dawnnet.org

9 Devaki Jain, 'Can Feminism Be a Global Ideology?', *Quest Quarterly* (Winter, 1978); Devaki Jain, 'Advances in Feminist Theory: An Indian Perspective', paper presented at the World Sociology Conference, New Delhi, August 1986.

CHAPTER 1

Development as if Women Mattered

Can Women Build a New Paradigm?

This lecture was delivered in 1983 to the Women in Development group of the Development Assistance Committee, Organisation for Economic Co-operation and Development, Paris. This was a group of women officials who represented various European aid agencies sponsoring development projects in the former colonies. They were preparing for the Third World Conference on Women, to be held in Nairobi in 1985. I had been invited to present a lecture outlining how these agencies could assist our countries in the field of women and development.

As part of the research that I was conducting along with my colleagues at the Institute of Social Studies Trust, I had found not only that existing development projects were inappropriate, but that the very framework of 'development' in use was flawed. Hence the question, can the lived experience of women create a new framework for planning and implementing development?

THE MICRO-EXPERIENCE: A CHRONICLE OF PERSONAL EVOLUTION, 1975–82

This presentation is more in the form of a quest in which I hope your participation will help not only clarify but realistically assess whether women can evolve another paradigm of development.[1] Of late, especially in the last one year, I have begun to feel that articulation and clarity emerge to a greater degree out of commitment rather than reasoning, out of endeavour rather than thought. It is with this frame of mind that I perceive women as a gender-based formation having the capability of creating an alternative paradigm by making it happen a fortiori, rather than by proving its logic theoretically, a priori.

This may seem like a strange, rhetorical statement, but it is meant also to reveal my own position or condition. The more I dissect and analyse and derive and pursue, the more I see hurdles ahead of any attempt to regenerate a just and peaceful society. The tunnel does not find an end through reason alone. But I believe—it is my real belief—that with faith in the ability of humans to change their destiny through their own will and collective determination, I see the potential of a united women's movement being a force in the world which can heal the divisions and thaw the confrontations, and perhaps even change the order—the economic and social order. I would like to share with you as briefly as possible the evolution of my own thinking, as I suspect that many of you would have had a similar experience, as also because I think it will help in my attempts to communicate my thoughts to you.

When I entered this field of women and their universal unequal condition, particularly in the 1970s, I used to talk of distributive justice. I used to take development and its virtues for granted and make statements to the effect that women, especially in the less developed countries (LDCs), were already integrated in development, were already participating in the economy at very high rates. What they were not getting were the fruits of development. Hence, just as there is a case for distribution between classes, there is a case for better distribution between the sexes.[2]

My next perception was that women could reach for and grasp a greater share of these benefits by organised assertion of power. Women could organise themselves and be organised by a sensitive identification of common critical issues among homogeneous groups, whether occupation-specific, class-specific or area-specific. This was only an endorsement of the kind of methodologies to build solidarity and self-confidence that had been talked about in the West as feminism, consciousness raising, bonding and grouping.[3] The achievements of the members of the Self-Employed Women's Association (SEWA) in Ahmedabad gave grassroots support to this proposition.[4]

A study of rural women's organisations in India,[5] and an expert group meeting on the same subject in Bangkok, made me realise the links between a macro programme for organising rural women to receive or reach for development and the political/ideological

framework. Would poor women's articulation as a separate formation be allowed in a military regime with, say, a strong theocratic or
patriarchal cultural tradition?

Another interesting analysis was the experience in socialist countries such as China and Vietnam. Women's groups consisted of local
members of the party—its women's wing. How far were these cells
able to articulate women's opinions? Were they very different from
women's church groups—for example, those dotting the Pacific Islands
where the church allocated jobs to these groups and used them for
its own purposes?

It appeared that the power and autonomy of women's groups
depended on how they had come into being—whether they were created by the establishment or had emerged out of women's consciousness. Their clout with the regime depended on their autonomy. In
Vietnam, the Vietnamese Women's Union had emerged out of women's
participation in the liberation war. The organisation was independent
and not 'set up' by the party. It nominated its representatives to the
Politburo. The party did not select and nominate women from the
women's wing, as it did in the USSR and China.[6]

Similar evidence emerged from the analysis of women's organisations in East European countries. Not being autonomous, even if these
organisations were ideologically consistent with the party, prevented
them from articulating their opinions as women.[7] Questions such as
'So where does this lead us?', or 'This situation is similar to the general condition of women, but what difference has socialism made?',
or, 'Given that socialist countries have achieved at least two major
demands of women—employment and some support services like
state-supplied childcare—where has that got them?' were discussed
at a conference on women in East European countries.[8]

Socialism has made one striking contribution to women, namely,
it has absorbed them in the workforce. In almost all these countries,
women are 50 per cent or more of the labour force. A second important
achievement is the free provision by the state of social inputs, especially
childcare facilities to release women for taking up work. Since these
are two of the first demands of women's movements, whether in rich

capitalist countries or in poor underdeveloped ones, it is worthwhile to know that these two great leaps forward have taken place in East European countries without any special effort by women.

However, as in most other economies, women have been concentrated in the low-skilled, low-paid tasks within occupations. Women are also not well represented in managerial decision-making positions either in economic or in political institutions. Even in Poland, the independent trade union solidarity, which has a very high rate of participation by women, does not have more than a few women on its executive or in any of its decision-making forums.

The question arose, why? First, the system regarded women as labour, and women were participating in the workforce in large numbers, but not as women specifically. The fact that, in spite of the provision of support facilities, women did not come into public policy areas seemed to suggest that attitudinally, socialists were not different from other men and did not perceive this aspect of inequality or the need for women to represent themselves. In other words, within the general notion of equality, the need for equality between the sexes was not strongly perceived.

East Germany, where there is affluence and socialism but where the divorce rate has been going up rapidly and there are many single-parent families, has been compared to Sweden, where there is affluence and a strong infrastructure provided by the state to support women, and yet there are high rates of divorce, delinquency and the use of drugs. It seemed that work and support services were important gains, but they did not release women from the binds imposed by historical and cultural attitudes associated with their dominant role as mothers. Again, autonomous women's organisations emerged as another necessary condition for women's status, whether under capitalist or socialist economies.

Women in Poland, queuing up for food and other essential goods, recognised that the distribution system had failed because of a distortion in investment. Food, no more produced in Poland, had to be bought in exchange for other goods. Any problem in the pipeline ceased to be a nationally resolvable problem and instead became a political problem between the Soviet satellite countries and the power centre, namely the Soviet Union. In other words, self-reliance in basic necessities seemed as important within the socialist zone as in the capitalist world for an individual country's autonomy. These experiences showed that the centralisation of economic power and economic decision making was critical, or as critical as the older issue of ownership of economic power, whether in private or public hands.

It also seemed that it was not the ends, namely work, social facilities, education, etc., but the means by which these were achieved that might make the difference and determine how much leverage or choice was available to women and men to decide the lifestyle they wished to adopt.

The third direction in which I worked was to improve the quantitative data available on female work, disaggregated according to class, culture and geophysical characteristics. This investigation revealed the sharp differences between the lifestyles, perceptions as well as needs of women from assetless households, and those that had any form of resource, whether it was a home or a pair of bullocks or a skill.[9] This led to the assertion that, in the theorising of women and development, the most important categorisation that should be made is that between the resourceless and all others. In India, everything—work participation, sex-based task allocation, disabilities, attitudes, nutritional status, access to opportunity, social attitudes, stigmas, customs, culture, and male–female relationships including marriage—vary across this dichotomy.

The tendency to see women as one group had imposed middle-class perceptions and values on the efforts towards women's liberation. Going down to the assetless, I noticed the sharpness of inequality between males and females.[10] Twenty-one per cent of Indian women work for a living, according to the 1981 census. According to quality statistics collected by scholars and others interested in women workers, this percentage is an underestimation due to various characteristics of female work, which make it difficult to net. The figure becomes even more of an underestimation if it is disaggregated according to the economic class of the women workers—the poorer the community, the higher the work participation rate of females and children.

Sometimes, as for instance in states like Rajasthan, amongst the landless, the female participation rate would be even greater than the male participation rate, in the range of 74 per cent compared to the male rate of 67 per cent.

There are many other kinds of evidence that point to this same phenomenon, namely that amongst the poor, especially the assetless, women work in the same if not greater numbers than men. For example, counting heads in any form of public works programme—whether drought relief or employment programmes like the Maharashtra Employment Guarantee Scheme—shows the predominance of females in these hard, unskilled jobs.

Another aspect of the same phenomenon is the existence of female-headed households—households not only customarily headed by females, but where a woman provides the sole means of support.[11] Small-scale surveys undertaken by SEWA, a 12,000-member organisation of street vendors in Ahmedabad,[12] surveys of assetless rural households undertaken by us,[13] a survey conducted by the Agro-Economic Research Centre of Andhra University in Visakhapatnam district and analysed by Prof. G. Parthasarathy,[14] all show the prevalence of such households as ranging from 20 to 50 per cent, the number increasing with the acuteness of poverty. In his J. P. Naik Memorial Lecture on 'Women and Rural Development', M. S. Swaminathan, director general of the International Rice Research Institute, Philippines, mentions a figure of 25 per cent of families in poverty as having women as their sole breadwinners.[15] Other indicators also emerged revealing that within this hard-pressed community of men, women and children, women and girl children were the most deprived.

The well-known Indian statistic of 935 females to 1,000 males, however unfortunate, hides behind it a grimmer scene. Again disaggregated according to economic class, on the basis of assets, this ratio falls to 800 and below, with the statistics on children being the cruellest of all. Small-scale surveys are beginning to reveal the havoc that takes place among female infants and children amongst the poor. A survey of 124 households in Kaira district, the home of Amul, revealed that the sex ratio amongst the children of the landless was only 774 as compared to an average of 905 for the total sample.[16]

Neglect of the female, of course, is a well-known phenomenon—less food, less healthcare. But what is less recognised is that physical strain under subnormal conditions of food and health affects poor women and their children in greater measure than men. Periods of high reproductive activity coincide with periods of high work participation amongst poor women, leading to coincidence with high mortality.[17] This characterisation of poverty with women as the poorest of the poor is not unique to India. Income distribution data classified by sex, not only from the 'South' countries but also data on poverty in ghettos in the 'North', reveal the same pattern.[18]

I had always heard that the sociological 'family' is the microcosm of the world or the larger society. I now realise how true this was of the economic family, for this economic household contains in it the economic characteristics of the larger world: namely, unequal distribution of economic power and the benefits related to ownership of capital, access, responsibility and gender. The fewer the resources in a family, the greater the inequality within it.

Another phenomenon of inequality that I pursued involved the differences in articulated needs between women and men in, for example, poor rural and urban communities. The well-known 'save the forest' movement in the Himalayas, known as Chipko (meaning 'to stick') because women embraced trees to prevent woodcutters from felling them, has many documented stories in this direction. For example, in one area, men wanted to plant fruit trees for earning cash income, while women wanted fuel and fodder trees. In another, men wished to give over community land for potato growing, whereas women wanted to save it for fuel trees.[19] In villages in which I have worked, while the community of men may have wanted a road into the village, the women wanted a local health centre.[20]

THE OBSTACLES TO THE MICRO: MACRO PROCESSES

Improved technologies in agriculture—for example, the use of weedicides, hybrid seeds, the shifting of land from food crops to cash crops, mechanisation of planting, processing—and similar changes in industry from the hand to the machine, have displaced women from breadwinning opportunities. At the social level, the formalisation of informal relationships—such as marital relationships as in the case of the Caribbean and the Pacific Islands, or tribals in India among whom education and exposure to modernisation changed perceptions of work sharing—as well as structural or institutional formalisation such as the introduction of built-up markets instead of traditional fairs, pinning down of land rights, and so many other formalisation processes have been causing havoc for women.[21]

In the Caribbean, in September 1982, the University of West Indies held a conference which embraced all the islands. Investment patterns triggered off by large countries next door, but with the collaboration of the dominant regimes, seemed to be the primary concern of the participants.[22] On a little island called St Kitts, with a population of 35,000 people, the story was the same as on the islands of the Philippines with a population of 46 million people. A multinational arrives and sets up a factory to produce garments; he offers well-paid employment to 200 women. The women give up existing income-earning activities, whether they are home-based or in the informal sector such as in the services, and join the firm. After operating the factory for a year, the entrepreneur decides to close it down as he does not find it viable. In closing it down, he gives notice to the regime but not to the employees, and is allowed to leave the country quietly. The closing down of the factory comes as a surprise to the employees. The regime says it is helpless, as the man has left the country.

In the Philippines, tourism and other industries are being promoted to encourage exports and bring some relief with regard to the negative balance of payments. The drive for exports is focused on building the tourist industry, which means luxury hotels and various forms of entertainment, which include prostitution.[23] The emphasis on these sectors, which open up such opportunities, also pre-empts other opportunities. Women are therefore sucked into these professions in a situation of unemployment and poverty. The unemployment amongst the men pushes women to find any source of income available. The debasement and exploitation faced by women have become so enormous that relief measures provided by health clinics and counselling seem ineffectual. The only way seems to be to redirect the economy away from cheap tourism completely.

Nawal El Saadawi of Egypt too cries of the destruction of her country's economy by the liberal import of goods from multinational companies (MNCs), which is destroying domestic production and therefore the expansion of employment opportunities within Egypt. At the same time, it has developed unrealistic consumption habits within her country.[24] Having heard and read about these experiences, I decided to gather together the various studies and experiences from all over the world which trace the difficulties faced by women to certain investment strategies and types of projects. I wanted to see if particular investment and domestic strategies could then be selectively identified as being women's enemies, and suggest an alternative package.

Raj Krishna, the Indian economist, analyses the global economic situation with special reference to LDCs.[25] Krishna documents the trend of increasing inequality both between regions as well as within regions of the globe. The present regimes of trade, aid, investment, technology and migration simultaneously contribute to this trend. Drawing policy implications for LDCs, he argues that the worst strategy of development is to rely on foreign direct investment, except in a few sectors, because MNCs usually take out more foreign exchange than they bring in and do not transfer core technology. Concessional aid or commercial borrowing is preferable. Import substitution and export diversification should be pushed to reduce the trade drain. Core technology transfer even at a high cost must be insisted on. And in all fora, freer immigration of LDC labour into rich countries must be demanded. He adds that an exploitative relationship prevails even between the dominant socialist countries and their satellites. Concentration of economic power is not a monopoly of capitalist countries alone.

But much further thinking on this subject with a specific focus on women has been done in a paper presented at the Expert Group Meeting in Vienna in September 1982.[26] The paper makes a similar point, showing how most of the macro fiscal and monetary policies of the globe are meant to impoverish poor countries, and further impoverish the poor particularly within poor countries, and within this, even more particularly, worsen the condition of women. The paper makes an excellent analysis of the deep and severe structural changes, mostly negative, that are taking place around the globe from North to South. It shows that these changes affect women more regressively than men, because of reduction of the budget for social and basic needs, the shift from organised production to informal production, as well as the shift from domestic market-oriented production to export-oriented production. The paper also shows that women's participation in economic sectors increases in both zones as a result of development. But in LDCs, this increased participation is at the cost of lowering real wages, increased physical strain on women, and general decline in women's self-reliance.

Therefore, whether it is an agricultural product development project, an integrated rural development project, population project or a health project, there are so many built-in strategies for transferring economic as well as political power to the dominant countries, increasing the dependence of all strata of poor such that women are only one group among the many sufferers. The Vienna paper cited above then proceeds to suggest that special arrangements must be made to avoid the specifically harmful effects on women, and that a 1 per cent budget be allocated specially for giving them these additional handicaps.

It is at this point that I have doubts. What would be the point of nudging women upwards relative to men, when the process itself is impoverishing the whole country and adding to inequalities across the world, and within each country? It would indeed be an extremely shortsighted policy.

ISSUES EMERGING FROM CASE STUDIES AND THE VIENNA PAPERS

Many more studies and analytical reports have emerged in the last few years. Some of these were presented at the Expert Group Meeting in Vienna, and there are those that have been brought together for the OECD DAC correspondence group on women in January 1983. These studies note that projects generally ignore women during conceptualisation, and hence tend to affect them negatively in implementation, sometimes even to the disadvantage of the project goals (see Appendix at the end of this chapter).

The macro analysis, whether in the form of case studies of industrialisation, global economic, fiscal and monetary arrangements, or food production and food politics, reveals that existing development strategies either contain, or become involved in through environmental pressures, and tend to exaggerate, global as well as national inequalities. Our exercises in integrating women in development, whether at the micro project level or at the national bureau level, tend to take this context as given.

There are projects to stimulate agricultural production, but, by ignoring women, such projects have not only hurt women's status and nourishment but also production. There is the project of investment in the manufacture of garments in Mexico.[27] Women are the main labour force in this industry. The conditions under which these women are employed are unjust—wages are low, there is no security of work, and the development of the power to strike is not allowed, nor is there any arrangement for social inputs. It is recommended that surveys, and involvement of women in the designing of projects as well as in decision making, would ensure that these mistakes are not made in the first instance, and that interventions could be designed to bring in some of these factors.[28]

Most of the present development strategies, especially the kinds of sectors in which investment has increased or where capital flows from North to South, tend to improve opportunities for absorption of female labour in employment. Whether it is garments, electronics or food processing, or a third sector which always expands with development, namely the tertiary sector, female labour is in demand.[29] One of the persistent demands of those engaged in the field of women and development has been greater employment opportunities for women. Looked at in terms of aggregates, certainly the present forms of capital transfer do respond to this, or do satisfy this demand. There may be some dissatisfaction with the terms and conditions of work of this kind, which lobbies can try to redress.

But the bigger issue, again, is employment at what cost? The impact of this kind of manufacturing process as well as the development of the tourist industry on women and their social condition has been powerfully presented. Obviously, we do not want employment at this cost. The question is whether we should integrate women with these processes. Even if a production programme is likely to impoverish the poor in a country, or increase the country's dependence, should women's development groups try to weave in women's interests? Is there a case for women getting a bigger share of a poisoned cake? Is there a case for designing methodologies by which poor rural women are part of the decision making, among the beneficiaries of an agricultural production project which ultimately is going to worsen the position of all the poor in that country, increase inequality, increase dependence and increase enslavement?

What seems to emerge is that since these policies are (a) bad for the country, and (b) worse for women, women must unite to protest against these policies, and by protesting avoid damage to themselves as well as damage to the country's autonomy. One should see in this a coincidence of women's interests in working against exploitative strategies.

These 'stabilising policies'[30] that are adopted by LDCs are not even good short-term solutions as they make very drastic changes in the economic and political structure, which are then very difficult to reverse. For example, the whole strategy of production for export creates certain structures and linkages which cannot easily be reversed; or strategies of production for domestic consumption. Hence, the argument that something has to be done while waiting for the revolution, which leads us to say, at least let us see that women get a better deal while some deals are being handed out, is shortsighted.

Another insight emerges from the Swedish International Development Cooperation Agency (SIDA) Sri Lanka Women's Bureau case study,[31] as well as the experience of the Danish health project in India. The Sri Lanka paper points out how the thrust in LDCs to provide income to poor rural women has meant the proliferation of income-generating projects which at some point come to a dead end because they have not been woven into the macro social economic programme of the country. One can produce too much of a commodity, or one can go into production on a scale where the raw material is unavailable or at a level of technology that cannot compete with the same product being manufactured at higher quality and lower cost elsewhere, and finally come to a head-on collision with national industrial policy which may not be interested in protecting that form of employment.

Compared to these kinds of Women's Bureau income-generating activities which plague LDCs, and which are supported by the UN Children's Fund (UNICEF) and other well-meaning organisations, commercially viable projects like free trade zones and investment by MNCs seem attractive. But they have their disadvantages also. Hence the need to look at the macro frame not only in LDCs but in the even bigger frame of global economic operations.

The report on the processes and problems of the Danish International Development Agency (DANIDA) project in India also reveals, in the field of health, the effect of macro constraints. The DANIDA project made sincere and very careful efforts to take note of the historical problems of health services for the poor, such as poor utilisation of services by those who needed it most, and built in many local inputs to develop the participatory system. However, established practices, the political instability of the state of Karnataka and its relationship with the central government, the general nervousness of the establishment in launching on a somewhat unpredictable participatory development course, as well as stereotypical perceptions of health delivery by the established official health machinery made for a painful, obstructive process.

The question arises whether in both these cases there might have been some possibility of bypassing or overpowering the obstruction of second- and third-level establishment cadres by co-opting support from outside the bureaucracy, from voices and lobbies which are able to influence the power centres but can speak for the poor, for women and for participatory development. It seems to me the whole issue of mobilisation of the women's lobby, the modern radical lobby which would have the skills for identification with the poor and their needs, which would be able to develop the articulation of poor women, was missing in the Sri Lanka as well as the DANIDA mechanisms. It is natural that it was missing in the former, as the Women's Bureau is part of the government. This shows that however well-linked the machinery is, by definition it cannot implement. It can facilitate design, but it tends to co-opt representation not only from the 'beneficiaries' but also from the environment that can speak for the beneficiaries.

This also reveals that however well-designed a project, co-option of entry points into the local decision-making process is as important as the design. It also shows that checklisting of the technical aspects of projects is only one aspect. Other social and political processes that go towards project design and implementation are equally necessary.

MY EXPERIENCES OF INTERVENTION IN PROJECTS AND DEVELOPMENT PLANNING: TWO ILLUSTRATIONS

The World Bank Sericulture Development Project

These are not constraints faced by donor/international agencies alone. Some lessons on the difficulties of intervening on behalf of women in a project, however influential and mobile one may be at the national, domestic level, is revealed by my experience with the World Bank Sericulture Development Project and the five-year plan exercise.[32]

The World Bank, in collaboration with the state government of Karnataka, is supporting a project to expand the output of silk. The project sets out its priority aim as employment. The basic thrust is on improving the quality of the cocoon through better breeding as well as feeding and rearing practices.

Initially, my interest was in examining the roles of women, since it is well known that women are deeply involved in this industry, and assessing whether the project design and implementation had taken note of this—or whether in some way it was negatively impacting women. Some inferences were drawn from a quick survey as well as a field visit by a group which included the district sericulture project officer, the women's development officer of the state, a local activist and myself. My concerns were expressed in a paper, and as a result a task force was set up by the state government to monitor the project, not only towards safeguarding women's interests, but also intensifying the benefits of the project by concentrating the state government's social development investment in the very areas where this economic programme would be intensified.

This became the necessary strategy as I found that this was truly a family occupation where men and women substituted for each other in various roles without too much traditional demarcation. Going further, however, I found that the design of the project was such that the larger the sericulture farmer, the greater the benefit. For the landless there was no special input; for the small peasant, adaptation to the new technology was too risky and therefore unattractive. The processing was also geared to the export market and therefore pre-empted certain types of weaving and knitting, as it was not competitive with world silk products. This also would push out male and female processors, replacing them with entrepreneurs and machines.[33] Another effect that was pointed out by an agricultural economist was the shifting of land from food crops to mulberry, thus destroying the access of peasant households to proximate food production and perhaps lowering the nutrition of women and children.[34]

The World Bank recruited a well-established social science research institute for monitoring and evaluating the project. Though they were an Indian group, they understood monitoring mainly in terms of the districts reached, staff deployment and production targets.[35] The employment and distributive effects as well as the possible quality of life changes were not priority indicators of this monitoring module.

I took up the issue with the India project officers at the World Bank in Washington, going from the vice-president through the evaluation department and the pre-investment project appraisal division, as well as the officer directly in charge of the sericulture project. They shared my concern but said this advocacy should be done by me at the project level and with the Indian government. They only responded to a country's demands and requirements. They were helpless. On the Indian side, the project is designed by an administrative officer with the help of his technicians with whatever perception he has of outputs and inputs. He may have entered the field in this sector recently, and might leave the project for another responsibility even at the project cooking stage.

In fact, the Karnataka project had already undergone two changes in its leadership. After two to three years of being on the ground, it still had not filled 2,000 vacancies. No survey had been done of existing shares in employment or income in terms of class, location or sex, nor was there any anticipatory study of the changes that could be expected in the forward linkages.

The state government officers who designed the project have no access to poverty inequality studies, methodologies of investigation, ideologies of participatory development, or information on how projects get distorted. The World Bank has these resources. The question that struck me then was, could not funding agencies include these modules in the very early stages of drawing up a jointly agreeable project? Or would this be considered wasteful, since it is a project oriented to export product growth, and 'people' are secondary?

A similar case study describes the development of *tasar* silk (largely tribal-grown), massively funded by SIDA through the Government of India's Central Silk Board.[36]

The Five-Year Plan Exercise

Our work in trying to dissect a five-year development plan and rebuild it with the interests of women closely knitted into the formulation of the plan also revealed the difficulties of drawing women into a 'bad' process. Since there has been a very lively debate all over the world that women must be integrated into the development plan, we took up this exercise. In India, during the formation of the last two plans, 1978–80 and 1980–85, women and related experts have been called in to make suggestions on how the plan could better incorporate women's needs and roles. It was found that the exercise could not be done at the discussion level, but would have to go deeper into looking at sectors, looking at the allocations within sectors, linking them to the performance and roles of women in that sector, and then trying to draw procedural and budgetary links between the plan for that sector and women. We decided to do this as a strictly technical exercise following all the steps which a state planning unit follows in drawing up the five-year plan.[37]

We chose a state, as usually the national plan attempts to be an aggregate of states' plans. Plans are made sectorally against a theoretical model of growth. The sectoral plans are then parcelled out into state plans with a great deal of professional as well as political negotiation on the state's shares not only of the budget but of projects. At the state level, plans are made with an eye not only on the central format but also on what are called departmental requisitions or demands. Ideally, the state plans are to emerge from district and subdistrict plans, but over the years most of the allocations and decisions in the state have been subject to Delhi's priorities and preferences.

Most Indian plans have had a strong statement on achieving full employment, on poverty alleviation, on distributive justice, on socialism. The reflection of these goals can be seen in the development of a dominant public sector, i.e., state-owned investment and production of what are called 'priority areas' for the economy, apart from the usual essential services. Poverty alleviation programmes have meant provision of basic amenities, provision of employment through public works sites, housing schemes and welfare schemes. Distributive justice is attempted to be achieved by fiscal measures as well as public investment and price regulation in essential commodities.[38]

The poverty line is set at US$300 per capita per annum. It has been common to have a lively discussion whether the number of those under the poverty line has declined or not due to the government's efforts and so on. Poverty is also described in terms of per capita nutrition consumption, and there is a debate currently going on regarding the various forms of measurement of nutrition, as well as the norms of calorie requirement. Just as the poor are an important target to be reached by plan development, within the poor, another group that is given a strong studied priority are the Scheduled Castes and Tribes.

We decided to take the whole gamut of all government expenditure which is especially directed towards people, particularly towards poor people, and see how far this has been utilised by the poor, and amongst the poor by women. For this we did a survey of nearly 2,000 households in two parts of a state, reflecting an advanced area in terms of social and economic indicators, and a backward area.[39] Our very first finding was that most of the decisions on what to do for an area were taken in the state capital without any response to the articulated needs of the area, even though the government itself, namely the district official machinery, may have put up their needs to the central state planning unit. We found that only 18 per cent of the allocation in a district was determined at the district level. In fact, this 18 boiled down to 12 per cent. The rest were blueprints made in the state capital (even at the national capital) sought to be implemented in the district whether relevant or not.

At the same time, we found that the needs of the majority of women could be articulated and responded to only with a decentralised system. For example, in the district of Mangalore in South Kanara, women earned from fishing or from rolling cigarettes. Those who earned through the processing and marketing of fish needed some covered shelters for marketing when it rained as well as certain amenities like crèches and toilets at their workplace, which was on the seaside. This had in fact been identified by the District Development Council and the scheme submitted in the district plan. But the state capital decided that what Mangalore needed was a cold storage for fish. This, of course, would help the classes engaged in large-scale fishing, namely trawler owners.

It struck us that the articulation of the needs of poor and disadvantaged groups can only be met and resolved if our ears are to the ground, which means decentralised financial and administrative power. We found, therefore, that even prior to weaving women into the plan, we had to argue against the methodology or process of drawing up the plan. It was the process which was wrong and would have to be righted before anything could be done about women.

The survey also revealed that women and men amongst the poor were not even aware of what are called 'poverty alleviation programmes'. The awareness was as usual confined to the middle classes, and to fill targets, the government extension agency responded to the articulation of these classes and met their goals. In this way, the intention of the government had been distorted by the government's procedures.

Thus, though we were able to improve the perception of the government and draw attention to what women were doing, we found it impossible to merely add the problems of women to a planning as well as decision-making, allocation-making procedure, which would in any case not have the methodology to reach the poor, let alone women. Both these cases show the identity between the interests of women and the interests of all the poor. In trying to point out the weaknesses in the World Bank sericulture project, I found that I was shifting focus from injustice to women to the bigger issue of injustice to the poor and to small agriculturists. The second issue became predominant, as one could see that the long-term effects of this would affect men and women among the low-resource classes very drastically.

THE BASIS FOR THE NEW PARADIGM

I had promised that I would present a new paradigm for development with justice.

What had seemed fairly simple to me initially seemed more complex with experience, but the basic logic of my reasoning remained. I had looked at the question of inequality between men and women, especially amongst the poor. I had found that this was the most pervasive inequality, and any attempt to redress this inequality would automatically be able to redress other inequalities.[40]

Gender inequality is different from other forms of inequality, such as those based on economic, racial, ethnic, religious or colour criteria. Inequality between men and women enters the so-called ultimate unit of social organisation, namely the household, the family. There can be inequality between sons and daughters, between a father and a mother. To my mind this is the most sensitive and basic inequality. It pervades class, caste, religion, colour, and the usual boundaries of homogeneous formations.

It was and continues to be my belief that attempts to redress this inequality, the very comprehension of the roots of this inequality, could show a path for reducing all other inequalities. This fact can be a value, a binding force for unity amongst women, just as it can and is a dividing force. It is binding because whatever their class, women have the experience of being subordinated to men within a family. At the same time, since women can be part of a section of society which is exploitative or dominating, this can divide women.

I characterised women in LDCs as largely invisible, non-monetised, subordinated, stigmatised, as yet unpoliticised, hence powerless and abused. Any attempts made to help this group or any attempts made by this group to extricate itself from this position, I thought, would automatically extricate all other groups who had some of these characteristics.[41] Employment in the informal sector in traditional economies is often non-monetised, invisible, bonded, abusive. So also are minorities, disadvantaged castes and so on. Strategies for women then would be strategies for all, I thought.

Hence I used to argue that designing and implementing policies and programmes with women as the primary focus would automatically generate responses and have implications which would take care of all the worst inequalities within a society.[42] Having arrived at this insight, it seemed to me then important to intervene in policy, in project design, to negotiate on behalf of women.

But looking at the macro forces at work, I found that this earlier model was too simple, though not entirely off the mark. It was not off the mark in that methodologies built around a goal of emancipating women and safeguarding their interests would take care of the emancipation of all subordinate groups. But the methodological change would have to go deeper than tinkering with distribution only, or shifting the ownership of means of production. Other questions need to be addressed, such as what is produced, with what type of technology, what form of organisation of production—factory-based, urban-based or putting-out—and how the product is chosen, that is, for whose benefit. In the selection of a product lies a value judgement on whose preferences are being catered to, whether the goods are for the consumption of the rich, for the consumption of those in the importing countries, or for the producers.

Apart from my own position, I found that most progressive groups in these poor, unequal societies were finding development almost a menace—and yet also a compulsive need. The question became, how to make development a route to justice? It seemed then that in reconstructing development we would have to start from base, or think from first principles. One possibility as yet unexplored was to build development from the experiences of women from disadvantaged social and economic categories, to evolve it experientially rather than intellectually.

Experiential Basis

Documentation of women—of their economic roles, their behaviour, their attitudes, their aspirations—has begun to reveal some interesting shared characteristics—for example, women's overwhelming desire for peace and support of movements for peace, or rejection of the accumulation of armaments. Women's sense of responsibility as well as care for each other and for survival, whether expressed in the poignant commitment of a woman from a lower-resource household to making any sacrifice, however physically dangerous and devastating to her health, in order to keep the family alive, or the kind of caring that women do in other social situations, whether in working together as women's groups or in their work styles at the workplace, have also been noticed. A sense of responsibility and a sense of care seem to stand out as psychological attributes of women. A rejection of hierarchy has also been noticed. Women prefer work styles characterised by equality and tentativeness.

In the developing world, especially in its traditional sectors, agrarian or urban, women find themselves functioning either in subsistence households or in the self-employed sector. This phenomenon is limited to non-socialist countries. In socialist countries, production for self-consumption is found in the kitchen garden, in peasant households in the Soviet Union, in China as well as in Vietnam. This seems to account for 40 to 60 per cent of the household's food consumption and reveals higher productivities than in the collective.

In industry, even though large parts of the economic sector are 'organised' in developed countries—socialist or capitalist—women still play a role in the household sector. Whereas in LDCs which do not have dominant organised sectors, women predominate in small, autonomous, micro production-consumption units.

Cultural and religious roots also influence women, for various reasons. Traditions of carrying on tradition prevail. In other words, women have links with the traditional base, sometimes deriving strength from it through their own networks, and through this maintaining some autonomy as women, while sometimes suffering through these traditions. I have elaborated on these characteristics and provided references to the relevant literature in my Padmaja Naidu Memorial Lecture.[43]

The question then is, can one build on these characteristics, and, if so, how? As I said earlier, the effectiveness or practicability of such strategies can be tested not through logic so much as through commitment and action. Even if we accept this first step, namely to build a strategy drawing from women's experience, situation and styles, it would need a prior philosophical or moral base. In fact, in my opinion, women and development work have suffered for the lack of an ideological base. Development has been ad hoc and lacking in direction.

Philosophical Basis

What would this philosophical base be? To my mind, the base would have to rest on individual autonomy and self-reliance. Many theologies and philosophies of West and East have reflected on the question of individual autonomy as well as the self. Names perhaps familiar to westerners are John Stuart Mill, even Spinoza and Kierkegaard.

The ethics of self-development and realisation as providing the strongest basis for a moral society is, however, not the popular idiom of today. Today it is the idea of collective ethics that prevails in the form of organisation and consciousness raising, which suggests the submersion if not sublimation of the individual. Whether we take communes in socialist or liberal countries or institutions like trade unions and associations or the family, the boundary is the group, not the individual.

In my opinion, this has led to a breakdown of morality. Ethics is asked of the group, not the individual, and this has tended to erode, allow the decay of, the individual's sense of responsibility. On the other hand, women still continue to take and face responsibility as individuals in the family. A revival of focus on individual morality—self-consciousness, self-control—might help replace any moral aggregations of irresponsible individuals with moral aggregations of responsible, moral individuals. It would also draw more of society to follow practices which women are already following.

For me as an Indian—familiar with Hinduism as a way of life—this emphasis on individual autonomy with the goal being self-realisation does not appear strange. This kind of belief system provided the basis for the non-violent freedom movement that Gandhi launched in India. However, while his use of non-violent resistance to liberate India is well known, his economic and political strategies which he saw as part of the freedom struggle are relatively little known.

I am elaborating on this, as the paradigm I am considering draws some inspiration from Gandhi's views—I want to show its operational power. To Gandhi, freedom from the British was only one step to freedom. For him, self-reliance meant not only liberation from foreign powers, but from internal domination of each other by classes and castes, or internal exploitation. The struggle had to build a self-reliant process right from the individual up to the nation. *Swaraj* (self-rule) was linked with *swadeshi* (production and consumption of domestic goods), and swadeshi with *swavalambh*, i.e., self-reliance.

Advocacy of self-made goods in order to prevent not only exploitation by foreigners but exploitation by the owners of domestic capital became a platform for Gandhi, upon which he linked together freedom for the country with self-freedom. He put forward these types of fact-based arguments in order to stimulate and motivate consciousness among all classes of Indians, that their interest lay in making themselves independent of the British. But he did not limit himself through this rhetoric to the simpler task of separating Indian sovereignty from British sovereignty. He tried to help society liberate itself from various forms of bondage, those imposed by outsiders and those imposed upon us by ourselves.

Goods which were made by hand, such as handspun (khadi), and by village cottage industries were retailed through alternative marketing networks such as the Gandhi Ashrams. Gandhi recognised that the commercial class and the state would not support this kind of process, and the best way to bypass them was to reach the consumer directly through ideological consciousness raising, to develop the circle between consumers and producers as mutually supporting groups.

He called these Gandhi Ashrams—namely the retail outlets—the 'barracks' where his 'army' was housed during peacetime. When there was need to come out for mass struggle, these shops were manned by one person while the rest courted arrest in *satyagraha* (non-violent civil disobedience). It is important to see the practical wisdom of these marketing networks which still exist in India. It is also interesting to note that the newly emerging networks of Gandhian women[44] are proposing to use and revive alternative raw material/market networks to sustain their outreach in rural areas with ideology-based employment for women and the poor.

For example, one of the greatest hurdles in Indian history is the caste system, which even today presents various forms of obstruction in our attempts at revolution. But within this caste system, there is the particular ill-treatment or ostracisation of those whom we call the Scheduled Castes, whom Gandhi called the Harijans (children of God), who are known in the English-speaking world as India's 'untouchables', and call themselves Dalits today. They are 'untouchable' in the sense that the castes would not like to socialise with them, eat with them, be touched by them, allow them to enter their houses. These communities usually live in separate colonies.

Instead of bombarding the society, which Gandhi also did, to change its heart, he put his finger on the critical reason for this ostracism or segregation. The Harijans were basically engaged in occupations associated with filth. Through the centuries they became those who cleaned human excreta, who removed the carcasses of animals, who flayed animals for leather, who ate pigs and rats and all the animals associated with dirt. They used their own hands and very simple equipment to scrape off excreta; they carried it on their heads in baskets to throw it in the farmers' fields. In a country with vast rural areas with no forms of modern sanitation, anyone who performed this kind of task and yet did not have the facility to bathe would begin to show physical signs of filth and smell.

One of Gandhiji's priority platforms, even as he talked of the boycotting of foreign goods, was that these Harijans must be liberated from such occupations, and he fought this battle on two grounds. He urged his class, his brotherhood and sisterhood, in Indian society to clean their own toilets. He made it a fetish that toilets would be cleaned by those who lived in the ashrams which he had created as part of his movement. At the same time, he tried to get municipal corporations to provide wheelbarrows so that the excreta need not be carried on the head. He had latrines dug wherever he could in the rural areas, and he made latrine maintenance, latrine cleaning, one of the fundamentals of what is now known as the Gandhian path to reconstruction. In other words, Gandhiji had the extraordinary sensitivity and imagination to put his finger on these critical spots for emancipation—whether of Harijans from the other castes, or of Indians from the British.

Similarly, in relation to women he straightaway saw that the assignation of roles to them was a result of the ignorance and lack of imagination of men. He said that women should be drawn out of the kitchen, women should be in the forefront of public life, that women had a highly developed sense of morality and responsibility which should be used in national development. Getting to the bottom of this situation, Gandhi urged women to shed their ornaments, saying that the ornaments that they wore were part of men's conspiracy to make them into ornaments which men held as their particular possession, which men used to display as their wealth.

Gandhi further suggested that food habits should be simplified, and that one should eat uncooked food or very simple cooked food, basic hand-processed grains and raw vegetables and milk. This was also to reduce cooking, one of the most bondage-inducing assignments in which women all over the world are enmeshed. While in an ashram, as in the kibbutz in Israel, or the communes of China, eating is a community affair, Gandhi went further than the community kitchen, urging changes in eating habits and encouraging people to go in for a less processed diet to reduce unnecessary time spent in elaborate cooking.

Concerned by men's use of women as slaves, free labour and sex objects, he even went as far as to tell women to refuse to participate in sex as a kind of non-violent resistance to the male tool of subordination. A whole generation of women who fought with him took the pledge of celibacy just to prove this point. They were not made into nuns, who are also celibate, but rather lived amongst men in cohabitation but rejected sexuality.

Some of these ideas may look extremist and old-fashioned, but Gandhi was reacting to what he felt was the terrible situation of Harijan and female subordination in a caste-ridden, hierarchical, unequal, widely dispersed society which had a heritage of so many cultures and religions that it required some amount of sharpness to heal and congeal into a beautiful mass. Though many of his statements on women, his do's and don'ts are jarring when read today, he seems to have intuited women correctly and also seen their potential as no political or religious leader in any part of the world has ever done. He perceived them as equal but different; he had an artless way of identifying himself with them totally. Issues such as prohibition, self-reliance through spinning of khadi and production for self-consumption, and the rejection of ritual in religion further responded to the main needs of the majority of women.

The Gandhian ethic of self-reliance insisted that each individual labour for his or her bread, produce as much as they needed and consumed. Consumption was to be totally controlled by production capability. Simplicity became a form of conservation, self-reliance, as well as of identification with the poor who were very simple for their lack of purchasing power of goods. Acquisitiveness could be a basis for aggression or injustice, so wants were kept minimal. Discipline of mind and body was made part of the preparation for non-violent struggle. Hence the insistence on a strict individual moral code. Thus,

Gandhian education, called 'basic education', insisted that children labour and learn through their labour. Growing food, spinning and weaving cloth, cleaning toilets (in a society where there was no automatic flushing system) became part of a schooling intended to remove disparities between classes and castes.

Gandhi's philosophy can be characterised as being pinned on the decentralisation of social, political and economic units. It avoided the tendency for dependence by postulating a production pattern which had as its starting point self-consumption on the demand side, and an available set of locally accessible materials on the supply side. This control of consumption to suit the production possibilities of those who had low resources or low skills and were assetless seemed a viable springboard for generating equality without centralisation.

The ethic of simplicity bordering on austerity has a special power in visibly poor, unequal societies like India. It not only provides a demonstrative identification with the poor, but allows a more even spread of scarce resources. As Gandhi saw it, it was also ahimsa, as there was less open aggression through monopolisation by the few of scarce resources. The importance of this package of ideas is that the masses of Indian women—the poor and the traditional—could assimilate it. It sprang from values they understood.

It seems to me that there is an interesting design here for women to consider. The process, the methodologies they follow for achieving emancipation should be so self-conscious and depth-reaching that they fundamentally reorder all economic and social relationships.[45]

IMPLICATIONS FOR THE WOMEN'S MOVEMENT

What are the operational implications of these two concepts, namely, building on women's experience, and the individual self-reliance ethic? The first implication that emerges is that the basis for women to come together on a united platform need not only be issue-based but can also be methodology-based. Very often issues by necessity vary between classes. For example, a crisis in the lives of the poorest women might take the form of an immediate need for nutrition, wages and water.

In another class, the priority issue may be the right to divorce. The affluent in developing countries may be looking for legal protection, property rights, better divorce laws, equal opportunity for holding decision-making posts, etc. And for the poorest, the issue may be how to prevent technological displacement from work, from income-earning opportunities, how to prevent eviction, decimation. Hence, issues which are very important for mobilisation at the micro level and an essential phase in building up women's solidarity and women's consciousness, leading to a feminist consciousness as the basis of the women's movement, do not provide a base for declassing women.

On the other hand, methodologies provide a common territory. What are these methodologies? First, the means that we use for achieving ends—whether we could co-opt non-violent techniques, peaceful resistance, and so on. Second, the methodology of production and distribution. Here I see the ethic of simplicity expressed as consumption restraint, consumption 'focus', as a powerful platform for solidarity amongst women.[46] Third, decentralised systems of management.

Before going further and listing the possible action points that can be drawn from my earlier steps, namely the philosophical base and the identification of methodologies, I think it is necessary that I share with you two other premises. First, I postulate that the women's movement, or an ideology-based movement for women (not necessarily only by women), is not only a precondition but a parallel stream or current necessary for the effects of development to have the characteristics of peace and justice. To put it even more specifically, the new paradigm would be dysfunctional unless it simultaneously promoted the movement along with development. In the language of feminist theory, development would mediate the building up of feminist consciousness. Matching it to a progressive language would mean that just as class consciousness is considered to be a necessary condition of class struggle, feminist consciousness would be a necessary condition for female emancipation. And the building of this consciousness has to be a part of the development process.

My second premise, or position, to describe it more specifically, is that many of the judgements made and inferences drawn by those who are reviewing development and women contain implicit values.

These implicit values are derived from earlier concepts, earlier analytical frames, and should be rejected if not questioned. As an illustration, many of the papers and case studies, including from the Vienna Expert Group, see home-based work, subsistence households, the dispersed putting-out system of work, adherence to religion and tradition as negatives.

For instance, in the paper on the SIDA Checklist Project,[47] it says that the assumption underlying the checklist is that the donor agency (and the recipient country) seeks to bring male and female farmers into contact with a monetary economy. There is enough evidence now—and many of these aspects I have elaborated on in an earlier lecture[48]—to show that these inferences are not conclusive. Some of these forms of work organisation, some of these links to culture can also be stimulated to yield positive results—including the subsistence household and self-employment, including religion or tradition and culture.

The assessment would have to be made against the kind of systems of human relationships that seem best suited to certain basic principles such as decentralisation, individual autonomy, self-reliance. In other words, if these two or three principles are the philosophical pillars of our paradigm, then such presumptions or implicit value judgements would have to be modified. The thrust would be on how to make these styles of work organisation or their cultural roots shed their negative aspects and to build on their positive features.

IMPLICATIONS FOR FOLLOW-UP BY DEVELOPMENT AGENCIES

To build the new paradigm, some action points can be derived for those who are interested in or belong to the forum of women and development.

First, our own work at the micro level—intervention on behalf of women in development projects at the design and evaluation state, stimulating this intervention through financial support, collecting data on women's roles, women's contribution and expenditure—should continue. It has increased our own knowledge. When we transfer this knowledge, it increases the knowledge of others; it awakens conscious-ness not only in our class of women but even among poor women as we attempt to reflect their lives to them. In other words, our own efforts have had some radiation effects in raising feminist consciousness at levels and in areas which had not been reached earlier.

Second, going beyond the micro area, analysis of the implications of macro strategies has to be undertaken and a strict identification list drawn up of macro policies which tend to hurt women specifically—as well as in most cases the poor and the disadvantaged. This may have to be done under at least two political categories. First, a list of initiatives and strategies which are part of the liberal economic system, such as the operation of MNCs, the impact of International Monetary Fund (IMF) loans, and 'free trade'. A separate analysis may have to be made of the economic impact of aid as also of trade policies with other socialist countries as well as non-socialist countries. If it is possible to identify certain strategies in those countries which create similar effects, then there could be a common agenda; if there is no common list, then that also can be an identification or analytical point.

Third, even if we have to limit ourselves to the so-called capitalist world and its operation, once we have clearly specified the actions which have an identified negative impact, some attempts should be made to mobilise women's opinion into one united forum against these strategies. One venue that comes to my mind is the 1985 Women's Conference. If all of us here and in other influential international lob-bies can agree on an agenda to oppose (rather than sing praises of) the new international economic order, then we can make this a platform for women's support.

Fourth, to go deeper into the causes, the sources of processes which create operations like MNCs and foster conditions which allow capital transfer to become a source of abuse of women and the poor, it may be necessary to look at systems. For example:

1. Analysis of the centralisation and decentralisation of economic power as well as economic organisation might go beyond the dichotomy of capitalism and socialism.

2. Second, the form of organisation of work, i.e., the debate between home-based production linked to collective structures and factory-based production: how do women respond to each of these forms? The potential for women's autonomy in either system, past experience, and certain kinds of exercises and reordering and restructuring could bring out the best of both systems. One might be able then to assess which is the preferred system.

3. A third issue concerns subsistence production and production for exchange. Again, the exercise would be to look at the experience, auditing the balance sheet between negatives and positives.

4. Fourth, there is of course the issue of ownership of means of production—how far this can be squared with equality and justice. In all cases, choices and judgements could be made based on empirical rather than theoretical study. Assessments could also be made against the perceptions of various classes and cultures and those of women regarding their own options. If this kind of further thinking, apart from opposing certain policies, can also be done in 1983–84, one might be able to go further and get wide-ranging global support for a creative alternative with specific categories, structures, concepts, projects.

To continue with the list of action points, a fifth strategy might involve greater stimulus to the development of informed women's opinion. This is not an easy task—and especially not an easy task for outside agencies. A case in point is the participatory research programme of the UN Research Institute for Social Development funded by the Swedish Agency for Research Cooperation with Developing Countries (SAREC). The aim of the research basically is to develop strength in people's struggle, especially in countries which have dominating or undemocratic regimes. The argument is that entering through a UN agency would 'launder' interventions of this kind which otherwise politically would be unacceptable to these oppressive regimes.

The idea that donor agencies stimulate progressive women's forums to articulate in the first instance objections and resistance to international economic arrangements which are exploitative, and at the same time create programmes which strengthen the economic and political power of the poor and the disadvantaged, might appear romantic. But the only reason why I proposed it is that the stimulus and the programme for women still have an ostensible aura of innocence. The most despotic regimes will have set up a bureau, even a ministry for women. Iran was a case in point. There is still a view, especially in Asia, that efforts directed towards women and children are an expression of the humanity and compassion of the regime. They are an indication of the regime's protection of the weak. Hence, even within despotic regimes, women working with the poor and the wretched amongst women and children are given softer treatment than, let us say, men working with workers. Women are not seen as a political force.

This space I think could be exploited by us. In other words, build the human resources of women in these countries, a kind of skill building as well as experience building, which can be done within national bounds in large countries which have some built-up resources of this kind, such as India, but also across countries where the resources are scarce or positive experiences are rare. This is one way of linking women's development with a women's movement through using research and training institutions.

Sixth, there is need for more research, analysis and dissemination of the connection between women and tradition. Living through the experience of women and development over the last 10 years—as a woman as well as an activist and social scientist—I am beginning to see the need not only for better understanding of tradition-created relationships in society, but also to use or build on these relationships for creating a just and peaceful society. Women almost all over the world, and especially in developing countries, have been the main carriers of tradition, be it in the form of religion or culture. There has been some study of the reasons why women predominate amongst the carriers of tradition, and usually the inference is that this happens for negative reasons. Women are motivated by fear, ignorance, lack of opportunity and lack of power, and hence cling to these legacies.

We also find, however, that women tend to be more sensitive to moral principles—more responsible and less dominating in general. This is not to forget that many women do not conform to this description. The evidence for this kind of psychological statement comes from so many writings and researches. It also comes from documentation of the kind of issues in which women participate in large numbers with great zest. For example, the majority of those who take part in peace movements are women. Similarly, women have been prominent in the use of the methodology of non-violence. Again, in India and elsewhere, women have come out in large numbers against injustices such as confiscation of land, shooting down of dissenters, cutting down of forests and so on. Providing security has been so much a part of women's historical experience that it has become almost second nature for women to care.

Is there some connection between these characteristics of women and women's attachment to tradition? Most religions of the world, in a sense, do talk of the spirit, in norms of goodness such as honesty, compassion, the universalness of mankind and womankind, and so on. It is true that religious organisations have tended to become alternative sources of power, often perpetrating discrimination and inequalities. But in a sense, religion might also evoke goodness. Is it possible that this lesson has, in some way, 'touched' women more than men?

A specific concern in this area would be the condition of women in Islamic countries. Discussion on this issue has become difficult, since the Islamic revival has also been used as a force against imperialism and colonialism. Most countries have found that the most powerful way to resist cultural domination and revive self-confidence in citizens is to go back to their roots. And usually in many of the Asian countries, these roots lie in religion. This has meant Buddhist revival in Sri Lanka and Islamic revival in Malaysia as also in the West Asian and North African countries—and the latest is Bangladesh.

If there are areas within the traditions generated by these religions which are particularly harsh on women, those who raise their voices for reform initially get put down as being unpatriotic. Women from these cultures have found it as hard to articulate their concerns as women from outside.

Basically, these six action points that I have listed appeal for some compassion and understanding of women's experiences and existing situation, especially in the LDCs. They are an appeal to stop the imposition of analytical techniques, concepts and categories evolved in other situations on these societies. The idea is to reject the existing economic order, not only in its concentration of economic power, but in its organisational basis and its philosophy.

The argument is developed out of the prior reasoning that earlier political frameworks, whether derived from socialist or liberal philosophers, have not been able to propel the globe towards peace, towards a just social and economic order. On the contrary, inherited ideologies, however modified and reoriented, continue to propel the world towards acute crisis—economic, political and moral. Apart from the build-up of arms and the threat of war, global inequalities have sharpened with the worse off getting further impoverished at the global as well as national levels. Moreover, none of these frameworks has a satisfactory perspective on women's subordination.

In the meantime, feminists have been active on several levels:

1. At the activist level, they have mobilised themselves, articulated needs, participated in struggles, and have even derived some concrete benefits as well as gaining social attention.
2. At the intellectual level they have challenged concepts, definitions and strategies being used in development, showing the inadequate, misleading knowledge and perceptions regarding women, and even pointing to methods by which these can be corrected.
3. Further, at the theoretical level they have also tried to analyse the roots of the female condition in order to give a perspective for action as well as to be able to generalise, go beyond the micro and provide a basis for the women's movement.

I suggest that while these efforts at all three levels have provided essential insights, cleared the undergrowth and developed a widespread basis for women's movements, such efforts are still trapped by inherited theories, methodologies and categories.[49] They accept earlier categories, earlier solutions and seek to make marginal modifications, or seek to bring earlier explanations of processes into their understanding of women's condition, for example, pointing out similarities between production and reproduction, between capitalism and patriarchy, and so on. The new paradigm has to be evolved and built on existing stimuli—religious, social and economic—amongst women, and linked through sisterhood globally.

APPENDIX: CASE STUDIES ON WOMEN IN DEVELOPMENT

A. Case Studies, SIDA Group, Stockholm:

(i)   'Case Studies: Kenya Rural Access Road Programme', Cr. no. 651.

(ii)   'Rada Integrated Rural Development Project: Yemen Arab Republic—Case Study', September 1982, presented by the Netherlands to OECD Paris, 26–27 January 1983.

(iii)   'Case Study: Unterstützung der Frauenselbsthilfe Organisation', Union Nationale des Femmes de Djibouti for OECD/DAC/WID Meeting, Paris, Der Bundesminister für Wirtschaftliche Zusammenarbeit, 30 September 1982 (Letter from Gudrun Graichen-Druck).

(iv)   Sarah McPhee, 'The Checklist Project: Project Evaluation Techniques and Women's Contribution', November 1982.

(v)   'A Case Study in WID: A Rural Development Project in Mali—Summary of a Recent Study', 13 September 1982.

(vi)   Riva Jolkboron, 'A Case Study of the Women's Bureau of Sri Lanka', September 1982.

(vii)   Mari Abelin, Sarah McPhee and Eva Poluha, 'Integrating Women as a Means of Rural Development: A Case Study of the Swedish CADU Project, 1976–1974', September 1982.

(viii) Marie-Thérèse Abela and Catherine Rambaud, 'Le projet "Aménagement des Vallées des Volta" (Haute Volta)—Impact du projet sur les femmes', 1982.

(ix)   O. Reveyrand and A. Correze, 'Note de synthese: L'impact des projets de développement sur les femmes dans la Province du Zou, Republique Populaire du Benin', 10–28 May 1982.

(x) Jeanne Bisilliat and Catherine Rambaud, 'L'impact du projet de développement intégré de DOSSO sur les femmes', June 1982.

(xi) P. Woodford-Berger, 'Monitoring Women: The Use of Checklists in Rural Assistance Programmes against the Background of Ten Case Studies', paper submitted to the OECD/DAC/WID Meeting, Paris, 26–27 January 1983.

B. Case Studies, Vienna Group:

(i) Branch for the Advancement of Women, Centre for Social Development and Humanitarian Affairs, Department of International Economic and Social Affairs, UN Secretariat, 'Resource Paper on Women and Industrialisation—Excerpts', Expert Group Meeting on Women and the International Development Strategy, Vienna, 6–10 September 1982.

(ii) 'Resource Paper on Women in Developing Countries and Monetary and Fiscal Matters in the Context of the International Development Strategy', Vienna, 1981.

(iii) 'Resource Paper on Women and Tourism', Vienna, 6–10 September 1982.

C. Others:

(i) 'Working Women and the NIEO', Special Memo, International Labour Organization (ILO).

(ii) Susan George, *How the Other Half Dies: The Real Reasons for World Hunger* (Harmondsworth, UK: Penguin, 1977).

(iii) Maxine Molyneux, 'Women in Socialist Societies: Problems of Theory and Practice', in K. Young, C. Workowitz and R. N. McCullagh (eds), *Of Marriage and the Market: Women's Subordination in International Perspective* (London: CSE Books, 1981).

(iv) Lourdes Arizpe and Josefina Aranda, 'The "Comparative Advantage" of Women's Disadvantages: Women Workers in the Strawberry Expert Agribusiness in Mexico', *Signs*, vol. 7, no. 2 (1981), pp. 453–73.

(v)   Pepe Roberts, '"The Integration of Women into the Development Process": Some Conceptual Problems', *IDS Bulletin*, vol. 10, no. 3 (April 1979), pp. 60–66.

(vi)   Diane Elson and Ruth Pearson, 'The Subordination of Women and the Internationalization of Factory Production', in Young et al., *Of Marriage and the Market*.

(vii)   Angela Cheater, 'Women and Their Participation in Commercial Agricultural Production: The Case of Medium Scale Freehold in Zimbabwe', *Development and Change*, vol. 12, no. 3 (July 1981), pp. 349–77.

(viii)   Carmen Diana Deere, 'Changing Social Relations of Production and Peruvian Peasant Women's Work', *Latin American Perspectives*, vol. 4, nos 1–2 (1977), pp. 48–69.

(ix)   Kate Young, 'Modes of Appropriation and the Sexual Division of Labor: A Case Study from Oaxaca, Mexico', in A. Kuhn and A. Wolpe (eds), *Feminism and Materialism: Women and Modes of Production* (London: Routledge and Kegan Paul, 1980).

(x)   Verena Stolcke, 'The "Unholy" Family: Labor Systems and Family Structure—the Case of Sao Paulo Coffee Plantations', paper presented at the symposium on 'Latin American Kinship Structure', Social Science Research Council, Ixtapan de la Sal, Mexico, September 1981.

(xi)   Fiona Wilson, *The Effect of Recent Strategies of Agricultural Change on the Position of Women: A Review of Literature on Latin America* (Copenhagen: Denmark Centre for Development Research, 1982).

(xii)   International Centre for Research on Women, *Elements of Women's Economic Integration: Project Indicators for the World Bank* (Washington, D.C.: International Centre for Research on Women, 1982).

(xiii)   Nadia H. Youssef and Carol B. Helter, *Rural Households Headed by Women: A Priority Issue for Policy Concern* (Washington, D.C.: International Center for Research on Women, 1983).

(xiv)   *Bringing Women In: Towards a New Direction in Occupational Skills Training for Women* (Washington, D.C.: International Centre for Research on Women, May 1980).

(xv)   Sarah Lund Skar, 'Fuel Availability, Nutrition and Women's Work in Highland Peru: Three Case Studies from Contrasting Andean Communities', World Employment Programme Research Working Paper, Rural Employment Policy Research Programme, ILO, January 1982.

(xvi) Jacquelyn Ann K. Kegley, *The Humanistic Delivery of Services to Families in a Changing and Technological Age* (Washington, D.C.: University Press of America, 1982).

D. Papers from India:

(i)   Edeltraud Drewes, 'Three Fishing Villages in Tamil Nadu: A Socio-economic Study with Special Reference to the Role and Status of Women', Working Paper BOBP/WP/14, Bay of Bengal Programme, Development of Small-Scale Fisheries in the Bay of Bengal, Food and Agriculture Organization and SIDA, February 1982.

(ii)   M. E. Khan, S. K. Ghosh Dastidar and Patanjeet Singh, 'Nutrition and Health Practices among the Rural Women: A Case Study of Uttar Pradesh', paper presented at the International Symposium on 'Problems of Development of the Underprivileged Communities in the Third World Countries', New Delhi, 2–8 October 1982.

(iii) H. Sethi, 'Redefining Political Power and Development', Background Papers on Action Groups, BUILD Documentation Centre, Bombay, 1982; Ajit Muricken, 'Action Groups: Agents of Change for Revolutions?', Background Papers on Action Groups, BUILD Documentation Centre, Bombay, 1982; John J., 'Critique of Action Groups', *Marxist Review* (August 1982), pp. 67–77; Dunu Roy, 'Between Dogma and Debate', in Harsh Sethi and Smitu Kothari (eds), *The Non-Party Political Process: Uncertain Alternatives* (Delhi: Lokayan, 1983); and material on workshop organised jointly by Lokayan and UN Research Institute for Social Development entitled 'Popular Participation: A Look at Non-party Political Formations', January 1982.

(iv)   Ashok Subramanian, 'The Small Step and the Great Leap: Issues in Managing Replication in Development Programmes', Working Paper, Indian Institute of Management, Ahmedabad.

(v)   T. K. Moulik and P. Purushotham, 'Indian Tasar Silk Industry and the New Technology: A Case Study of Modernisation of Conventional Technology and Its Field Suitability', Indian Institute of Management, Ahmedabad (also other papers on technology projects).

NOTES

1   For other writings on a similar theme, see: Björn Hettne, 'Development Theory and the Third World', Swedish Agency for Research Cooperation with Developing Countries (SAREC) Report, Stockholm, 1982; Aant Elzinga, 'Evaluating the Evaluation Game: On the Methodology of Project Evaluation, with Special Reference to Development Cooperation', SAREC Report no. 1, Stockholm, 1981.

2   For example, see Devaki Jain, 'Women and Poverty Eradication', *Mainstream*, vol. 16, no. 9 (29 October 1977), pp. 21–23; Devaki Jain, 'Women and Development: A Two-Sector Model', *Social Action* (New Delhi: Council for Social Development).

3   Devaki Jain, Nalini Singh and Malini Chand, *Women's Quest for Power: Five Case Studies* (New Delhi: Vikas, 1980).

4   Ibid.; Devaki Jain, 'The Self-Employed Women's Association', in *From Dissociation to Rehabilitation: Report on an Experiment to Promote Self-Employment in an Urban Area* (Bombay: Allied, 1975), p. 32.

5   Devaki Jain, Nalini Singh and Abha Bhaiya, 'Role of Rural Women in Community Life: A Case Study from India', Report of the Expert Group Meeting, *Economic Bulletin for Asia and the Pacific*, vol. 29, no. 2 (December 1978).

6   Ibid.

7   Devaki Jain, 'Changing Status of Women in East Europe: Report of the Conference on the Status of Women in East Europe', *Economic and Political Weekly*, vol. 17, no. 8 (February 1982), pp. 275–77.

8   Ibid.

9   Devaki Jain and Malini Chand, 'Patterns of Female Work: Implications for Statistical Design, Economic Classification and Social Priorities', paper prepared for the National Conference on Women's Studies, Bombay, April 1981 (mimeo, ISST, New Delhi).

10 Devaki Jain, 'Indian Women Today and Tomorrow', Padmaja Naidu Memorial Lecture, Teen Murti House, New Delhi, November 1982.

11 Ibid.

12 *SEWA Marches On* (Ahmedabad: SEWA, 1981).

13 Devaki Jain and Mukul Mukherjee, 'Women and Their Households: The Relevance of Men and Macro Economic Policies—An Indian Perspective', paper prepared by ISST for ILO, 1984.

14 G. Parthasarathy, 'Rural Poverty and Female Heads of Household: Need for Quantitative Analysis', paper presented at the Technical Seminar on 'Women's Work and Employment', ISST, New Delhi, April 1982.

15 M. S. Swaminathan, 'Women in Rural Development', J. P. Naik Memorial Lecture, Centre for Women's Development Studies, New Delhi, September 1982.

16 'Milk Maids of Kaira', in Jain et al., *Women's Quest for Power*, chapter 3; J. D. Sethi, 'India's Biological Decay', *Indian Express Magazine*, 5 December 1982; Lincoln Chen, Kamla Puri Sabharwal Memorial Lecture, Lady Irwin College, New Delhi, December 1982; C. Gopalan, 'Population: The Qualitative Dimension', inaugural speech for the Indian Association for the Study of Population, 26 December 1982.

17 Jain and Chand, 'Patterns of Female Work'.

18 Gloria Steinem, Ms. Foundation for Education and Communication; Mahar Mangahas and Teresa Jayme-Ho, 'Income and Labour Force Participation Rates of Women in the Philippines', Discussion Paper, School of Economics, University of Philippines, 1976; Amartya Kumar Sen, 'Food Battles', Coromandel Lecture, India International Centre, 6 December 1982.

19 Anil Aggarwal, 'Try Asking the Women First', *Indian Express*, 20 July 1982, p. 6; interview, Radha Bhatt, Lakshmi Ashram, Kausani, Almora district, Uttar Pradesh, March 1981.

20 'Qualitative Findings', Rural Household Study, ISST, New Delhi, 1976.

21 ISST, 'A Case Study in the Social and Cultural Implications of Tasar Production for Tribal Communities', New Delhi, August 1982; T. K. Moulik and P. Purushotham, 'The Predicament in Silk Industry', Indian Institute of Management, Ahmedabad; Vina Mazumdar, *The Role of Rural Women in Development*, Report of an International Study Seminar, Institute of Development Studies, University of Sussex, 5 January–10 February 1977 (Bombay: Allied, 1978).

22 Conference on 'Women in the Caribbean', University of West Indies, Barbados, September 1982.

23 Devaki Jain, 'Asian Women: In Search of an Identity', paper presented at the conference on 'Role and Rights of Women in Asia', Asian Students Association, Manila, 28 August–4 September 1982.

24 Nawal El Saadawi, Conference on 'Women in the Caribbean'.

25 See, for example, Raj Krishna, Lecture at the India International Centre, New Delhi, December 1982; also see Raj Krishna, 'The Inequity of the International Economic Order: Some Explanations and Policy Implications', mimeo, Manila, November 1982.

26 UN, 'Resource Paper on Women in Developing Countries and Monetary and Fiscal Matters in the Context of International Development Strategy', Expert Group Meeting, Vienna, September 1982.

27 See the studies cited in the Appendix to this chapter, part B (Case Studies, Vienna Group).

28 Mari Abelin, Sarah McPhee and Eva Poluha, 'Integrating Women as a Means of Rural Development: A Case Study of the Swedish CADU Project, 1976–1974', SIDA Group, Stockholm, September 1982.

29 See the studies cited in Appendix to this chapter, part B (Case Studies, Vienna Group).

30 UN, 'Resource Paper on Women in Developing Countries'.

31 Riva Jolkboron, 'A Case Study of the Women's Bureau of Sri Lanka', SIDA Group, Stockholm, September 1982.

32 ISST, 'An Assessment of Women's Roles: The Karnataka Sericulture Development Project', mimeo, Bangalore, 1982; ISST, 'Integrating Women's Interests into a State Five Year Plan', submitted to the Ministry of Social Welfare, Government of India, September 1984. See also the discussion in chapter 10, this volume.

33 Moulik and Purushotham, 'The Predicament in Silk Industry'.

34 Soedjatmoko, Nehru Memorial Lecture, Nehru Memorial Museum and Library, New Delhi, 13 November 1982.

35 Draft Report, UN Educational, Scientific and Cultural Organization (UNESCO) Regional Expert Meeting on Women's Studies and Social Sciences, New Delhi, 4–8 October 1982.

36 ISST, 'A Case Study in the Social and Cultural Implications of Tasar Production'.

37 Devaki Jain, 'Women in the Sixth Plan', *Yojana*, vol. 35, no. 19 (16–31 October 1981).

38 Planning Commission, *Fifth Five-Year Plan, 1974–79* (New Delhi: Government of India).

39 ISST, 'Integrating Women's Interests into a State Five Year Plan'.

40 Jain, 'Women and Poverty Eradication'; Devaki Jain, 'Are Women a Separate Issue?', *Populi*, vol. 5, no. 1 (1978), pp. 7–15.

41 Jain, 'Asian Women: In Search of an Identity'.

42 Jain, 'Women and Poverty Eradication'; Institute of Social and Economic Change, 'Monitoring and Evaluation of World Bank Sericulture Project', mimeo, Bangalore.

43 Jain, 'Indian Women Today and Tomorrow'.

44 Jain et al., 'Role of Rural Women in Community Life'.

45 Jain, 'Indian Women Today and Tomorrow'.

46 Ibid.

47 Sarah McPhee, 'The Checklist Project: Project Evaluation Techniques and Women's Contribution', SIDA Group, Stockholm, November 1982.

48 Jain, 'Indian Women Today and Tomorrow'.

49 Ibid.

CHAPTER 2

Advances in Feminist Theory

An Indian Perspective

By 1986, the women's movement had experienced two World Conferences, which meant getting to know women from other parts of the world as well as the varied ideologies and terminologies being used by women's movements elsewhere. Feminism had entered the scene as a new and revolutionary idea, but was still mainly confined to the US and the global North. It was viewed with suspicion in Southern countries that tended to lean ideologically towards the Soviet Union and the left. Even within the women's movement in India, there were questions regarding the assumptions underlying feminist thinking. In this lecture, I present the debates that were happening in India around the term 'feminism' and the ideology it represented. I also offer a proposal on vocabularies, how they too have come from the North and tend to distort contexts, while other vocabularies drawn from our own contexts can be so enabling.

In this paper, I present a perspective on the Indian debate on feminism, the scope of which will be restricted by my own limitations, that is: (*a*) my experience of the debate; (*b*) the limited reading I have done; and (*c*) my ideological or philosophical preferences/biases. I suggest:

1. That feminist theory—as distinct from feminist practice—is still not a body of knowledge in India. This statement implies that feminist practice is widespread in India, which I maintain it is.
2. That in India and perhaps in other similar countries, the reflections or even early statements on theory are emerging from the empirical field: from activist knowledge and dialogue. The theory is grounded in users' language; it is derived as a response to the needs of grassroots activists.
3. That the goal of exercises in theory building is predominantly to find a basis for solidarity—feminist solidarity, a united women's movement, a common politics.

Summing up, I would suggest that feminist theory in India is defined by feminist practice and feminist goals. I shall illustrate this using various types of empirical evidence: a conference; a study (in process); a networking process; a book; and a man.

A REGRET

It would have been feminist, it would have been a true reflection of the Indian feminist way, if I could have discussed this paper with different groups and presented it as a collective view. But alas, I could not, because I did not start writing the paper till quite late—one more of its shortcomings. I gratefully acknowledge the tireless assistance of Madhu Garg, Jaya Sharma and Shikha Goel of ISST in preparing this paper.

Before I offer the illustrations I referred to, I would venture to list what in my view are the 'advances' in Indian feminist theory in recent years. They are all interlinked and may appear repetitive:

1. A self-confidence revealed in the wider acceptance of the term 'feminism', when earlier the term 'women's movement' was current, accompanied simultaneously by an affirmation of its cultural/political context, with content moulded for Indians by Indians. Put negatively this would read, 'accompanied simultaneously by a rejection of definitions, of context, of preoccupations developed in the West'.
2. A quest to derive the roots—the explanatory variables—of the female condition in India from religious, cultural, historical and economic forces and trends; thus, a consideration of terms such as 'intra-household' instead of 'patriarchy', and so on. This means looking at subordination in a context wider than gender relations— perhaps in terms of power relations in general.
3. A search for a platform for building unity as part of the collective empowerment process so as to deal with national crises—social, economic and political.
4. Bringing in development and its impulses as factors to be dealt with, and thus, through a process of consultation, seeking to design a feminist development, or a feminist framework for appraising

development. The effort has been to reconstruct theory, to give visibility and legitimacy to the modes of production and exchange which predominate in India, to build a new normative science to assess them, and thus reconstruct development.

5. A slow, cautious selection of local issues/observed phenomena to support a kind of 'renaissance', a strengthening of existing economic and social arrangements as culturally suited modes. Included in this sweep are some aspects of women's roles, women's work styles such as home-based or hand-driven work, the idea being to enhance or legitimise some aspects of our particular place in the firmament. In this process of reflection and revaluation, there is full awareness of the dangers of romanticising the past or conservative practices.

6. Finding a place for women's voices in South–South economic and political alliances, especially the Non-Aligned Movement (NAM), the six-nation disarmament initiative. This involves a process of conscientisation of the powers/policy makers with regard to the importance of gender differentiation, as well as giving gender considerations legitimacy in Third World politics. It also involves theorising in the language of the South: fitting gender consider-ations into the frame, and thus influencing that frame.

I now discuss some empirical bases for an Indian feminism.

A CONFERENCE

In offering some glimpses of a feminist theory, my first resource is the national conference held in December 1985 in Bombay, called 'Perspectives for the Autonomous Women's Movement in India'.[1] Some 85 women's groups and several individuals from different parts of the world attended the conference. All of the participants, about 300 in number, came at their own initiative and expense. The conference was structured so as to have two workshops per day. Presentations were made in the morning, and subgroups for each workshop were formed for discussions. A plenary session was held towards the end of the day for a general reporting to all the participants. Cultural programmes, plays and audiovisuals followed. The last day saw a variety of small workshops suggested by the participants.

The method of convening this conference was feminist—through several prior consultations on the venue and themes, with decisions being taken by a group of representatives of women's groups. Attendance was self-supported and self-motivated; the roles of moderator, rapporteur and so on developed at the conference itself. Crisp formulations such as the following came out of the meeting:[2]

> The term feminism needs clarification. Do you accept that sexual bondage is a stronger one than the class bondage? Is it possible to bring all women together on the same platform? Or should there be separate demands for separate classes? What is meant by reformism—the act of counselling?

> Cohesiveness and richness come out of private activism, while validity comes from public activism. Therefore, there is always pressure to participate in public activism. This often forces a group to resort to public activism in a rather traditional form.

This discussion then led to the whole issue of defining feminism. While some felt that feminism as a tool was sufficient to explore oppression and inequalities in all their forms, others disagreed with this perspective.

> Who is a real feminist? Some members felt that at times women became feminist chauvinists who look down on women who have to do house work, child care, etc. These middle class, articulate women tend to dominate groups. And in such groups, if expected behavioural patterns are not visible then they question the feminism of the others. This opinion was not shared by many. However, some women continued to argue that women's organisation is not non-class organisation. The women's organisations have neglected the class issue in the same way as left political organisations have neglected the gender issue. This has led to the exclusion of [a] large mass of poor women.[3]

The principal concern of the conference was alliances—understandably a natural preoccupation in a plural, multiple-religion, multiple-caste, multiple-language, multi-party, unequal but secular, democratic nation. Not only alliances with existing external forces—political parties and ideological movements—but also alliances within, that is, of women with women as individuals, of women's groups of one kind, say activist, with women's groups of another kind, say researchers.

Women's groups claiming to work as collectives had often empowered individuals, or, conversely, had exploited them. Similarly, feminist research had been no better in its motivations and interests than the inherited, man-made research. Dichotomies such as activist versus researcher, class versus caste persisted. Where was the breakthrough?

No movement—left, reformist, Christian, Gandhian—had been able to accommodate women's voices. If all existing political forces are not appropriate vehicles, then what? 'We need our own politics' is the answer. 'What is that politics?', asked this large, non-party political formation.

The other strong concern was consolidation. The two—finding a politics, and consolidation—are of course closely related quests, but not the same. Consolidation of this dynamic, self-conscious, widely dispersed, representative women's movement has become a real preoccupation in its every part. Simple aggregation does not make it into a political force. Yet the potential is there. A tantalising situation. The need for consolidation is vivid because of the happenings in the Indian polity. Reassertion of separatism. Violent expressions of hidden angers over language, religion, caste and gender differentiation.

Why this sliding back to 'old' barriers? This issue has been brought out poignantly by feminists like Kumari Jayawardena in analysing the ethnic conflict in Sri Lanka.[4] Ethnic consciousness has overpowered class consciousness, she says. One reason is the scramble for a piece of the pie—a mix of unattainable and untenable consumerism on the demand side, and accelerated but distorted growth of output on the supply side. In the midst of these shattering experiences, feminist consciousness seems to flicker like a lamp still alight before getting snuffed out.

At the conference, Kumari Jayawardena described the spontaneous way women from different classes, religions, politics in Sri Lanka had taken a united stand against the ethnic riots through peace marches, peace actions. The group then suggested that feminist consciousness was alive—was today replacing class consciousness and class solidarity as the focal point for progressive causes. The burning question again became how to prevent feminist consciousness from withering away or being subordinated, as has happened with class solidarity. What can we learn from the history of the deterioration of class consciousness? How to resist the decline? Again, consolidation seems to be a first step, and consolidation needs a politics—a common frame, theory.

What theory can enshrine this quest? Tracing the roots of the tangible unity, the solidarity that seemed present in the room—but which escaped agreement when expressed. Feminist theory in India has to find an answer to these questions. This conference was a beginning.

A STUDY

The report of the Committee on the Status of Women in India[5] had pointed out the numerous ways in which women in India suffered discrimination and subordination. But neither that report, nor work done thereafter, had come to grips with the problem of what constitutes an unambiguous improvement in the status of women of a nation, community or region, and what variables are crucial to determine the direction of the change. So far, status had often been measured by any one of several kinds of social indicators, depending on the model used with regard to concepts of status and positive changes in status. A view of the available data suggested that not all these indicators move in the same direction for all regions at all times.

Other curious paradoxes exist in India—the worship of goddesses by men and women (learning, wealth and power are all worshipped as goddesses in religious traditions) on the one hand, and on the other hand the nutritional deprivation of women in society. Outsiders notice a sense of self-confidence, vigour, an ease in occupying powerful positions in Indian women, and a sense of resilience and androgyny in men. Yet, as Lakshmi Lal shows, this is not the complete picture.[6] 'This breast of yours, unfailing, refreshing, bearing treasures, giving of largesse by which all that is choicest in the world is nourished, you may nourish, O Saraswati.... You have given birth to a hero and thereby attain heroic stature.' Thus ends an ancient household rite, described in great detail in the *Brihadaranyaka Upanishad*, for obtaining a male child. It is in fact the only point in the whole proceedings, starting with the actual act of intercourse and ending with the placing of the son in her lap, at which the woman receives a measure of affectionate attention. She is simultaneously deified too, in the true Hindu manner. She is, to use a modern managerial euphemism, 'kicked upstairs'.

Then there was the Indian freedom struggle which saw the vivid participation of Indian women, without the usual backsliding noticed in other experiences of struggle. That Gandhi moulded the modes of that struggle had its own ripple effects.

The study under discussion attempts to pull together these threads as explanatory variables.[7] After the first round of scanning the data, especially the linkages between sex ratios, work participation and literacy rates, Nirmala Banerjee, the researcher, suggests:

> Women's status is dependent on a complexity of socio-cultural factors most of which interact significantly with each other. It is essential to understand these interactions between the forces and to allow for them in designing policy measures for improving women's status.
>
> The pattern of regionwise variations in levels of women's status can be described as cultural in the sense it is expressed in terms of cultural practices and taboos. However, it is not random, but is based on economic forces which in turn were determined by ecological factors. This cultural pattern of Indian women's status falls into five broad categories corresponding to five broad basic types of economic situations or ecosystems in the country.[8]

Banerjee finds that once the country is divided into these various economic types, important indicators of change have remained 'constant'. In other words, the women's movement and the development interventions put together have not had any impact on the situation of women. What a fact to face!

Banerjee calls these types 'traditional cultural categories'. She hopes to unlock some of these doors, through workshops on cross-cultural marriages, oral histories of women stratified across class and language, and finally forge the links. One waits with bated breath to see where that leads us in reaching the roots of our power and our subordination—the quest for theory.

A NETWORK TO GAIN MACRO
PERSPECTIVES ON DEVELOPMENT

The DAWN network initiated the process of analysing poor women's experience of development in the Third World in the context of the macro situations in these regions, like the food crisis in Africa, debt in Latin America, poverty and hunger in Asia.[9] Such analysis revealed both the impoverishing nature of 'development', but also the validity of the several strategies pursued by poor women. Empowerment of poor women, it seemed, did not need intervention; rather, they needed to be left alone, not to be crowded in but offered territory into which they could step. Activism was to listen to them; research was to learn and reveal; development was to facilitate their steps.

The roots of this devastating development—which emptied oceans of fish, tribal lands of forest, deprived women of wages and food, and created the enslavement of the South by the North—seemed to lie not merely in the evil intentions of the North, but also in the existing theories and practices of development in the South—the language and legacy of the North. Observing the various forms of social, economic and political processes in our countries, we can identify some modes of production which are not only the predominant modes, but whose strengthening could in fact provide a new form of organisation of production and exchange, giving us certain positive values.

For example, self-employment is perceived as a less worthy form of employment than wage employment, by different ideologies, administrations, as well as labour itself. However, it is the pre-dominant mode in our country, especially amongst the poor, and provides certain inbuilt securities if properly nurtured. However, the sense of inferiority and guilt inherited as part of the colonial legacy compels us to abandon this mode of employment when in fact we should enjoy it. Dispersed production entails not only decentrali-sation of power, not only less human congestion perhaps, but also more control over lifestyles. It is a point of intense debate whether home-based work, given the exploitative mechanisms which exist, is not a further intensification of female household subordination. Yet experiences from Africa as well as India show that within dispersed work patterns, alternative arrangements are possible so as to reverse the trend from exploitation to empowerment. Such an inversion of the pyramid can in fact be the thin end of revolutionary processes. Accepting existing structures and trying to debate within them seems old-fashioned.

'Formalisation' of every institution and process is another concept and value which needs reconsideration. An organisation must be registered, title to land must be clarified, and so on. Why? Formality makes for rigidity; often it overpowers democracy, openness, and closes options. Resilience may be necessary to avoid not only conflict but aggrandisement. Labour that is not employed in a factory for a wage is called 'informal'—when in fact it is as procedurally bound as wage/factory labour. There are so many such legacies that need reordering to make our economic and social cultures look interesting, useful and potentially rich—which indeed they are. Gandhi was one leader who plucked at these strings.

It is my view that the modes of not only economic but also social and political exchange that are derived from our own histories and cultures have been neglected and overpowered in the theory building that we have inherited from the North. However, the poor, and amongst them especially women, have in fact survived in spite of the 'attacks' of development because they are still operating in those indigenous modes.

Often, these old modes are branded as 'feudal' or 'primitive'; these very descriptors are suggestive of unwanted characteristics. Yet there is an outcry of alarm and concern when, because of these lenses, various culturally homogeneous groups and processes such as the tribal way of life or island societies get destroyed. It is this inconsistency that has to be looked at again. 'Old' structures which have built-in unequal and oppressive elements can perhaps be cleansed of their oppressiveness without necessarily destroying that core in those structures or processes which has provided the self-generating inner power of these societies over time. These deep links between history, society, culture and economy have been ignored by the globally popular development strategies, including 'women and development' strategies.

The usual argument is that to improve the level of living we need growth, and growth creates structural imbalance whether in socialist or capitalist countries. In these processes some sacrifices are made. It is presumed, in socialist countries, that the sacrifice is made by property owners, and in capitalist countries by the working class.

In the alternative development programme, what is challenged is the very process as well as the goals. Most revolutions talk of structural change, usually based on production and its ownership and organisation as linked to class, and are limited to transforming power relations. The alternative path also requires structural change, but in values, concepts and implementing processes. Therefore, there is a need both to build theory as well as to practise the theory through individual evolution as well as collective action.

A BOOK

An inter-religious feminist conference titled 'Women, Religion and Social Change' was organised in 1983 at Harvard University. Later brought out as a book, *Speaking of Faith*, by the Indian feminist publishing house Kali,[10] it adopts the view that while discrimination against women exists in all faiths, since women are the primary practitioners, there must be a strengthening and bonding aspect in religion, along with all the other baggage of discrimination and bigotry. What is it? Feminist theory for an Indian, a Hindu or Muslim, may have roots in religion and may build on that relationship.

While Christology and feminism have begun to engage each other, this has not happened to the same extent with non-Christian religions. It needs to, and is beginning to happen. Fatima Mernissi has published a book called *Women in Moslem Paradise*.[11] A collection of such profiles of women in Hindu, Buddhist, Christian and other religious traditions can reveal what paradises are not and also what they can be.

In an essay in *Speaking of Faith*, I showed that religion can empower women given the context and the method.[12] I illustrated this with Gandhi's practice of meeting tradition halfway, so that those who had been caught in its web could step out. In my article, I referred to the use of *bhajans* (hymns) and *sarva dharma* (referring to all religions) prayers to reveal both the divisive and the educating roles of religion. I showed how following an ethic of self-effacement could be a step to annihilating differences of all kinds—gender, class, caste, religion, 'me' and 'thou'. Becoming the other in a conflict situation was part of an etiquette derived from religion. Gandhi's form of secularism (sarva dharma) was not agnosticism, but acceptance that there were many paths to the Divine. I went on to suggest that women were the best vehicles for providing this leadership in religious practice, thus leavening, healing and sublimating conflict-ridden societies.

But today these views are met with doubt. Women's condition of oppression perhaps leads them to extremes rather than moderation. I don't know. What I know is that the women's movement cannot be a bystander to these pre-existing strands in India. It will have to discover and stimulate religious sentiments of tolerance and forgiveness. We are distracted because we can see women only as victims of religious wars. We must see them as antagonists of that war. We must open our eyes and walk with these religions. Since women are the main vehicles of social change, and the main practitioners of religion, in the study of women, religious consciousness has to be included.

Women have been the main practitioners in every religion. Religion has often been their only support—a deity in place of the mother left behind; a court of appeal since there is so much domestic oppression; a source of courage when fear dominates. The majority of women of all classes would be orphaned without religion. But if they are the principal practitioners, could they provide an alternative culture of religiosity? How do we get this new culture of religion to become all-pervasive and wipe out the old oppressions? We also need to look at the roles of women during religious wars: whether they stoked the fire or doused it. One hears of both types of behaviour.

The dialogue across faiths expressed discontent with concepts like patriarchy and sexuality. It paused at motherhood and fertility—power politics in social dynamics. Another fountainhead for theory building.

A MAN: GANDHI

While earlier, the linkages between Gandhi and Indian women were not seen positively except by those who worked with him, both his personal as well as his political behaviour are now being examined from the feminist perspective. Gandhi has emerged almost unscathed from this scrutiny, as his programme not only for women but for the society and economy of India is life-saving and freedom-giving.

The quest for the feminist ethic lands me in Gandhian territory every time, from wherever I stand—development, religion or politics. To me, feminist theory for India could be built around Gandhian thought, and every experience I have listed above leads me to the same view. In Bombay, where the participants asked how to operate a model where individuals did not misuse informal or collective groups for self-empowerment, I would say it is the individual's ethic. In analyses of the root causes of inequities, insensitive development, I would remember Gandhi's views on decentralised production and exchange, restraint in consumption, and so on. Gandhi always seems relevant and useful.

All ideological training—communist, Christian, Islamic, Hindu—demands self-development. But this is ridiculed by the modern person and especially feminists, as they feel it only legitimises what they have been enduring, namely, suffering. Why see it that way? If women are strong as individuals, it is because of these experiences. They already engage in personal development processes as it has been their strategy for dealing with their societal situation. I suggest, let us maintain that strength—but autonomously. Let us change the bathwater, and keep the baby.

If feminist theory emphasises the individual's self-discipline, her self-conscious evolution, it only carries on what women are already doing as responsible individuals. Though this needs thinking through—and I hope to be doing that through the processes of both reading and dialogue—I would like to suggest that there is a key here to shifting feminist analysis from female/gender subordination which leads us to patriarchy, to just human or personal subordination, another domain of discourse. Subordination of one individual by another, whether based on race, religion or gender, could be seen as limited awareness in the oppressor of the oppressed. It reveals his ignorance, blindness, lack of imagination, lack of personal evolution into 'higher', more sublime levels of consciousness.

Gandhi was working on this question when he practised the idea of taking on the consciousness of the identity of the other—the 'adversary', or the person who is subordinated or victimised. Simply stated, this involves putting yourself in the other person's shoes, seeing it from the other side—the worm's-eye view. Gandhi's method of handling conflict non-violently was based on his attempts to efface the reason for the conflict at its root, namely, separate identities or separate consciousness.

Thus he wore clothes like the rural poor, lived in the houses of the 'untouchables', travelled in the mode of the poor on foot (*padayatra*) and, when necessary, by economy (third-class) rail compartments. This has been mocked at as a joke, because when VIPs try to do this, it causes more fuss than demonstration. But I am here looking at: (*a*) the mind and hope behind the effort; and (*b*) the fact that Gandhi tried this even before becoming a 'VIP' because of the mass appeal of his attempts, so there is a legitimacy in these ideas.

There is an emphasis here on the mental, that is, the attitude, the frame of mind. Both the subordinated and the subordinator are in a mental state of incomprehension. When the subordinator gets into the shoes of the subordinated, he understands, he can be enlightened to give up his oppressive acts. The subordinated is afraid, hostile. By coming close to the subordinator, he or she loses fear, opens the doors of communication.

To believe in the validity of such attempts requires faith in the human being. For Gandhi who saw God in every person, this was no problem. But to us, it may seem like hocus pocus. However, Ramchandra Gandhi, the philosopher, has elaborated in more scientific and erudite terms this concept of merging one's consciousness into another's and the validity of this in analysing conflict.[13]

For religions, cultures, societies and economies like India—highly unequal, facing onslaughts from the inside as well as the outside— where separating gender subordination from the numerous other forces operating both ways, both attacking and resisting—to trace the source of conflict in the mind, in the consciousness, rather than in the body seems to offer relevance, appropriateness. I think this has to be further probed by us using other disciplines, including psychology, theology and so on.

The source of the angry, uncontrolled competitiveness that we see expressed in monopolistic assertions, in movements like 'sons of the soil', linguistic chauvinism or religious-territorial assertions, it is often suggested, is the style of development and its thrust on physical output, surplus generation, export, consumerism. Consumerism planted in a society brought up on deprivation and on sharing and mired in all kinds of inequality is like a holocaust. Gandhi foresaw the potential violence of consumerism and concentrated on using consumption as the lever for guiding the economy. Women have been conscious of the role of consumption, and there have been many efforts at dampening consumerism, another vital and major preoccupation of the Indian feminist.

REVIEW

I had an opportunity to quickly glance through the two other papers that are being presented on the panel, namely, 'Deconstructing Patriarchy' by Deniz Kandiyoti and 'The Gendered Nature of Social Structure and Culture' by Joan Acker and Karen Ericksen Paige.[14] I was delighted to find that both papers are asking for the 'deschooling' of certain thought processes. Acker and Paige emphasise the need to open up sociological investigation across disciplines to understand the influence of culture on the status of American women. They ask for a blending of the humanities with the social sciences. Kandiyoti wants to look at patriarchal bargaining as it operates in different cultures and to reassemble from empirical knowledge a more positive, non-residual concept of patriarchy.[15]

In many ways, what feminists in the Third World are doing is to dismantle not only the concept given to them by Western feminists, but also the understanding of social and economic processes that is being given to them by what is called the 'dominant discourse', the classical capitalist or socialist framework. They also are in the process of reconstructing. Thus, these echoes are in some way in harmony.

Social science concepts would need a new language, which by itself would generate new values for certain phenomena. For example, substitute the words on the right for the words on the left and we begin to see a change in the perception of what is and what ought to be:

For current	Read new
subsistence	self-reliance
seclusion	female socialisation
decentralisation	local organisation
home-based work	household enterprise
home	workplace

It is amazing how pervasive are the theoretical concepts from which almost all development strategies are derived. We in the developing world, who make so many attempts to unite—for example, as the Group of 77, NAM, programmes of South–South co-operation, as 'poor countries', 'former colonies'—to resist the exploitation and the enslavement which have become part of the global political economy, however, derive even our strategies for change from the countries that we are resisting or that are dominating us.

This problem or phenomenon is most crisply stated by Partha Chatterjee in *Nationalist Thought and the Colonial World*. 'Orientalism *created* the Oriental,' he says, quoting Edward Said's description of Orientalism as 'an enormously systematic discipline by which European culture was able to manage—and even produce—the Orient politically, sociologically, militarily, ideologically, scientifically, and imaginatively during the post-Enlightenment period.... In every case, there is a paradigm derived from the understanding of European history in the post-Enlightenment period.'[16] In other words, whichever political theory we in the developing countries adopt—capitalism or socialism—we cannot move towards independence because we pursue the strategies and structures of our masters, and therefore necessarily have to depend or link ourselves to them.

Why is this so? Because we have neglected to derive a positive normative theory which legitimises as well as gives value to our own modes of production, exchange, our own modes of social organisation and stratification—our own modes of political participation. How well this matches a paragraph from Kumari Jayawardena's book *Feminism and Nationalism in the Third World*:

> It has variously been alleged [in the Third World] by traditionalists, political conservatives and even certain leftists, that feminism is a product of 'decadent' Western capitalism; that it is based on a foreign culture of no relevance to women in the Third World; that it is the ideology of women of the local bourgeoisie; and that it alienates or diverts women, from their culture, religion and family responsibilities on the one hand, and from the revolutionary struggles for national liberation and socialism on the other. In the West, too, there is a Eurocentric view that the movement for women's liberation is not indigenous to Asia or Africa, but has been purely a West European and North American phenomenon, and that where movements for women's emancipation or feminist struggles have arisen in the Third World, they have been merely imitative of Western models.[17]

The field in India is fertile for building an original feminist theory, and, as I see it, its goal and its process would be based on building a well-grounded solidarity.

As an Indian woman, I feel great sadness these days that our country, which withstood so many onslaughts of every kind in the past, is violently agitated right now. It seems to be in a trauma which could lead to the breakdown of many institutions and behaviours that have survived so many shocks. I firmly believe that only women can control and deflect this agitated nation into healing, constructive paths. To do that, we need to bind together with a common perspective on solid moral foundations. The source materials I have used for this presentation give me hope that we will.

APPENDIX: DIALOGUES WITH FEMINISTS FROM THE NORTH

A North/South conversation, Athens, June 1986:[18]

'But why do you women in the so called Third World separate your-selves? We are struggling against the same system of patriarchy and against the same dominant discourse,' said a Dutch feminist to me.

'But', I said, 'we are struggling against two dominant discourses—the one you are struggling against and the one you are generating. They are strong, powerful, highly disseminated discourses with which you flood us. We need to consolidate, know ourselves before we join you.'

'What is your stand?' she asked.

'We don't know. We know it is not only the "male" nor is it "impe-rialism, capitalism, Zionism". It is something else. We will find out by dealing with it,' I said.

I am giving below some quotations, denoting those with which I feel identity and those with which I do not, as illustrations of distance and nearness.[19]

Examples of Distance

- 'The focus of feminist consciousness is the troubled response to the male and the low perception of self.'
- 'Feminism has unmasked maleness as a form of power that is both omnipotent and nonexistent, an unreal thing with very real consequences.'[20]
- 'And in all this, do we forget that we have swallowed the old paradigms, been raised in the same woman-hating culture? We ourselves have learned to associate women with nature, dark skin with dangerous knowledge. In a part of us, we are afraid of the knowledge that we have inherited from masculine societies. We fear female power, in ourselves and in others. And we fear separation.

We do not like another woman to think differently than we do. We confuse ourselves and our own integrity with that of other women, whom we confuse with our mothers, whom we confuse with nature. That which in society has created conditions which imprison us also determines the shape of the dialogue we have between us, the shape of our efforts toward liberation. Just as society has separated the idea of "woman" from the idea of "knowledge", we cease to be able to accept our own thoughts, feelings, and sensations as a source of authority. We too, long for an ideology which will erase our own experience.'

Examples of Nearness

- 'What I know from the political theory of liberation is that where an old paradigm exists, a new paradigm can come into being.'
- 'I believe that we are shaped by circumstance and that we shape the circumstances around us. In my own mind I experience the same dualism which haunts civilisation; between psychological thinking and political thinking. Yet, I cannot give up either vision, because both to me are equally true and experienced as such every day, every moment.'
- 'Feminism stands in relation to Marxism as Marxism does to classical political economy: its final conclusion and ultimate critique. Compared with Marxism, the place of thought and things in method and reality are reversed in a seizure of power that penetrates subject with object and theory with practice. In a dual motion, feminism turns Marxisms inside out and on its head.'[21]

NOTES

1 National Conference on 'Perspectives for the Autonomous Women's Movements in India', Forum against Oppression of Women, Bombay, 23–26 December 1985, *A Report* (Bombay: Forum against Oppression of Women, 1985).
2 Ibid.
3 Ibid.

4　Kumari Jayawardena, *The Rise of the Labor Movement in Ceylon* (North Carolina: Duke University Press, 1972).

5　Government of India, *Towards Equality: Report of the Committee on Status of Women in India* (New Delhi: Department of Social Welfare, Ministry of Education and Social Welfare, 1974).

6　Lakshmi Lal, 'You Have Given Birth to a Hero', *Times of India*, 25 May 1986.

7　Nirmala Banerjee, *A Case Study Reviewing Indian Women's Experience of Development in a Historical Perspective—Using Demographic, Economic, Cultural and Political Variables* (Calcutta: Centre for the Study of Social Sciences, 1986).

8　Ibid.

9　See Sen and Grown, *Development, Crises and Alternative Visions*.

10　Diana Eck and Devaki Jain, *Speaking of Faith: Cross-Cultural Perspectives on Women, Religion and Social Change* (New Delhi: Kali for Women, 1986).

11　Fatima Mernissi, *Women in Moslem Paradise* (New Delhi: Kali for Women, 1986).

12　Devaki Jain, 'Gandhian Contributions towards a Feminist Ethic', in Eck and Jain, *Speaking of Faith*, pp. 255–70.

13　See Ramchandra Gandhi, *I Am Thou: Meditations on the Truth of India* (Pune: Indian Philosophical Quarterly Publications, 1984).

14　Joan Acker and Karen Ericksen Paige, 'The Gendered Nature of Social Structure and Culture', paper presented at the International Sociological Congress, New Delhi, 1986.

15　Deniz Kandiyoti, 'Bargaining with Patriarchy', *Gender and Society*, vol. 2, no. 3 (1988), pp. 274–90.

16　Edward Said, quoted in Partha Chatterjee, *Nationalist Thought and the Colonial World: A Derivative Discourse?* (Tokyo: Zed Books, 1986).

17　Kumari Jayawardena, *Feminism and Nationalism in the Third World in the 19th and Early 20th Centuries*, History of the Women's Movement Lecture Series, part II (The Hague: Institute of Social Studies, 1982).

18　Devaki Jain, 'Alternative Development for Women: Five Page Summary', Women's Studies Summer Program, Mediterranean Women's Studies Institute (KEGME), Athens, 1986.

19　Extracted from Devaki Jain, 'Dialogues with Feminists from the North: A Conversation', mimeo, Athens, June 1985.

20　Catharine A. MacKinnon, 'Feminism, Marxism, Method, and the State: An Agenda for Theory', in Nannerl O. Keohane, Michelle Z. Rosaldo and Barbara C. Gelpi (eds), *Feminist Theory: A Critique of Ideology* (Chicago: University of Chicago Press, 1981).

21　Ibid.

CHAPTER 3

The Leadership Gap
A Challenge to Feminists

As president of the Indian Association for Women's Studies, I was obliged to address a conference which took place in Mysore in 1993. The members of the association were largely scholars from the women's studies departments of various universities, but there were also leaders of activist organisations who had engineered ground-level change. By the time of this conference, the association had been functioning for almost 11 years.

I used this opportunity to share what has been a refrain for most of my life, that the women's movement, whether in the form of women's studies or activism or working through the state, needs to redesign theories and practices across the board, drawing from experience based on study or ground-level change. We seemed to be always acting, not building theory, ideas which could change the very road on which we were travelling. I referred to the extraordinary brilliance of women on the ground in collectively addressing their challenges and overcoming their difficulties with innovative ideas of struggle. I appealed to the scholars to learn from these collective efforts and the ideas behind them, and to recreate these ideas in development design.

It is my hope that this conference will make a breakthrough, remove some of the roadblocks that hold us back from providing leadership in society and state, not only in India but across the whole world. Or to put it in another way, I hope it will enable our creativity to play its role in global governance. I suggest:

1. that 'theory'—a set of analytically useful constructs—is a necessary condition for solidarity, for effective practice, and for legitimising practice.
2. that there is enough gender-differentiated evidence across all disciplines, especially relating to practice or methods, to justify the evolution of theory, of intellectual efforts, of exercises systematising

the knowledge that we have gained from our work and our feminist discourse.

3. that while there is, however heterogeneous and fragmented, a worldwide women's movement, it has not evolved into providing what in simple terms can be called a women's opinion on national or global issues, policies and ideas.[1] The women's movement does not have political clout, which sometimes leads us to the extreme of saying that there is no women's movement, that there is no justification or legitimacy for a women-based formation.

I would argue that there is an urgent need to search for an ideological, theoretical perspective for the movement. Put conversely, the missing link is the ideology/theory that will bind the movement. This ideology has to move away from current political ideologies and develop from women's experience of politics in the broadest sense, namely, within families, the society and the economy. I would go further. This ideology is feminism; we need not shy away from the word. By shying away from the term we continue to be fragmented, even suspicious of each other.

I would also suggest that there is a dangerous vacuum in ideological leadership in the world today, and argue that this lack of a framework is partially responsible for the unsettled and chaotic state of our nation and the world.

THEORY AND PRACTICE: A FEMINIST VIEWPOINT

From its inception, IAWS has been an organisation for scholars and activists. It has denied the categorisation of ourselves into these two conventional groups.[2] In some ways, IAWS has redefined the scholar as an activist and the activist as an intellectual. 'We (the women of the Sanghas) want time to think.'[3]

Angelique Savane of the Association of African Women for Research and Development (AAWORD), speaking to Aruna Roy at the first meeting of DAWN in 1984, argued that scholars in the women's movement, being the voices, the reflectors of action, are activists. Action, she said, had taught her what she knew. She pleaded with Aruna that it was unwise and unnecessary for activists to alienate themselves and their work, or to alienate those who were not working at the grass-roots level—the so-called desk workers—from practice, by drawing attention to these distinctions or making much of these distinctions of location and the form of work. It could be suggestive of inverted snobbery, and women's solidarity needs to supersede these false, dividing hierarchies, she argued. Feminism? Could this be a characteristic of feminism? Could this rejection of dichotomies be feminist ideology?

The women's studies movement can establish that Practice is the school for Theory. And Theory is an instrument for the Practitioner, the activist. The characteristics of the women's movement, of IAWS, of this gathering, reveal this better than any other formation. Experiences of many ground-level organisations of women have given the particular flavour to IAWS of being a network, an instrument for empowerment of a broad-based kind, a mutually reinforcing process, a school of learning.

What is missing is the construct of solidarity. Feminism? Our journeys as academics and grassroots workers have been deeply intertwined with learning, complementing each other's capabilities, differing politically and evolving out of the differences. We have found an identity through our similar but different routes to working for and with poor women workers. We have come to this partly through the negative route, namely, discovering that the 'enemy' was the same, what can be called the common areas of hurt and hostility. Whether it was a mass-based organisation or a development research and design centre, the experience of the outside was the same, and the internal problems of growth and harmony were the same.

We need to build on such analysis, such reality, to articulate this 'finding' with greater self-confidence and solidarity in forums outside ourselves. I would like to suggest that we make this another element or construction of feminism.

CONVERGENCE OF CONCERN: SOME ILLUSTRATIONS

In the many national and international forums in which I have participated, particularly in the last two to three years, I have found this sense of a common concern and a common focus. I know this must sound like wishful thinking if not naiveté, but let me provide the evidence and then we can see whether I am fantasising.

Evidence I

The ICSSR held a meeting at Trivandrum, 16–29 April 1989. It was a kind of review, a stocktaking of women's studies, under different subject categories. Susheela Bhan had organised it, and I remember the excitement in the room when Neera Behn, Kamala Ganesan and I found that we were all leading up to the same three suggestions from our varied experiences, whether of subject matter, place of work, age or ideology. Each of us felt that our review revealed the following:

1. That the theory, the intellectual heritage to which we belonged, be it economics, sociology or politics, or other concerns, was inadequate to explain, to 'model' what our empirical work revealed. Definitions were inappropriate; behavioural theorems, or what can be called the reasoning, the logic, were incorrect, and the predictive and policy interpretations were therefore incorrect as well as being inappropriate.
2. That we need to work on reconstructing these intellectual paradigms, brick by brick, so that we can understand the phenomena we observe in generalisable frames, seek legitimacy for these frames and roll back some of the classical reference works.
3. That we need to plumb the depths of our own disciplines with greater vigour before coming to interdisciplinary discourse. Recognising the interdependence, we still felt that for success in the battle against inherited wisdom, intradisciplinary work was as critical as interdisciplinary work.

The response to all this was the common platform. We believed that all was not well with the male empire of wisdom. Only through mutually supporting efforts, only through superseding or suppressing our tendency to pick on each other's analytical frames, only through avoiding labelling, denouncing or alienating each other, could we build over this experience a house, with windows open, which would bring women's wisdom, differentiated and unique, into the arena of influence that was evading it.[4]

Evidence II

Maithreyi Krishnaraj, whose absence from this conference is a real deprivation, has written more than once on the need for consolidation, even more on the value of consolidation. She recognised the potential boundary-shaking tremors contained in the broad canvas of thought and action that makes up our community.

> When we do attempt curriculum reform, I find that we have not faced squarely a major dilemma, namely the theoretical structures of the disciplines themselves and their inhospitability to radical departures.
>
> Women's studies can add facts and insights to the discipline but their marginalisation has something to do with the fact that empirical work and critical concepts will be an appendix to the main disciplines unless we simultaneously mount discipline critiques. Such critiques have been mounted in the West and several books have come out, but in India, we are just beginning this exercise.
>
> Much of the research and scholarly material that is available today are studies of impact of development and fit an interdisciplinary course than within particular disciplines.
>
> What I feel is the need for both types of endeavours, an interdisciplinary, integrated course as well as inputs into disciplines. As for the latter, I feel we need to do more work on consolidating the research output, assess it, re-evaluate it, identify and clarify both implicit and explicit frameworks used before we can incorporate this mass of information meaningfully into an existing system. Here is the biggest task awaiting us.[5]

Evidence III

At the global summit in Dublin in 1992, two feminist heads of state, President Mary Robinson of Ireland and President Vigdís Finnbogadóttir of Iceland, spoke from the same perspective as the rest of the conference participants (people like you and me) on the need for identifying feminist methods, whether in political or economic leadership.[6] They posed questions that were self-critical, asking in what way their presence in such positions of political importance was making a difference either to their societies or to societies in the rest of the world. While they in their personal behaviour contained the seeds of that difference, it seemed unclear what precise difference they were making, unless it was simply the fact of their own presence.

The question arose in our minds: are there special characteristics that make up women's behaviour and that get reflected when women lead? Some suggested characteristics of women's leadership emerged: non-hierarchical, responsive, mediating, pro-equity and so forth. But unless we give this bundle of qualities legitimacy by giving it the label of, let us say, feminist leadership, as different from other forms of leadership, we cannot preserve or expand it or argue in favour of having women in leadership roles. Thus, emphasis was laid on definition, agreement on the boundaries, articulation of this identity or difference, as necessary conditions before launching on advocacy for bringing women into leadership. In other words, without that basic bundle, or theory, or conceptualisation or identification, merely asking for more women in leadership positions was not either valuable or efficient, or even moral.[7]

Characterising women's behaviour in this way also carries with it the danger of romanticising, recalling the anti-suffragists in the USA in the 19th century who thought of women as closer to nature than men and possessed of a kind of superior morality. Women were identified with nurture as against the brutality of the market economy. They were identified with the home, seen as a space of refuge and civilisation. If women were to enter the public sphere by exercising their voting rights, men feared that civilisation would collapse.

I have taken some time with this particular issue because I think it makes a strong case for two things: brainstorming on the qualities that give identity; and the need for agreement.

Evidence IV

A young woman Christian pastor from Korea, Chung Hyun Kyung, spoke in Bangalore. She characterised religions in Asia—Buddhism, Hinduism, Islam and so many others—and linked her characterisation to an Asian mode of worship derived from an Asian mode of life, Asian culture.[8] She was trying to find a way to provide a Third World affirmative stance, but through the medium of religion and culture and regional solidarity. In her search for building a strong political base in these fragile countries overrun by political, religious, economic and military pressures from the North, for finding a way to help the people to derive strength from their own histories and resist this domination, she found this thread of faith from which she had woven a carpet.

The carpet seemed extremely relevant and legitimate. Because religious faith is such a vital part of human expression and emotion, especially in the old civilisations, Chung's carpet seemed in some sense even more legitimate than the economic or political carpets that we try to put on the floor. Therefore, instead of ignoring it, she addressed herself to it, and in her experience and her study found much to build on.

Srilatha Batliwala has referred to this same point, that in our preoccupation with economic and political empowerment, we have forgotten the spiritual needs of people, especially women.[9]

Evidence V

One can give dozens, if not hundreds, of examples of other gatherings where women have resolved to build new bases of solidarity, of resistance to the dominant modes, and for the questioning of categories. I think, for example, of a meeting of the Mahila Samakhya Sangha in Bijapur (in 1991), and of a meeting of SEWA in Ahmedabad (1993), of a meeting in Vienna on 'Women in Extreme Poverty' organised by the Division for Advancement of Women (1992). I remember a DAWN meeting in Fiji (1992), one in New Delhi convened by the National Commission on Women on the new economic policy (January 1992) and one on the 'Politics of Gender' in New Delhi (February 1993). Wherever we gather, what seems to be uppermost in our minds is the need to think together and to assert our special position, whether we call it a perspective, a method or a priority. At the same time, we are hesitant because we neither have a name for it, nor do we have a common viewpoint.

Evidence VI

In the book world, the list of titles that suggest the same need or quest can be endless. I shall refer only to three illustrations since I reviewed them and know them well. Two were co-edited by Leela Dube: they are *Visibility and Power: Essays on Women in Society and Development*, and *Structure and Strategies: Women, Work and Family*; Dube also wrote the preface to a third volume, *Finding the Household*, edited by K. Saradamoni.[10] All these works come to the same analysis and vision. They try to remove the mist from the male lenses that have been peering into the world and society within it.

Women know the 'business of living',[11] and they can teach this to the rest of society. Women can save and re-circulate cash/credit.[12] They can self-examine and critique their context. But alas, the world is not listening. This great flood of useful knowledge, sensitively and passionately created, remains private, silent and peripheral, like the domain in which, by and large, women live.

I would characterise women's scholarship as follows. The integrity of scholarship and activism around the business of living, as women do it, is such that there is a deep inhibition against rhetoric, oversimplification, skirting issues, pretending. There is also a reluctance to dominate. Hence, it is often found that women's discussions and debates do not end too easily in consensus but in open-ended agendas, in questions, giving autonomy to those involved to choose their outcome. The tendency is to remain heterogeneous, to differentiate.

CONSTRUCTING THEORY FROM PRACTICE

In recent years, we seem to have moved away from the exercise of defining feminism through analysis of the causes of subordination. Whichever route we took in that analysis, we came to patriarchy as the source of all our subordination. We thus spent much reflection on patriarchy and how to deal with it. We then went into the whole issue of family and the household.

What seems to be coming out of the discourse of the last few years is something else. It involves building theory from practice, from what can be called the phenomenon, as we observe it (and the ideas and expression of women is part of this phenomenon), and responding to it. It is the reverse process of giving activism pride of place, priority in the sequence of cause and effect. This is typical of the inclination of feminist analysis to upturn hierarchies.

The Anveshi report on the anti-arrack action by women in Andhra is an illustration of this trend. The article begins by asking: 'Can the agitation against arrack by women in several districts of Andhra Pradesh be viewed as yet another phase of women's ongoing struggles against patriarchy and its articulation in society? Or do they present features which point to the need for new perceptions of women's concerns?'[13] Taking indices from the Anveshi report, I have attempted a characterisation of 'spontaneous' collective actions by women in the form of a chart to see what patterns emerge (see the Appendix at the end of this chapter). The chart lists the struggles waged and describes the issues that generated these struggles and the methods employed.

Commentary on the Chart

In reviewing these actions, some patterns and a few characteristics of feminist capacity for collective action emerge.

1. *Issue:* It is usually a gut issue, one that directly attacks livelihood, income, the family's security.
2. *Response:* The response is derived from local idioms, both in language and in action—the use of kumkum on the elephant's trunk in Assam, of cooked rice in Andhra, and so on. Self-developed language and action generate instant solidarity.
3. *Area of action:* Both the struggle and its redressal are localised.
4. *Outcome:* Success in stopping the assault on women's livelihood and well-being has been possible where the action has been able to spread. For example, the movement against arrack in Andhra was a local redressal mechanism, a phenomenon limited to urban settings.

However, the Khirakote struggle did not lead to what could have been a review and revision of limestone quarrying in the fragile Himalayas. Nor did Chipko actually end in a forest felling ban as desired and demanded by the movement.

I also think there are some necessary conditions:

- The 'bed' on which such actions can sprout: the existence of some social homogeneity around caste, ethnicity or religion, similar to the earlier successes built around economic class.
- The presence of an 'awakening air'. I use these words since others maintain that the actions are spontaneous. I suggest that there is a pre-spontaneity, a consciousness-building fertiliser in the soil.
- The accessibility of a focal point, an external structure or organisation that facilitates the broadening, networking, understanding and building up of power.

Next, Some Questions

How to sustain these collective activities? In Manipur, the women remain vigilant guardians and continue to sustain their power. So too the women of Manek Chowk via SEWA. In Assam, that formation does not exist. The Khirakote struggle did not spread or stop the quarrying, although the women themselves have formed a local women's group with power in the local village process. Do we have a role to play as focal points offering networking and support for local actions?[14]

Should this question of how to help sustain these activities be asked at all? Or should 'maintenance' of that collective strength and spirit be left to chance, to local opportunities and impulses? It is increasingly felt that this is not a relevant role for us, nor even a viable programme; that the ground level is taking the initiative, revealing more serious solidarity and is better left alone; we can only corrupt it or co-opt it. There is also the more basic question about dominance, that it is 'a problem of humanity and no revolution has ever abolished it'.[15]

Local action, action that starts from below, suggests that local, proximate organisations, institutions for redressal, are more meaningful instruments for women to assert their 'political' choices. Does this suggest that as scholar-activists, we have a role in gaining widespread support for decentralised systems and ensuring a fair space for women's movements to come 'up' into decision making?

My reading and my instinct tell me that both backup and follow-up are necessary conditions for the outcome to be significant and for women's sacrifice and battle to be rewarding. The 'backing up' need not be in the form of a leader; like bicycle racers, these women need pick-up vans; they also need services and a network, and a public relations structure.

In other words, I come back to my old point. Analysis, understanding, consolidation of experience, identification of method, its characterisation and then its formalisation, followed by an action support agenda against the frame of macro policies, the larger context, all need to be undertaken. These are responsibilities, duties we owe to the spontaneous expressions of women's solidarity to enable their arrival in the political arena.

I recognise the difficulties of having commonly held viewpoints on any issue on the basis of gender. Because I recognise the importance of caste and class differentiation, of religion-based differentiation, of other differentiations in the world, it is easy for me to slip into the position which overwhelms our gatherings, namely our heterogeneity, and therefore the rationality of not being able to come together.

And yet we do come together. Why? Perhaps because these encounters reveal that we are, at least potentially, an important force. I speak of force not in the sense of exercising authority but in the sense of illumination, a power, a thrust.[16]

It is for this reason that I am coming to the conviction that we must give it a name, and I would unhesitatingly call it 'feminism'. Maybe we could say that feminism is a method; feminism is a set of qualities; feminism is women's experience of dealing with political, economic and social issues; feminism is built on equality, and so forth.[17] But we just have to give it a bundle of characteristics and then name it.

ECONOMIC LEADERSHIP: A SERIOUS CRISIS

Perhaps this construct is what is necessary just now. Most of the inherited wisdom, derived as it is from classical logic, classical constructions of theory and reasoning, is being threatened and in some sense has been dismantled. This is not to say that the Aristotelian virtues do not still have intrinsic value. But as fountainheads of guidance for societies, the classics have lost their legitimacy. We must develop new classics out of the history of the last 80 to 90 years. I do not propose to dwell on why we need to reconstruct theory from this century's experience; the uniqueness of the century has been written about elsewhere.[18] It has been traced to the phenomenal advances in science and technology and the phenomenal destruction of the planet. There is something alarming in seeing so much destruction and division and conflict scattered all over the earth's surface in both its natural and its human expression.

Serious contradictions exist between rhetoric and reality in global management. In the regions of the world where liberal ideology has an empirical base—Europe, the United States and the Pacific Rim—efforts to manage not only their national but their regional unions on the basis of liberal, unregulated transactions have come up against roadblocks, imposed by national as well as by sectoral and sectional interests. There is recession in the rich countries and strong differences of opinion on trade and fiscal strategies. The disabled condition of the East (that is, the old USSR and its satellites in Europe) has added to the debate about political and economic management, about what the state can promise and what it can take responsibility for.

For example, what kinds of rights are granted? And if they are granted, who ensures that those rights can in fact be availed of? If the state guarantees rights, whether it is the right to life or to information, the rights of the child or of minorities, how is access to these rights to be provided except through state machinery? The question is not so much how much market and how much state, nor even where market and where state, but by which instruments the intentions can be realised.

The reality of unemployment, and the resurgence of violence around the world especially on the basis of race, ethnicity, gender and age, have revived interest in governance; this includes the management of political economy, the relevance of national boundaries, the problems posed by interdependence and the interlocking of economies. It also includes the implications of politics for economics, especially if politics is seen as including the expression of social interests or concerns.

The idea of 'self-reliance' is gaining ground, moving from collective self-reliance to subnational self-reliance, which is expressed in ethnic assertions of priority in importance or access to national resources. Self-management, self-government, even self-employment—all these terms have been the political language of poor countries for many years, more as a form of staving off dominance by politically and economically powerful countries; now these terms have gained prominence in the North and are being expressed by ethnic and other sectional assertions to safeguard their own self-interest.

Interestingly, such a narrowing of interests clashes with, or points in the opposite direction from, the rhetoric of 'globalisation', 'liberalisation' and even 'privatisation'. Self-reliance often requires highly managed 'borders', both economic and political. 'Highly managed' tends to require strong government regulatory powers.[19]

In other words, a primary issue in the richer countries is how political institutions should play their role in keeping with the traditional role of the state as one of providing peace and security to its citizens. Here in the South, political and economic leaders are finding it rough going. We have two kinds of poverty: the old and entrenched, and the new, emerging out of interdependence and from structural adjustment programmes. Politicians and economists are hamstrung by the conditionalities: their private sector is not as free as the liberal philosophy describes; their capacity to produce competitively and to export is dependent not only on the buoyancy of the rich countries, but also on the legal and political structures of the South that inhibit inward and outward flows of technology, labour and products. They are operating in a highly regulated world market, but under injunctions based on the fantasy of a free market.

Their situation is in a sense an enlarged picture of the local domestic and subnational marketplace within poor nations. The market has its own power structure. The powerless poor must operate in a market against the powerful rich.

There is urgent need for a theory that can respond to this phenomenon by drawing from practice, from the critique of the current leadership by those actors who care for social justice, for security in civil society, and for environmental protection. This is an empty space which needs to be filled. It is my view that this can be done by women as a formation that challenges all the classical assumptions. The disarray in the world needs a political and economic reconstruction. In this area, I believe, the potential for leadership lies with us.

The process of preparation for the two UN World Conferences—on Population in Cairo in 1994 and on Women in Beijing in 1995—offers us an opportunity to outline an agreed agenda for action, a programme for reconstruction of our societies and the state. There will be so many gatherings, papers, books, ideas, recommendations. Can we extract from the process a simple minimum agenda, backed up by a theoretical/ideological base which would give it power in the mainstream?

In preparing for this meeting we, the executive committee, and the committee of coordinators have tried to generate a process which could be called 'towards consolidation'. The co-ordinators have met several times to discuss their formats and to allow intersections between sub-themes, to see where we appear at the end of discussion. I hope this will facilitate our work here.

I would like to take this opportunity to thank all of you, old and new members, for gathering here, those who voted us into the committee, the principal organiser of this Mysore conference and her colleagues, the co-ordinators, the executive committee members, the founders and nurturers of IAWS, the funders and facilitators of the association and its activities. On behalf of the executive committee and myself, I apologise for failures that you may already have noticed and those that might be coming up.

APPENDIX: INDIAN WOMEN'S COLLECTIVE ACTION CHART

Place	Nellore	Khirakote	Imphal (city)	Manek Chowk (city)	Assam	Manipur
Year	1992–93	1982	1989–90	1993	1980	1979
1. Issue	Arrack (local or country liquor)	Quarrying, traditional market	Relocating, rebuilding	Relocating vendors	Eviction from land colony	Liquor
2. Action base	Village	Village	Market	Market	Housing colony	All-state
3. Basis of social homogeneity	Dalit/Muslim	Kumaon tribe	One tribe (Maithei)	Occupation (vegetable vending)	One tribe	Maithei
4. Technique a. Turned back (through 'sit-in')	Jeeps	Donkey carriers	Police and corporation	Police, jeeps and corporation	Elephants	Men
b. 'Dramatics'	Cooked rice thrown in front of arrack sellers	Reducing width of donkey tracks, so they fall	Slept in market at night with lanterns and mosquito nets	Slept on pavements all night	Worshipping elephants to distract from their destructive role	Patrolled streets at night with lathis (sticks)
c. Slogans	No jeep to carry sick but jeep to carry arrack	Girls have no road to go to school, but donkeys have.	From women's market to outside dukandars' (shopkeepers') markets	Cars for the rich but no 'shop' selling space for poor (as the space was earmarked for a car park)		

Place	Nellore	Khirakote	Imphal (city)	Manek Chowk (city)	Assam	Manipur
5. Men's behaviour	Low profile: two-way support (no gender conflict at village level)	Low profile: supportive (no gender conflict at village level)	Nowhere in the picture	Supportive (locally)	Low profile: supportive (locally)	Men were the object of attack. Retaliation.
6. Support a. Initial impetus	Literacy primer (curriculum)	Gandhian padayatra (travel on foot) visiting houses, letting people speak up	Historical strength of women's collectives in Manipur	Trade union method/Gandhian satyagraha	Gandhi Ashram's extension to assisting rights movement	Historical strength
b. Focal point	Jana Vignana Vedika	Building confidence to think and act Lakshmi Ashram	NUPILAN	SEWA	Gandhi Ashram	NUPILAN
7. The state's controlling instrument	Auction of liquor/giving of licences	Auction of quarries/giving of licences	Urban development traffic nuisance	Urban development traffic nuisance	To develop land	Liquor shops licensed
8. Outcome	Arrack auction sales stopped in Andhra Pradesh	Quarry closed even at a loss to contractor of Rs 1 lakh (court order)	New market project abandoned. Old market to be renovated in consultation with the women.	Court order. The pavement (entitlement). Manek Chowk belongs to the women vendors.	Don't know.	Prohibition bill brought into Assam (but no follow-up)

Source: Created by the author based on her experiences at various field visits.

NOTES

1 Devaki Jain, 'Women's Opinion on National Issues: Need of the Hour', *Indian Express*, 11 January 1990.
2 Maithreyi Krishnaraj, 'Taking Stock', paper presented at 'Women's Studies and Higher Education: A Symposium', Centre for Women's Development Studies, New Delhi, 1991.
3 Srilatha Batliwala, oral presentation on Mahila Samakhya, 1991.
4 International Workshop on Women's Studies, ICSSR, Trivandrum, 16–29 April 1989.
5 Krishnaraj, 'Taking Stock'.
6 Global Forum of Women, Dublin, July 1992.
7 Devaki Jain, 'Women: New Vision of Leadership', Opening Plenary, Global Forum of Women, Dublin, 9–12 July 1992.
8 Chung Hyun Kyung, 'Theology in the Context of Religious Pluralism and the Search for a New Spirituality from an Asian Feminist Perspective', Bangalore, August 1992.
9 Srilatha Batliwala, *Empowerment of Women in South Asia: Concepts and Practices* (New Delhi, Food and Agriculture Organization, 1993).
10 Leela Dube, Eleanor Leacock and Shirley Ardener (eds), *Visibility and Power: Essays on Women in Society and Development* (New Delhi: Oxford University Press, 1989); Leela Dube and Rajni Palriwala (eds), *Structures and Strategies: Women, Work, and Family in Asia* (New Delhi: Sage, 1990); K. Saradamoni, *Finding the Household: Conceptual and Methodological Issues* (New Delhi: SAGE, 1992).
11 This was a phrase used by Leela Dube.
12 See, e.g., the work of Ponna Wignaraja on women's economic activity.
13 Anveshi, 'Reworking Gender Relations, Redefining Politics: Nellore Village Women against Arrack', *Economic and Political Weekly*, vol. 28, nos 3–4 (January 1993), pp. 87–90. Based on a report by Anveshi, Hyderabad, 1991.
14 Devaki Jain, 'The Natural Power of Women', in *Sarla Behn Smriti Granth* (New Delhi: Himalaya Seva Sangha, 1984). New Delhi.
15 Edwin Ardener, 'The Problem of Dominance', in Dube et al., *Visibility and Power*.
16 Devaki Jain, 'Power through the Looking Glass of Feminism', paper presented at the symposium on 'The Gender of Power', Leiden University, 1990.
17 See Kamla Bhasin and Nigat Said Khan, *Some Questions on Feminism and Its Relevance in South Asia* (New Delhi: Kali for Women, 1986).
18 M. A. Sreenivasan, *Of the Raj, Maharajas and Me* (New Delhi: Ravi Dayal Publications, 1991).
19 Devaki Jain, 'Women in Extreme Poverty', Expert Group Meeting, Vienna, 1992.

CHAPTER 4

Minds, Not Bodies

Expanding the Notion of Gender in Development

By 1995, women's movements and the UN had been supporting the quest of women for justice for 20 years. So the Beijing Conference in 1995 was a landmark, illustrating the consolidation of knowledge and strength by the movements. There was an air of celebration. The UN, basically the United Nations Development Programme (UNDP), the development wing of the UN, wished to present an award to two persons recognised for their leadership, one from the North and one from the South. I was the one chosen from the South. The two awardees were to address the entire congress on ideas for the next decades. I emphasised the importance of showcasing women's intelligence, shifting the focus from merely the physical to the intellectual. I argued that women's reasoning, and the ideas that emerged from their lived experience, needed to be converted into the macro frameworks of development, moving the focus from concern about women's health and other inputs to showcasing their ideas.

BRADFORD MORSE

It is a privilege for me to be associated with the Bradford Morse Memorial Lecture Series and to participate in its inauguration. The connection with Bradford Morse has a very special meaning for me as an Indian. We in India think of Bradford Morse as a partner in the struggle for justice, in the struggle for a kind of development which is enabling and not disabling.

Morse's report to the World Bank in 1992 on the social consequences of the Narmada dam provided powerful support to those engaged in a life or death struggle against the dam. If those with power would merely behave with the integrity and courage that Bradford showed when he gave his judgement on the Narmada dam—'that the project as it stood was flawed, that resettlement and rehabilitation of all those displaced by the project is not possible under prevailing circumstances, and that the environmental impacts of the project have not been properly considered or adequately addressed'[1]—that would be almost all the enabling environment that we need to generate the just development that we seek. So much depends on the moral sense of the individual, and yet we spend so little time and energy on providing the foundations for creating more such morally sound individuals.

It is also worth recalling the factors that enabled Bradford Morse to conclude that the project was flawed, which then was followed by the World Bank withdrawing support to the project and the events that followed this judgement. One of the critical elements in this process has been the existence of a mass movement called the Narmada Bachao Andolan (NBA) (Save the Narmada Struggle),[2] which started nearly nine years ago. The movement is broad-based, well-informed on technical facts, and persistent. It is part of the wider field of mass-based struggles in India which are redefining, rethinking and recasting development.[3] So the first critical element has been the NBA, representing the most immediately affected people with facts, figures and voices, for Bradford Morse and his team to talk to as one of the interested parties.

Among the most articulate and thoughtful leaders of this movement is a woman in her forties, Medha Patkar.[4] Before leaving for Beijing, I asked Medha for some recollections of Bradford Morse, as she had had many meetings with him. She said with a soft laugh, as if recalling Bradford Morse brought a touch of happiness, of affection, and I quote:

> He was a very peculiar man—he was an administrator and yet genuinely believed in consulting people, in people's participation in their development. He was very bulky, could not negotiate the slopes and footpaths which led to the villages threatened with submersion—but the villagers said 'lie down on the cot and close your eyes, when you open them you will be in our village'—and bodily carried him as on a stretcher to the villages for listening to evidence…

… which Medha said he listened to, and listened with genuine respect.[5]

And that is the second critical element in this episode of Bradford Morse, a classic example of a powerful official, international figure, a former administrator, being 'peculiar' enough to respect people. Medha used the word 'peculiar' because she found it an impossibility that an administrator could believe in people's views and judgements.

Do we see any elements here to be incorporated into our various indices and necessary conditions for a just development? Yes. On the one hand, the existence of a strong, mass-based, well-informed groundswell of resistance organisations—what I would like to call, using typical economist jargon, the 'demand side'. On the other hand, an exemplary administrator—sensitive to moral issues, respectful of people's minds—the 'supply side'.

I would like to carry this story one step further. What has happened since? The struggle of the NBA against the construction of the dam goes on, only now the World Bank is out of it. Contractors and those who need power and water away from the site are still fighting for the dam. And the andolan continues to fast, to file cases in the Supreme Court of India (the federal and highest judicial authority). That's our Indian story. But according to Medha, an arrangement exists now in the World Bank, a panel to which people affected badly by any project supported by the Bank can send petitions. That arrangement, if it is working, is a real achievement, an encroachment by 'the space of struggle' into the belly of the World Bank, an enabling measure for all the world—wow!

In this lecture, I will continue to dwell on these two themes: 'just' development as struggle; and the role of exemplars as a critical element for achieving 'just' development. I will link these themes to women's experience, women's actions.

In the last 20 years, since the first World Conference on Women was held in Mexico in 1975, there has been a flood of literature, a great leap forward in understanding, and a tangible change in the consciousness and solidarity of the worldwide women's movement. I will, however, limit myself to a few experiences of struggle and a few recent documents for illustration, analysis and proposals. I suggest:

1. that women's struggle provides the substance as well as the method of just development;

2. that to break through the hard rock of gender inequality, we need to shift our attention to gender difference from the body to the mind;
3. that women's struggles also provide the ethical underpinnings for economic reasoning;
4. that political restructuring is key to economic growth with justice;
5. that women's political leadership can provide the necessary condition for just development;
6. that it is not enough to draw attention to the abysmal gaps between men and women, nor to show the links between social and economic development, or the link between women's empowerment and 'effective' change;
7. that it is not enough to add on women's empowerment, or to build in gender equity through reducing the gap; it is necessary to break down the central structures of power, to replace their politics with the leadership of exemplars;
8. and that to do this we need both 'sides' (supply and demand), continuing my imagery of the play of the two critical elements I referred to in the Morse story—affirmative, unified, competent, issue-based struggle organisations on one side, and sensitive power structures on the other. This would involve:
   (i) the conscious convergence of the women's movement into a unified platform, backed by a feminist ethic on the one hand; and
   (ii) morally sensitive, democratic, transparent, accountable development agencies on the other.

WE ARE MINDS, NOT BODIES

Women who are toiling at the ground level against the heavy odds of not having quality basic amenities, and with fragile if not negative sources of income—no 'bread, water and salt', to quote Dr Nelson Mandela[6]—are constantly engaged in collective struggle in the countries of the South. Michael Jackson's new song 'Scream' could be about them. They are screaming, not crying; they have been pushed beyond crying for attention to their terrible situation. Their food and water sources, their raw material and fuel sources, their personal security, whether in relation to so-called extension services or in relation to armed and unarmed conflict, are all diminishing, and they are not finding a way out of this deterioration. Even the minds of their children are moving away from them, being filled with desire for unachievable lifestyles and with the values of violence, while the bodies of their children are forever their responsibility.

A review[7] that I undertook of women's collective action in India reveals their strength and courage (see the Appendix to chapter 3). Spontaneous, mass-based resistance struggles in India—over Chipko in the Himalayas, arrack in Andhra, vending space in Ahmedabad, drinking in Manipur, land in Assam and so forth—reveal that when there is a threat to livelihood, to social peace (or when there is household violence), women rise like a wave, mobilised through their individual experiences, as if they had hi-tech signalling systems, and resist the 'enemy' by placing their bodies on the line.

Another aspect of these collective struggles is women's choice of issues and methods. Women usually mobilise around gut issues that directly attack their livelihood, income, their families' security. The response is derived from the local idiom, both in language and in action—the use of a *lehnga* (skirt) in Rajasthan; of kumkum on elephants' trunks in Assam; of rice in Andhra; and so on. These are instances of self-developed language and action which generate instant solidarity. Both the struggle and its redressal are localised.

Putting their bodies on the line, women hurt themselves in order to reorder development. Yet women—especially women in poverty—are usually seen as bodies, as needing inputs into their bodies, including food (nutrition), health, fertility interventions, shelter, and security from physical assault/violence against their bodies like rape, female foeticide, dowry murders. This is a reality. Yet every action of women—domestic, local or global—is an expression of their mind. These actions reflect women's intellectual and cultural capability, their individuality and creativity, their sense of responsibility. Women are the subjects. But in conventional development images and analyses, not enough attention is paid to their minds. They become the objects of the development agenda.

Medha Patkar describes what she calls the difference in *mahol* (a Hindi word meaning 'atmosphere') that is tangible when women are present in a march, a satyagraha or other public action. I asked her what this 'difference' was. She said, they have a look of determination and seriousness in their eyes; they reveal in their eyes that the struggle is for life (a fight against death), they persevere even when the men want to give up. They say let us finish what we have come to do. They don't stop for the toilet or for tea. They want to get on with the action. She said the whole atmosphere gets charged with their seriousness and fearlessness, their honesty and sincerity. She used the word 'inspiring', a reflection of their minds, and, in comparison with men, an effacement of their bodies.

Women's struggles against real threats to their life and liberty have also had muted results in the larger arena. An extraordinary struggle in India, one that is perceived as successful, as influencing election platforms, as having politicised women's choice of policy, is the anti-arrack movement in Andhra Pradesh.[8] Since the first major victory for these women, namely, compelling the state government to impose total prohibition on both the manufacture and consumption of liquor, there have been other outcomes. Political parties have mobilised the 'other party', those who were earning livelihoods through brewing liquor—many of whom were women in liquor-brewing families—and have made it a conflict of interest between women. Liquor has re-entered the villages in other forms, packaged in bags and therefore not requiring a vendor's shop. Most of all, no woman from the struggle has been included in the political structures, though it was yielding to the women's demand to ban liquor that provided voter support to the party that won the elections. There are hundreds of other experiences of struggle, equally illuminating and equally problematic.

GENDER RELATIONS

Some of these 'struggles' (or offers of resistance) are in the spirit of rebellion against imposed codes of conduct/stereotyping of gender roles and the consequent operation of gender hierarchies. These rebellions have almost always been denounced, if not effaced, by patriarchal/authoritarian power structures. *Nushuz* is a concept in Arabic which labels a woman who is strong and deviant as mad, as a means of getting her out of the way.[9] In Ghana, a strong, successful woman is labelled a witch, for the same reason—to remove her from the scene.[10] We all know about Joan of Arc, who, it is said, was burned as a witch because she threatened the 'male' order. Thus, changing the hardened hierarchies in gender relations is not easy, even though women have struggled against it from time immemorial, and across histories and cultures.[11]

However, there have been examples of successful collective rebellion by women against gender codes and hierarchies. An article by Marjorie Topley describes an interesting case from 18th-century China, that of the Golden Orchid Association:

> For years thousands of women silk-workers vowed never to wed. They swore friendships to each other and lived in pairs or groups in 'vegetarian' halls or monasteries devoted to the cult of the goddess Guan Yin. These women liked to be free to move about, detested to 'become the slave of a man' or a 'human machine of propagation', and abhorred the loneliness of marriage and its lack of economic independence. Life in the associations offered the members the possibility of a career in religious affairs and political status not open to married women. Their resistance was collective, involved the construction of a female counter-culture—an act of rebellion.[12]

What has been the response to these signals or messages from women's struggles and rebellions? Feminists have been struggling with these rigid imageries of strong or bold women as dangerous, as needing to be eliminated. Saskia Wieringa, in her recent volume *Subversive Women*, says:

> Women's acts of resistance, of self-affirmation, as social actors in their different historical and political contexts, are already in themselves subversive to existing power relations; but women have been 'subversive' also in another sense: in circumventing and denying the various, distinct and multi-layered verses in which their subjugation is inscribed and in replacing them with their own verses.[13]

In her analysis of the implications of the struggles that she reflects on, Wieringa observes that '"difference" is thus no longer an essential quality, but a location of politics.' I was happy to see both in the *Human Development Report* (*HDR*) of 1995, and in the book by Jean Drèze and Amartya Sen on social opportunities,[14] the emphasis on affirmative action—which may be regarded as part of the demand side—as a necessary element in redressing the widespread and pernicious discrimination against women, the inequality between men and women.

But I see no reference to the supply side, namely, the exemplar provided by Bradford Morse. I hope that the bold and beautiful men and women from powerful international agencies, sitting here or striding with their ever-so-long legs into our villages and cities, will note this aspect of the human index, namely the role of the individual and his/her moral sensibility. The *HDR* talks of missing women, dropping out of life in infancy because of a hostile environment with low or no value placed on their existence. What about missing ethical individuals, dropping out of our arenas of governance also because of no or low value accorded to building a decent, virtuous human being? Can the memory of Bradford Morse encourage the powerful to respect struggle as a political choice for development and not consider it a negative factor? Or, to quote Medha, can they be persuaded to believe in the consultative process? Can these individuals provide the enabling environment based on personal ethics, such as Bradford provided, for people-led development?

GANDHI'S RESPONSE

Gandhi—I mean the Mahatma—had a universal response to the denouncement of women who deviated from patriarchal fixities, the stereotyping of male/female roles and codes of behaviour. He suggested to women that they resist this male order, and refuse to marry, to have sex, refuse jewellery, and even refuse to cook. He believed that such collective resistance by women would be the only way for them to liberate themselves from the chains of gender apartheid.[15] An entire generation of women who fought with him took a pledge of celibacy just to prove this point. They were not nuns, who are also celibate, considering themselves married to God. Rather, they lived among men and with men in cohabitation, but rejected sexuality.

Not surprisingly, as Gandhi was a great believer in harmonising and equalising, he persuaded men to cook, sew, clean dishes, knit—do what are called 'women's jobs' in an attempt to alter mental perceptions of the differences between men and women. 'More often than not a woman's time is taken up, not by the performance of essential domestic duties, but in catering for the egoistic pleasures of her lord and master,' he wrote. 'To me, this domestic slavery of the kitchen too is a remnant of barbarism. It is high time that our womankind was freed from this incubus.'[16]

Some of these ideas may seem extremist and old-fashioned, but Gandhi was reacting to what he felt was the terrible fact of female subordination in a caste-ridden, hierarchical and diverse society. He perceived women as equal but morally different. In the ashrams or collectives that Gandhi built, roles were constantly transposed to dismantle such hierarchies. For example, everyone—men, women and children—had to do manual work as well as 'meditational' work, so that intellectuals or the educated would not look down on manual labour. Brahmins had to lift night soil to challenge the stigma of untouchability attached to the task of night soil lifting. Persons belonging to diverse religions had to recite the prayers of all religions—a Hindu would read the Quran, or a Christian would read the Hindu prayer. Thus, Gandhi sought to efface distance through muting the kind of differences that connote hierarchy.

I am fascinated by this technique as it illustrates how much these gender-related hierarchies are in the mind. It suggests to me that a critical factor in changing the relations of power between men and women is to emphasise the difference between them, not only in their biology and its consequences, but in their moral, methodological and intellectual ways. I do not suggest that these differences are physiologically fixed, but they do emerge from the difference in women's life experience.

In the indexing and ranking presented in *HDR 1995*, Scandinavia comes first from the point of view of gender equity, because Scandinavian men take an equal share in the burden of domestic chores, with paternity leave and so on. I wonder whether the mental bending, the disciplining of the mind to perceive these chores as not lowly, the removal of mind–body hierarchies, has also taken place? Or is it a mere mechanical changing of places? Only bodies not minds? I would be interested in knowing this. Can the poorer countries afford the Scandinavian system of social security? Would not Gandhi's approach of 'confusing' gender roles be both stronger and more feasible?

There is also a deeper, more pervasive hierarchy based on this mind–body categorisation. The mind of course is seen as superior to the body (*cogito ergo sum*, as Descartes famously observed). For years, activists were seen as good at doing things, and then there were the intellectually skilled who wrote or analysed, derived, theorised. Then there was also the hierarchy amongst non-governmental organisations (NGOs), including women's groups, of the North and South. We in the South were great organisers of action, and our comrades or sisters in the North would write up for us, or help us with formats and training modules, concepts, frameworks and networks. Technical assistance flowed from North to South. We were the bodies and they the minds.

From reviewing women's collective struggles, I sum up the following differences in the 'quality' of women's collective action: avoidance of conflict, pre-empting injustice, strength when it comes to the basic needs of the family, learning through doing, tentativeness, consulting, sharing, caring, undoing hierarchies and rebuilding informality. These are some aspects of a 'women's ethics' that seem to emerge out of the review of the life experience of women.

Empowerment of women, overcoming gender-based oppression, needs women to be perceived differently, by women themselves as well as by development analysis and programmes. Feminists can play a role in illuminating the special qualities and ethics of women and politicising the worldwide women's movement around these attributes. Development agencies and personnel can also play a role in reorganising their understanding. There is a need to overturn the logic of economic reasoning so as to accommodate the urgency of women's condition.

THE 'BUBBLING UP' THEORY OF GROWTH

If we take the signals emerging from women's struggles, and the analysis of poverty and inequality not only in *HDR 1995*,[17] but also the *World Development Report 1995*,[18] then it does seem clear that the engines of economic growth in operation today are inappropriate for achieving the stated objectives of economic growth. Gandhi offers an alternative that I have called 'the bubbling up theory of growth'. According to this line of reasoning, the criterion by which any political choice for economic change is made is whether it improves the condition of the poorest person. If we deal with the removal of poverty first, then the rest of the model follows.

In many countries with large populations like India, removal of poverty acts as a spur to demand, and therefore a stimulus to growth. I suggest that poverty eradication is the best engine of growth, and that by dealing with the last first, economic regeneration will bubble up, as economic prosperity has never trickled down.

My second example is an illustration from India: India's grassroots women leaders. Many of you would know that in 1993–94, India amended her Constitution to bring in elected local self-government based on multi-party competitive politics and universal franchise. The amendment introduced an element of what is called 'affirmative action', or 'positive discrimination', by 'reserving' 33.3 per cent of the places on the councils for women. India also reserved over 15 per cent of the places for Dalits—those social classes in India who have been discriminated against for centuries. India has already held elections for these local bodies at the rural level and is about to hold elections for the municipalities at the urban level. One million women are beginning to enter this arena of formal politics, traditionally occupied by men, by taking their places in local self-government bodies. Their statements suggest that they had been watching the men from 'behind the veil', as it were. Watching and knowing what such participation means—namely, power, control, negotiation, heat, dust and dirt.

Though the majority of these women are totally illiterate, and have entered the political sphere for the first time, often dragged in by men who don't want to lose their seats and therefore use the women as proxies, once they have seized power, women are beginning to exercise it. Even sceptics in the media have begun to take note of this transformation. For example, a magazine called *India Today*,[19] which we see as the Indian equivalent of *Time* magazine, has not only carried a full, illustrated piece on these women, but expresses an unqualified admiration, if not awe, for the way women are dealing with development, and, most importantly, with power, and within power, with gender relations. Every elected woman in any part of the country who has been interviewed has said that she will now redress the injustice done to her by men. It would be patronising to call this natural feminism. These women are deeply conscious of the fact that in order to redress the relationships of power, including those between men and women in their own houses, political power and participation in political spheres are critical. Men and their habits and attitudes seem to be their major concern and first arena of attack. The scent of power they are enjoying is often expressed in terms of having control over men.

There is a danger that this initial excitement may be dissipated by the pernicious and all-pervasive pressure of patriarchy and bureaucracy. These feminists can be shaped into unpaid development workers by being 'trained' to mimic the bureaucracy, or worse still, they could be shaped into men.

POLITICAL RESTRUCTURING IS KEY TO ECONOMIC GROWTH WITH EQUITY

The Indian illustration of women's political participation demonstrates more than the fact that women are aware of and ready for politics. It has implications, again for both sides—the feminist movements as well as development structures and agencies, in the fields of both theory and practice.

First, the experience reveals that women's presence in political power structures, in formal governance, does begin to knock at the historically embedded disdain and disregard for women. This point is recognised by *HDR 1995*, and is strongly carried forward as one of the points in its five-point agenda: initiating specific measures to move towards a 30 per cent threshold as the minimum share in decision-making positions to be held by women at the national level, in order to reach an ultimate target of 50 per cent. India perhaps could have had a better ranking, even first, in this index if it had included proximate, democratic political bodies.

Second, we need to recognise:

- that the government into which women are brought, say with 30 per cent reservation (as the HDR recommends), would be more 'empowering' for women if it was 'proximate', which means a system of local self-government.
- that women find proximity to government very enabling, both in terms of their style of functioning as well as their need for services, including redressal.
- that these women want to participate in political parties, regular elections, and to compete at the hustings and win. They feel that this is more empowering than 'nomination'.
- that these women bond as women, superseding party, class, caste and religious barriers, and need that identity to challenge men's disdain and oppression.
- that these women are more confident that they can transform politics than the elites or national-level politicians.
- that political decentralisation has to be matched with economic decentralisation. The new women politicians of India are handicapped by the mismatch between their political domain and the economic domain. Alternative economic institutions like co-operatives and self-help groups—all part of the worldwide contribution of women to alternative development—would need to be encouraged to 'replace' the large, untamable corporate institutions.

These findings suggest that we cannot see the issue of women's participation in decision making in a sanitised, anaemic way. Such participation has to be accompanied by many other 'items' from both the demand (feminist) and the supply (structure) side. First, we need to replace the concept of decision making with the concept of leadership. One could be part of a decision-making process and not be powerful enough to influence the decision. Leadership has a hierarchical significance. The feminist movement needs to stake its claim to leadership not only on the grounds of gender but also those of ethics. Second, feminists need to come up with at least a minimal agreement on identity, on the qualities of women, to develop it into a legitimate philosophy and disseminate it in many ways so that women politicians can strengthen their sense of feminist leadership. On the supply side, it would be necessary to reformulate propositions in development theory.

DECONSTRUCTING THE DEVELOPMENT MONOLITHS

On the supply side, as I just observed, there is a need for the monolithic institutions of development to deconstruct themselves, and, by reinterpreting their meaning, to create space for women's leadership and the ethics that such leadership embodies. The UN system depends on centralised structures, as it needs to deal with strong central governments for its accountability to be processed. In working at the national level, the UN clones itself in the national governments in the form of focal points and departments. These continue to be regarded as the necessary national machineries for women's advancement or empowerment (a recommendation based on the forward-looking strategies articulated at Nairobi, being followed up in the draft Platform for Action at this conference). However, these focal points are embedded in hierarchical, patriarchal bureaucracies, and thus are not able to generate the impulses for change that women's empowerment and gender equity require. Furthermore, they can be set up with great fanfare and visibility even in the most authoritarian and opaque political regimes.

There is a deep faultline in the process of management in the UN system. As a colleague at DAWN (a Third World women's network), Gigi Francesca from the Philippines, put it: 'The globe and Eurocentricism are the two key ideological forces in the world today.'[20] Activists and women at the grassroots whom we wish to empower are baffled, if not angry, that the UN and other international institutions set up to bring peace and justice are not overpowering these dinosaurs.

Most of the energy of women activists participating in UN meetings is used up in resistance and attack.

National governments and national spaces are the appropriate arenas for change to take place. Machineries and processes for women's empowerment need to evolve from struggle, from legal facilities, from politics. Development agencies like the UN should go beyond 'adding on' gender to learning from women and to creating spaces for women's leadership. Women are already involved in struggle and rebellion. What they need is exemplary support from all of us.

EXEMPLARS

The notion of exemplary individuals might trouble us, because social movements are seen as collective, altruistic and strategic. But I think women's experience of collectivities, except the feminist collectivity, has been painful if not oppressive. The feminist collective, however, is different because the members are feminist, with a particular ideology and an ethic. Feminism can teach us that exemplary individuals are necessary constituents of just collectives.

Today, the collective ethic is predominant. Terms like 'organisational strategy' and 'consciousness raising' really suggest the submersion of the individual. Whether we consider communes in socialist or liberal countries, or we consider such institutions as trade unions or the family elsewhere, the unit is the group, not the individual. An ethical position is asked of the group, not the individual, thus tending to erode the individual's sense of responsibility. Women, however, still assume and face responsibilities as individuals in the family. Women's traditional ethical norms are neither individualistic nor group-centred. Rather, women seem to consider the individual in the context of the group.

Gandhi had a formula for this problem, too. During his political struggles, he needed strong 'soldiers' for resistance. He argued that they had to be morally trained individuals in order to sustain the collective struggle. The collective, in his view, is the expression of its moral individuals.

To conclude, when I am asked to give a lecture that will illumi-nate the UNDP's quest for empowering women, for gender equity, I am assailed by the contradiction between this genuine interest and the reality as seen from the ground, and the implementation of that genuine interest. There are so many women's voices reverberating in my head. I wish I could bring them all here to this room. I can never forget an evening at the Kennedy Auditorium at Harvard University when my sister Achola Pala Okeyo of Kenya, delivering a memorial lecture, started her talk by just reading out about 20–30 names of African women social scientists, as if she were reading out a roll of honour. In her own subtle way, she was communicating to the very high-profile community of development specialists in the room, including Professor John Kenneth Galbraith, that there were as many women specialists in development in Africa as at Harvard. I wish I too could list the many hidden struggles so that all those brilliant women who fought them could be telling us what the women's agenda for the 21st century should be. Sometimes, though, rolls of honour are very troubling. Most awards for heroism are given posthumously. A heroic child, woman or man has to die for the cause before the world recognises their courage and wisdom. I hope we who have gathered here in Beijing won't wait that long.

NOTES

1 Bradford Morse and Thomas R. Berger, *Sardar Sarovar: Report of the Independent Review* (Ottawa: Resource Futures International, 1992).

2 Narmada Bachao Andolan, 'We Will Struggle Comrades: The Struggle of the People of Narmada Valley', July 1994. The NBA is a significant part of the wider *andolan* (struggle) in the country for rethinking development. The thousands of men and women involved in this andolan are farmers, workers, the Dalits (the socially oppressed) and the tribals who have been uprooted in the name of 'development' and 'public interest'. The Narmada Andolan is attempting not only to protest the destruction of the means of sustenance of the affected families by resolute resistance, but also to redefine development as such.

3 Ashish Kothari and Rahul N. Ram, *Environmental Impacts of the Sardar Sarovar Project* (Pune: Kalpavriksh, December 1994). The Karnataka Raithara Sangha, a farmers' organisation, has similarly been agitating successfully against mul-tinational presence in seed manufacture and trade, and especially against

patenting. The organisation is now focusing on fast food chains such as Kentucky Fried Chicken. It argues that the entry of MNCs in these areas is exploitative and detrimental to the health of both people and the planet.

4 Well known in the world of development and struggle, winner of the Right Livelihood Award and other public honours.

5 Conversation with Medha Patkar, 18 August 1995.

6 Nelson Mandela, Inaugural Speech, Cape Town, South Africa, 9 May 1994.

7 Devaki Jain, 'Leadership Gap: A Challenge to Feminists', Presidential Address, IAWS Conference, Mysore, 1993 (reproduced as chapter 3 in this volume).

8 Anveshi, 'Reworking Gender Relations, Redefining Politics'.

9 Fatima Mernissi, 'Femininity as Subversion: Reflections on the Muslim Concept of Nushuz', in Eck and Jain, *Speaking of Faith*.

10 Elizabeth Amoah, 'Women, Witches and Social Change in Ghana', in Eck and Jain, *Speaking of Faith*.

11 Feminist Review Collective, *Feminist Politics: Colonial/Postcolonial Worlds*, no. 49 (Spring 1995), pp. 1–137.

12 Marjorie Topley, 'Marriage Resistance in Rural Kwangtung', in Margery Wolf and Roxane Witke (eds), *Women in Chinese Society* (Stanford: Stanford University Press, 1975), pp. 86–88. See also Eck and Jain, *Speaking of Faith*.

13 Saskia Wieringa (ed.), *Subversive Women: Women's Movements in Africa, Asia, Latin America and the Caribbean* (New Delhi: Kali for Women, 1995).

14 UNDP, *Human Development Report 1995* (New York: Oxford University Press, 1995); Jean Drèze and Amartya Sen, *India: Economic Development and Social Opportunity* (New Delhi: Oxford University Press, 1995); see also Amartya Sen, 'Population Policy: Authoritarianism vs. Cooperation', John D. and Catherine T. MacArthur Foundation, International Lecture Series on Population Issues, New Delhi, 17 August 1995.

15 'Apartheid of Gender', *Times of India*, 21 August 1995.

16 Pushpa Joshi, *Gandhi on Women* (Ahmedabad: Navajivan Trust, and New Delhi: Centre for Women's Development Studies, 1988); Jain, 'Indian Women Today and Tomorrow'; Jain, 'Gandhian Contributions towards a Feminist Ethic'.

17 The *HDR* of 1995 echoes what women worldwide have pointed to with deep concern and anguish—the pauperisation of women, the disproportionate increase in their numbers amongst the poor. Of the 1.3 billion people living in absolute poverty, about 70 per cent are women. UNDP, *Human Development Report 1995*.

18 There are risks that workers in poorer countries will fall further behind, as lower investment and educational attainment widen disparities. Some workers, especially in Sub-Saharan Africa, could become increasingly marginalised. And those left out of the general prosperity in countries that are enjoying growth could suffer permanent losses, setting in motion intergenerational cycles of neglect. There is a substantial risk that inequality between rich and poor will grow over the coming decades, while poverty deepens. World Bank, *World*

Development Report 1995: Workers in an Integrating World (New York: Oxford University Press, 1995).

19 *India Today,* 'From House Keeping to City Cleaning'. See also Devaki Jain, 'Panchayat Raj: Women Changing Governance', Gender in Development Monograph Series #5, UNDP, New York, September 1996.

20 Statement by Gigi Francesca at a pre-Beijing consultative conference convened by DAWN in Barbados, 1994.

CHAPTER 5

Indigenising Feminism

By the turn of the century, the term 'feminism' had become much more commonplace in India as also in other developing countries. But in the early 1970s, when the idea of feminism emerged in India, it generated a degree of turbulence. The first response was rejection, partly due to a misunderstanding that feminism as an assertion of women's identity was anti-male. However, after that first 'shock response', another kind of response emerged. It was argued that feminism as an idea was not necessarily birthed in the West, that it was a philosophy or concept within the women's movement in South countries also. This paper was presented at a panel on 'Indigenous Feminism' at a conference organised by the Asiatic Society of Mumbai on the occasion of the 50th anniversary of independence. Many scholars on the panel, especially those based in Indian languages, quoted the literature to reveal the presence of other varieties of feminism. In this essay, I take up these challenges coming from Indian scholars and trace my own journey with feminism.

Feminism has constantly been evolving. It has been described, bound, unleashed and enacted in many ways, and has been elastic, flexible, mutated, searched for, found, doubted. Sometimes it is said that there are as many feminisms as there are cultures. The concept of many feminisms is not plastic: it suggests separate pieces, not a soft, malleable whole. In the desire to be inclusive, accommodating, reverential to difference and diversity, in the concern for avoiding/rejecting the rigid, authoritarian characteristics or shades of patriarchy, of male regimens, defining feminism tends to become a chase, a quest. So sometimes it is said that feminism is a quest, not a platform; a vision, not a practice.

But feminists abound, and the claim to being feminist made by the articulate is comprehensible both locally and globally. At another 'less articulate' level, feminist expression—both in thought and action—is identifiable and identified, whether it is self-acknowledged or 'judged' from the outside as feminist. Can these two phenomena be viewed together? Can there be a dialogue if not convergence? Is there a need for such dialogue or confluence or construction?

This paper will give consideration to these questions by attempting to use the lens of the aspirations and perspectives of women—poor, less visible, disadvantaged or deprived women. Without such an ideological lens, the discourse, it is suggested, can become an infinite inquiry, a journey without end. However fascinating and fair the journey, however kaleidoscopic the landscape, the openness might even vaporise it.

DEFINING FEMINISM

The theme of the panel—'Indigenous Feminism: Concepts, Achievements and Problems'—already presupposes a concept or a philosophy which can be termed 'indigenous feminism', and thereby posits different feminisms—Western, indigenous, and so on. There has been a political need for such affirmation of different streams. Vidyut Bhagwat's paper,[1] recalling feminist expression in India from the 13th to the 18th centuries, is a vivid example of the fact that feminism was not born in the West. The concept of feminism has been emerging over the last two to three decades, partly out of the need for 'naming' the varied expressions of women's collective strength. The concept is part of a language that avoids defining feminism too narrowly, or affirming that there is a universally acceptable ideology called 'feminism'. Kumari Jayawardena, in her book *Feminism and Nationalism in the Third World*, explains it thus:

> It has variously been alleged [in the Third World] by traditionalists, political conservatives and even certain leftists, that feminism is a product of 'decadent' Western capitalism; that it is based on a foreign culture of no relevance to women in the Third World; that it is the ideology of women of the local bourgeoisie; and that it alienates or diverts women, from their culture, religion and family responsibilities on the one hand, and from the revolutionary struggles for national liberation and socialism on the other. In the West, too, there is a Eurocentric view that the movement for women's liberation is not indigenous to Asia or Africa, but has been a purely West European and North American phenomenon, and that where movements

for women's emancipation or feminist struggles have arisen in the Third World, they have been merely imitative of Western models.[2]

My dialogues with Northern feminists at a meeting in Athens in 1985, pre-Nairobi (the Third UN World Conference on Women), is another illustration of this 'need' (see chapter 2, Appendix on 'Dialogues with Feminists from the North'). Another stream comes from feminism and knowledge. Feminism and feminist practice want to reconstruct knowledge, but the very process, the very concept that feminism wishes to reconstruct requires a more universal or specific identity for feminism, which also poses a problem.

There is an immense body of literature in this area. However, in sum, the dialogue (all this discourse is in the form of dialogue, as there can be no conclusive orthodoxy) is between those who see difference and its articulation as an important characteristic of the feminist movement, and those who attempt a common identity. Coming as it does from a foundation of oppression, discrimination and injustice, feminism necessarily is idealistic—and this very idealism inhibits it from practising exclusion, hence from defining boundaries. But within all this accommodation is also the concern that the unified stands, unified actions and notions of solidarity built around womanhood will evaporate.

FEMINIST EXPRESSION

It is my perception that feminist theory—as different from feminist practice—is still not a body of knowledge in India. This statement implies that feminist practice is widespread in India. In India and perhaps in other similar countries, the reflections or even early statements on theory are emerging from the *empirical* field: from activist knowledge and dialogue. The theory is grounded in users' language, is derived as a response to the need of grassroots activists.

The goal of exercises in theory building is predominantly to find a basis for solidarity—feminist solidarity, a united women's movement, a common politics. Thus, the 'dialogue', or interlocking, is already in process. But theory tends to emphasise 'difference', while activism looks for unity of 'common' elements.

Therefore, once we enter into those passages of this journey where the theoretical debates are going on, there remains no doubt that the process of setting up the basis for united actions is inhibited. On the other hand, if we take a definition of feminism which is built around practice and not around 'isms', built through women's ways and methods of handling things, there is a possibility of offering what can be called a 'common minimum programme' on which we can build solidarity, in other words, some kind of standpoint.

Glimpses of such a feminist theory might be gleaned from some of the discussions in which I have participated. My first resource is the national conference on 'Perspectives for the Autonomous Women's Movement in India' held in Bombay in 1985.[3] The method of convening this conference was feminist: there were several prior consultations on the venue and themes, and decisions were made collaboratively by representatives of the various women's groups. Attendance was self-supported and self-motivated, and all roles, such as moderator, rapporteur and so on, developed at the conference itself. The discussions dwelled on the need for clarifying the term 'feminism' and the possibility of developing a common platform.

A principal concern that emerged at the conference was the possibility of forging alliances—a natural preoccupation in a diverse, unequal, but secular democratic nation. Participants debated the potential of forming alliances not only with external forces, such as political parties and ideological movements, but also alliances within the women's movement, including between activists and researchers.

The other strong concern was consolidation. Consolidation of this dynamic, self-conscious, widely dispersed women's movement has become a real preoccupation in its every part. Simple aggregation does not make it into a political force. It was suggested that feminist consciousness was alive, and was replacing class consciousness and class solidarity as the focal point for progressive causes. But how to prevent feminist consciousness from withering away, as has happened with class solidarity? Again, consolidation seemed to be a first step, and consolidation needs a politics—a common frame, theory.

What theory could enshrine this quest? How could we trace the roots of the tangible unity and solidarity that seemed to be present in the room but escaped agreement when expressed? Feminist theory in India has to find an answer to these questions. This conference was a beginning.

My second illustration is drawn from the thinking behind the founding of DAWN,[4] a Third World women's network which brought in macro perspectives on women and development.[5] The DAWN network was established to undertake analysis of poor women's experience of development in the Third World in the context of the macro situations in their regions. Such analysis revealed the impoverishing nature of 'development' as well as the validity of the several strategies pursued by these women. The analysis critiques the commonplace argument that to improve the level of living we need growth, and growth creates structural imbalance; some sacrifices have to be made in the process. The alternative development programme envisioned by DAWN challenges both the very process as well as the goals of such 'development', stressing the need for fundamental change in values, concepts and implementing processes.

DAWN brought debates on political economy into the discussion on women and development, emphasised class, that is, poor women's perspectives as well as the crucial importance of macro policy, and questions of method or process. Thus, it could be suggested that DAWN, in arguing for a feminist development paradigm, suggested an ideological undercurrent for the use of the term 'feminist', namely, identification with means and processes more than goals. The means, almost naturally, are democratic, open, accountable and representative institutions.

My third illustration is an inter-religious dialogue amongst feminists titled 'Women, Religion and Social Change' organised at Harvard University in 1983.[6] What emerged from this dialogue was the view that discrimination against women existed in all faiths; yet, since women are its primary practitioners, there must be a strengthening and bonding aspect in religion. The conference opened up avenues for thinking about the interplay between feminism and religion.[7]

In a contribution to the edited volume that came out of the conference,[8] I suggested that religion could empower women given the context and the method. I illustrated this using Gandhi's manner of drawing on tradition so that those caught in its web could step out while retaining the core values of individual ethics and morality of self enshrined in every religion. I referred to Gandhi's use of bhajans and sarva dharma (all religions, or every religion) prayers to illustrate both the mobilising and the educating roles of religion. Following an ethic of self-effacement can be a step to annihilating differences of all kinds—gender, class, caste, religion, 'me' versus 'thou'. I suggested that women were the best vehicles for providing this leadership in religious practice, leavening, healing and sublimating divisions in conflict-ridden societies.

FEMINIST DIALOGUES

There are several moving illustrations of women engaged in struggle and women in grassroots organisations needing some form of 'unity'. For example, the chronicling of women's participation in the national struggle in Palestine by Amrita Basu,[9] and further by Islah Jad,[10] brings forth what has been an almost worldwide phenomenon, namely, 'the heroism of women in struggle' not being matched by concrete improvement in their status. Jad shows that as a result of this negligence by the leadership, as a result of not acknowledging in post-liberation times the work of women pre-liberation, there was deepened feminist consciousness among the women's committees. They began to realise the necessity of both returning to the women's programme and creating new women's agendas.

While the uprising had brought together women from different 'spaces', the feminist consciousness arising out of the neglect drove them to draft a women's bill of rights. It is to be noted that the preamble says, 'We, the women of Palestine, from all social categories and various faiths…'; it is inclusive, because of the recognition that unity was necessary to overcome male domination. The document continues:

... including workers, farmers, housewives, students, professionals and politicians, promulgate our determination to proceed with our struggle to abolish all forms of discrimination and inequality against women, which were propagated by the different forms of colonialism on our land, ending with the Israeli occupation and which were reinforced by the conglomeration of customs and traditions prejudiced against women, embodied in a number of existing laws and legislations.[11]

This is the reality, and it is from this reality that we have to judge the discourse, the dialogue between feminist theorists and practitioners. It is from this perspective that we have to see the importance of defining and giving substance to both the sense of a feminist consciousness and a feminist method. 'The relationship between identity and activism is difficult to establish. Moreover, identity itself is neither uniform nor monolithic. Often, women's experiences of their identities as gendered subjects may not assume a feminist form.'[12] Thus, Naihua Zhang reports that since the 1980s, Chinese women have challenged the androgynous ideals of the past by emphasising their femininity.[13] In the United States, the growing consciousness that identities are multiple rather than singular has often led women to emphasise race, ethnicity and sexual orientation as much as gender. 'As a result, identity politics flourishes at the same time that a unified women's movement has declined.'[14]

Christine Sylvester puts it this way:

One [trend] features feminism settling into its many philosophical and identity differences and defending an absence of consensus as appropriate for this era. Following closely on this first tendency is considerable feminist worry about issues of power and solidarity in a fragmented era and accompanying debates about the merits of this versus that specific feminism. The third tendency is in the direction of effecting some feminist amalgamations that merge or cross-fertilize the differences....

I would like to see a new trend emerge that takes the current emphasis on difference and turns it into 'something else' that is 'not an ascribed trait' or a feminist 'lifestyle' but 'a politics'. I would like more emphasis on methods of speaking in, through, and across differences—methods by which different identity feminisms and geospatial locations within them become mobile in ways that juggle and cross borderlands.[15]

Similarly, Barbara M. Cooper writes of the politics of difference in women's struggle in Niger:

> Women in Maradi share with women in feminist struggle elsewhere the necessity of living and working with what Ann Snitow has referred to as the 'recurring feminist divide': 'In feminist discourse a tension keeps forming between finding a useful lever in female identity and seeing that identity as hopelessly compromised'.... Maradi women draw upon their common position as women while simultaneously calling into question the unity and stability of the category 'woman'. They have played subversively upon the local category 'married woman' in order to make possible greater female public visibility, but their invocation of that category inevitably reinscribes local norms that stigmatise female sexuality outside of marriage.[16]

FEMINISM AS A 'METHOD'

One of the most fertile territories for pursuit on this journey to ascribe boundaries to feminism is the issue of method, or 'ways'. While even this has been contested, it can be linked to another discourse on theories and practices—how theories can be built around a practice, and practice often gives content to theory. For example, an interesting dialogue amongst feminist scholars which took place in Baroda on 9 and 10 August 1997[17] brought forth papers on movements such as the Periyar movement in south India. Periyar, or E. V. Ramaswamy Naicker,[18] initiated a movement to build the self-esteem of the down-trodden. He emphasised rationality, the mind, over the heart and emotion. He posited radical views on the roles of women, supporting their singleness as well as their autonomy in the lives they wished to lead. Periyar challenged Gandhi, arguing that Gandhi's attention to the spirit and appeal to emotion, love, forgiveness and so on was a facade for sustaining the unjust social structure of India, whether the injustice was based on caste or gender.

In retrospect, from the perspective of 1997, it was also suggested at the same seminar that Periyar's ideals have become so corrupted in today's Tamil Nadu that his idea of a rational society has been converted into a Tamil fundamentalism of the most limited kind, actually lead-ing to OBCs oppressing the Dalits. Periyar's ideal of motherhood has been distorted into the image of the Tamil nation as mother, therefore circumscribing women's autonomy. In other words, his principles, in practice, have been misrepresented.

On the other hand, for all the ambivalence of Gandhi's principles, their practical and moral value still persists. Could this be because Gandhi's theory, built from practice, met Indian aspirations halfway? Gandhi's this-worldly approach to revolution was especially appropriate to women's experience. He demonstrated this during India's freedom struggle. Women were significant participants in economic struggles, including the boycott of foreign goods such as textiles, and the Salt March. For women in the independence movement, spinning meant self-reliance and identification with the unskilled and unemployed.

In their biographies, many women leaders of pre-independence India have described how Gandhi's call to satyagraha (literally, 'truth force') opened the door to them for their own liberation from oppressive social modes. The code of his ashrams included simplicity in dress and reverence for women. The rules of the ashrams made it possible for women to 'come out' of the narrow worlds of their homes to participate in a wider community.

In a sense, Gandhi met Indian tradition halfway. He directed it away from its established 'structures' and towards its changing 'dynamics'. It was just this method of meeting tradition halfway that facilitated the emergence of women from the grip of orthodox tradition. However 'reformist' or 'middle-path' such an approach may seem, it is tactically effective, because it provides vehicles and options for change.[19]

'FEMINISM' AS IDEOLOGY

Many attempts have also been made to see if ideological—besides methodological—content can be given to feminism, apart from formulations such as 'method is ideology.' One such approach is standpoint theory, which suggests that being a woman develops a point of view—a view from where you stand as a woman. This standpoint overrides the divides of location, time and social stratification. Helen E. Longino put it this way:

> The problems of knowledge are central to feminist theorizing, which has sought to destabilize androcentric, mainstream thinking in the humanities and in the social and natural sciences. Feminist standpoint theory has been one of the most distinctive and debated contributions of contemporary feminist thought to the theory of knowledge. While some feminist theorists extend its range to natural phenomena, the theory was developed in a social science context and has been advocated primarily by feminists in one or another of the social sciences or by feminists emerging from the Marxist tradition. Provisionally, standpoint theory reflects the view that women (or feminists) occupy a social location that affords them/us a privileged access to social phenomena. This root notion has had various expressions, ranging from the romantic idea that women come, by nature or social experience, to be better equipped to know the world than are men to the more modest proposal that a social science adequate for women must proceed from a grasp of the forms of oppression women experience. Associated with standpoint theory was the concept of successor science, a science that would supersede male-centered science. Since feminist standpoint theory was introduced in the 1970's, postmodern theorizing, which calls into question not only the very possibility of knowledge but also the possibility of the category *women*, has influenced a growing number of feminist thinkers.[20]

Again, for 'feminists' located in poor, unequal countries, the ideology seems obvious—an ideological commitment to the removal of poverty and injustice (inequality, discrimination). For me, feminism is contained in Gandhi's 'Talisman', which says, 'Whenever you are in doubt, or when the self becomes too much with you, apply the following test: Recall the face of the poorest and the weakest man/woman whom you may have seen and ask yourself if the step you contemplate is going to be of any use to him.'[21] Gandhi referred to the poorest man as *daridranarayana*. I would change this to *daridranarayani*, the final *-i* giving it a feminine gender.

TOWARDS THE 21ST CENTURY

Today, as the 21st century is coming upon us, the 'corner' from which I view the world is somewhat influenced by the threats that I see. The

21st century offers a challenge, and demands greater solidarity and more politically significant collective action.

The 21st century has been anticipated and characterised in many ways, positive and negative. Information technology has crossed all barriers—those of national boundaries, corporate empires, intellectual empires. So in a sense it has levelled things. We have also seen an increase in social fragmentation, apart from the affirmation of social diversity, its acceptance. Difference, pluralism, multiple identities and self-determination are keywords. Feminists associate themselves with these affirmations of rights and movements, including movements safeguarding the ecology, as well as with the celebration of diversity and self-determination given their cultural aspiration for democracy, for space, for equality, for a discrimination-free society. Yet this very current also mutes the power of broad-based solidarity. Feminists would argue that while difference needs accommodation, unified action on issues is possible when necessary.[22]

However, other aspects of the coming century are horrific and cannot be contained by periodic spontaneous actions. They require careful, systematic, well-organised, strategically planned, transactable opinion and pressure to resist, to push back. What are these horrors? The threatening erosion of nature—and therefore greater disease, imbalance between soil, air, water and humans. The possibility of new mutants in humans and plants. The fragmentation of society and its old foundations—family, community, class and so on, individualisation. The overpowering economic influence of 'unaccountable' finance and its warlords—leading to an abrogation of national sovereignty and thereby the accountability of nations to their citizens. A world order without a world, the footlooseness of all peoples, cultures, economic giants and lilliputs, and therefore a blurring of purpose and responsibility. And last but not least, an increase in disparities between people—rich and poor, men and women, different places, leading often to conflict.[23] Hence, a more warring society, even if the wars are little and local. A shapeless planet in an awesome century.

In such a situation what seems necessary is intense counter-mobilisation with the clear purpose of retrieving/reclaiming the earth, water, air, humanity, justice, culture, order—identity, responsibility.

The women's movement can do this; women are the largest stakeholders for a healthy planet—giving life, they do not want it corrupted or wasted. But they require sustained, organised action with agendas—not only for women, but for society, state, market. Today, it seems that there is a case for finding some form of similarity within these differences.

To some extent, Beijing showed that it is possible to 'feel' a sense of unity as a woman based on what can be called a common background, even though such statements have been legitimately challenged in feminist discourse.[24] Some of the forms of the 'sense of unity' experienced at the Fourth UN World Conference on Women include:

1. A united sense of *political will*—as if the entire worldwide women's movement, including those who were spokespersons for women at the official conference, were one 'Big Mind' ('Big Mind' is a Japanese Zen concept) and were determined to bring women into formal political leadership.
2. Related to the first point, a new consciousness which could be called a *political consciousness*. This is not only about politics but about a consciousness—a feminist consciousness, the idea that women's perspectives, women's struggles, are a political issue.
3. The third point is what I have called *reversing relationships*,[25] or the idea that power centres for change are shifting from the government not only to the market, but also to civil society. The abrogation of sovereignty by the state, and the increasing pace of an undefinable, autonomous and unaccountable process called globalisation, are provoking reaction from citizens' groups. These elements could be summarised as Beijing's 'Big Mind'.
4. The fourth aspect was a sense of discomfort with the concept and march of globalisation.

In India, the issue confronting us is not only the daily interaction with acute poverty, inequality, deprivation, but also cruelty and violence, especially to women and children. The statistics, however inadequate they are, make it impossible to relax as a member of the women's movement. Yet no significant dent has been made by women in public or private policy in relation to women, girls and infants.[26]

In this context, it seems important to develop an identity within the multiple identities around the consciousness of women. I give below some women's voices—some who seem angry with men, some who want to fight with men, and some who want to affirm that women have different ways than men. I suggest that these are very similar to the voices I have heard in Latin America, Africa, USA, UK, Scandinavia, apart from Asia. I suggest that based on this 'similarity', we need to unite in action, and that action has to be supported by thought and literature which extol the common consciousness of women as women. Therefore, we need to go back to narrow definitions of feminism like the one with which I started.

> Forty-five year old Kempamma works in a coffee curing shed in Chikmagalur in Karnataka. Packing coffee seeds into sacks, 'What do they know?' she says, pointing to her male supervisors, 'we are to do nothing but bow our heads all our lives. I have a sick child, I am late, I am not given work—the family eats nothing that day. I bow my head. The union strikes for better wages. We starve for 15 days and we go back for 10 paise more—I bow my head.' Like a swan dipping into water, Kempamma demonstrates her words, bending her head down to touch the floor, with her hand on her forehead.[27]

> Haseena Begum and many others like her, live in the Jama Masjid area, but are also distributed across Delhi, Agra, Lucknow and many other cities and villages. They are Zardozi workers. At a meeting of SEWA, Delhi where the women were discussing the fact that their daughters came home with babies as their men divorced them, she said—Ya Allah, why did you create men?[28]

In rural Ahmedabad district, the eminent women workers' union SEWA had a project for rural women, associated with the equally famous National Dairy Development Board, known for what is called the 'white revolution'. A woman who was being trained and shown the technology of artificial insemination, after the class was over, drew aside the young technician who was demonstrating how the cattle stock could be upgraded. She asked him if there was a similar technique by which she could have higher-quality children, as their menfolk in the village were weak and useless. She came from a social category where women covered their heads and never spoke to a man except through the sari veil!

Here are some voices of women in local government:

> I am a better representative of the people than men. I can always be found in the kitchen or the yard: whereas men cannot be traced—they are in the liquor shops or in cinema halls or loafing in the town.
>
> —Suman Kolhar, Vice-President, Bijapur, Karnataka[29]

> I inherited a ward nursed by my husband, but now the people come to me, not to him, as I am accessible.
>
> —Ms Naik, Mayor, Ponda, Goa[30]

> 33% is not enough. We should have 50%. The men treat us with disdain, we need the strength of numbers.[31]

> Train the men—not us. Train them to step back, give them psychological training in relinquishing power.[32]

> Many thought that being a woman, I could be pushed over and they could drive from the back seat. But after a few months, that feeling has changed.
>
> —A. K. Premajam, Mayor of Kozhikode[33]

Are these indigenous feminists? Or feminists?

Thus I come back to my earlier proposition, that the cutting edge for both defining as well as giving purpose to the notion of 'feminism' is the grassroots, and the 'real' need of women from the masses. Classifications such as 'indigenous' and 'Western' do not, in my view, serve any purpose. I would even deny such 'differences'.

The difficulties of using 'woman' as an identity are present in all cultures and circumstances. Whether we engage in subterfuge like the women of Niger, consolidate feminist consciousness like the women of Palestine, or combine our agendas like the women of panchayati raj institutions (PRI) in India, there is in my view an underlying gender-derived identity. Feminist consciousness presupposes consciousness of the identity of woman as woman.[34] Feminist method is a form of affirming that women have specific ways of dealing with power, with structures, with ideas.

There is a crying need for women to unite on issues. A documentary on the Andhra women's anti-arrack struggle released by Friedrich Ebert Stiftung is titled *When Women Unite*—there is no need to say more. Leadership, especially in governance—political, economic and cultural—is in an abysmal state. 'If women unite...' can be the most significant factor of change in the 21st century. But it is a big 'if', unless feminist consciousness and 'woman' are seen as the basis for identity.

NOTES

1 Vidyut Bhagwat, 'Maharashtrian Bhakti: Women's Voices of Protest from 13th to 18th Century', paper presented at the panel on 'Indigenous Feminism: Concepts, Experiments, Limitations', conference on 'Cultural Transformations in Post-colonial India', Asiatic Society of Mumbai, 1 October 1997.

2 Jayawardena, *Feminism and Nationalism in the Third World*.

3 Forum against Oppression of Women, *National Conference on 'Perspectives for the Autonomous Women's Movements in India'*. See chapter 2 in this volume for a detailed discussion of this conference.

4 DAWN was founded in August 1984 in Bangalore by a group of women representing all the regions of the world.

5 For more on DAWN, see the discussion in chapter 2.

6 Eck and Jain, *Speaking of Faith*. See chapter 2 for a discussion of the conference.

7 See, e.g., Mernissi, *Women in Moslem Paradise*.

8 Jain, 'Gandhian Contributions towards a Feminist Ethic'.

9 Amrita Basu, 'Introduction', in Amrita Basu (ed.), *The Challenge of Local Feminisms: Women's Movements in Global Perspectives* (Boulder, CO: Westview Press, 1995).

10 Islah Jad, 'Claiming Feminism, Claiming Nationalism: Women's Activism in the Occupied Territories', in Basu, *The Challenge of Local Feminisms*, pp. 240–46.

11 Ibid.

12 Charmaine Pereira, 'National Council of Women's Societies and the State, 1985–1993: The Use of Discourses of Womanhood by the NCWS', in Attahiru Jega (ed.), *Identity Transformation and Identity Politics under Structural Adjustment in Nigeria* (Uppsala: Nordiska Afrikainstitutet, and Kano: Centre for Research and Documentation, 2000).

13 See Basu, *The Challenge of Local Feminisms*, p. 17.

14 See Basu, 'Introduction', p. 17.

15 Christine Sylvester, 'African and Western Feminisms: World-Traveling the Tendencies and Possibilities', *Signs*, vol. 20, no. 4 (Summer 1995), pp. 941–69.

16 Barbara M. Cooper, 'The Politics of Difference and Women's Association in Niger: "Prostitutes", the Public and Politics', *Signs*, vol. 20, no. 4 (Summer 1995), p. 853.

17 National Seminar on 'Early Years of Indian Independence: Women's Perspectives', IAWS, Baroda, 9–11 August 1997, organised to mark the first 50 years of independence.

18 See V. Geetha, 'Periyar, Women and an Ethic of Citizenship', paper presented at the National Seminar on 'Early Years of Indian Independence: Women's Perspectives', IAWS, Baroda, August 1997.

19 Jain, 'Gandhian Contributions towards a Feminist Ethic', p. 285.

20 Helen E. Longino, 'Feminist Standpoint Theory and the Problems of Knowledge', *Signs*, vol. 19, no. 1 (Autumn 1993), pp. 201–12.

21 See Devaki Jain, *Minds, Bodies and Exemplars: Reflections at Beijing and Beyond* (New Delhi: British Council Division, 1996).

22 Devaki Jain, 'Note for Anti-Arrack Meeting', India International Centre, New Delhi, 18 April 1997.

23 UNDP, *Human Development Report 1997* (New York: Oxford University Press, 1997).

24 See Jain, *Minds, Bodies and Exemplars*.

25 Drawn from Naila Kabeer, *Reversed Realities: Gender Hierarchies in Development Thought* (London: Verso, 1994).

26 See S. Sudha and S. Irudaya Rajan, 'Intensifying Masculinity of Infancy Sex Ratio in India: Preliminary Evidence from the 1981 and 1991 Censuses', T. N. Krishnan Memorial Seminar on 'Development Experience of Southern States in a Comparative Perspective', Centre for Development Studies, Thiruvananthapuram, 9 September 1997.

27 Jain, 'Indian Women Today and Tomorrow', p. 7.

28 Quoted in Kabeer, *Reversed Realities*.

29 Devaki Jain, 'The Poverty Thing', presented at a special event organised by UNDP, New York, 20 May 1997.

30 Ibid.

31 Ibid.

32 Ibid.

33 Ibid.; see also 'From House Keeping to City Cleaning', *India Today*, 30 April 1997.

34 Since the time this piece was written (1995), feminism has, of course, expanded to include the LGBT community. But in 1995, the feminist identity was still understood as being limited to women.

CHAPTER 6

Challenges for Women in India in the New Millennium

The impending birth of a new millennium generated interest among organisations like the UN as well as among women's networks in discussing what possibilities the future might hold for different categories of people, in this case women. I ventured to address this interest, albeit in a somewhat deflating mode, as these big ideas and goals had only meant big themes like the Millennium Development Goals, which became initiatives 'of the state, by the state, for the state'. The idea of goal setting had not seemed productive in my opinion in engineering the kind of really revolutionary change that seemed to be required. Hence, I plunged into a review and analysis of the work done so far, and reflected on what precautions the women's movement needed to exercise as it moved ahead.

The new millennium, the 21st century—these terms as they are thought or uttered have a ring of promise, adventure, modernity, the scientific age. Within that vision there can be ideas on how to land social segments like women on cloud seven, or in a grand future. Plans could be made to ensure they are not left behind, as dead before their time, or as obscurantist in a rational milieu, or oppressed or deprived when others are free and endowed.[1] Given the trend, say in the last 20 years, we would then assess what the situation might be after three to five years, or another 20 years. In the two decades between 1975 and 1995, the UN met four times for its World Conferences on Women. These were called 'women's decades'—initiated in 1975 in Mexico, continuing in Copenhagen in 1980, Nairobi in 1985, and in Beijing in September 1995.

However, this essay will not proceed along the lines of such a framework. It does not regard the new millennium as holding promise, adventure, rationality, or the rainbow's end. In some respects, the millennium does indeed hold out promise, for instance, in the capacity of information to cross all barriers and level hierarchies; the affirmation of social diversity; the celebration of difference, pluralism, multiple identities. Yet, in other ways, the millennium presents prospects that are horrifying, in the form of looming ecological disaster, increasing social fragmentation, the loss of sovereignty and resulting decline in the accountability of governments to their citizens, increasing disparities among people.

In such a situation—where disparities and conflicts are increasing, where national resources are under assault, where power has moved into unchallenged spheres such as international financial institutions and MNCs, and where two 'women's decades' with action plans and follow-up mechanisms have made attempts to usher in justice to women in a unipolar world—it is clear that women's situation cannot be redressed merely by social inputs, merely by trying to level them up with men. In fact, women themselves—if their voice in local as well as worldwide forums is taken as 'witness', as evidence—have recognised that their situation as well as the nature of the world can change only when they lead, only when relations of power change. So even they are moving out of the mode of voicing 'demands', towards claiming actual power. This essay argues that it is only shifts in the relations of power between genders, and leadership by those who are 'oppressed', that can build equity. It suggests that it is only through political restructuring that there can be growth with equity.[2]

The challenge then before women in India, as they enter the new millennium, is to affirm their leadership in the political economy—but with a 'new' politics.[3] What seems necessary is not the policy of 'interventions' for women in the conventional sense, but women's political action, intense counter-mobilisation with a view to retrieving or reclaiming the earth, water, air, humanity, justice, culture, order. For this to happen, a sense of identity and responsibility is required. The women's movement can enable women to come together, drawing on an identity which supersedes class, race, religion, age and other divides.

WOMEN'S ASPIRATIONS AT THE END OF THIS MILLENNIUM

Why this shift in the aspirations of the worldwide women's movement from making 'demands' to claiming power? Any review of progress made in terms of women's position in society vis-à-vis any indicator—political, economic or social—shows that change, if any, has been slow and partial. The UNDP's *HDR 1995*[4] marshalled data from all over the world to provide stark illustration that after two decades of global attention, women are still deeply discriminated against, and, whatever measures of outcome are used, women's contribution to society and economy is still ignored, as indeed is their voice in governance. The report says:

> In both the developing and industrialized world, men receive the lion's share of income and recognition for their economic contributions—while most of women's work remains unpaid, unrecognized and undervalued.

> Women work longer hours than men in nearly every country.... Of the total burden of paid and unpaid work, women carry on average 53% in developing countries and 51% in industrial countries....

> In industrial countries, roughly two-thirds of women's total work burden is spent on unpaid activities, and one-third on paid activities. For men, the shares are reversed.

> In developing countries, two-thirds of women's total work is also spent in unpaid labour. But less than one-quarter of men's work is unpaid.[5]

The passage above dwells only on the economic aspect. The data on social aspects are even worse.

This review at the global level is matched at the national level. In India over the last three to four years, secondary and primary data have begun to reveal the sharp disparities between males and females in everything, from survival—living and dying—to participation in decision making, whether within the household or at the global level. Many researchers have been engaged in trying to define the 'status' of women, measure it, give the measures a hierarchy of importance, and then assess the progress made in women's quest for equality and justice.[6] Here I shall refer to only one of the many reviews, as it attempts to pull together the various discussions even though it is a relatively 'old' (1990) exercise.[7]

One of the strongly held propositions in the decades 1970–90 was that women's economic position—based on ownership of assets, wage, income levels, and so on—was the crucial component of their status, if status was defined as an amalgam of well-being and freedom from injury such as ill-treatment of any kind, from discrimination in food and healthcare to actual beating and rape. Our exercise set out to test this and other hypotheses, such as the idea that economic growth can take care of inequity, or that public investment in social infrastructure can reduce disparities.[8]

In looking for a critical variable which could reflect the prevailing situation and track the trends, the sex ratio, namely the number of women per 1,000 men, was selected. But data on work participation rates and anthropological information on regional characteristics in India with reference to women's treatment were also gathered, however inadequately. The findings of this research, yet to be formally published, revealed that whatever the public policy might be in terms of investment in social infrastructure, however vivid women's voices, and whatever the extent of women-focused work undertaken by government structures, regional characteristics determined by a complex structure of elements kept the sex ratio constant. In other words, social hierarchies established by tradition superseded all other interventions and inputs in terms of their impact.[9] To quote from the report:

> In arguing that the particularly low ideological position of women in parts of India cannot be explained by their relative inability to participate in the work force, we are by no means suggesting that economic independence is not important for improving women's position. Certainly, partaking in productive work probably gives women some additional autonomy and therefore significantly improves their actual well-being. But in this paper our concern is with the families' attitudes and behaviour towards their baby daughters in the first few years of the latter's lives. These attitudes in their turn are likely to be largely determined by standard social perceptions regarding women's worth in that particular society.
>
> We argue that there are some special, culture-specific reasons why Indian societies appear to react fairly regularly in this particular way, viz. by degradation of their women, to the growth of social hierarchies. The

reasons probably lie in the particular historical combination of social and of course economic forces which made the society in Indo-Gangetic plains one where patri-local, patriarchal, extended kin joint families became the rule: where pressures of demand for labour gave inordinate importance to women's reproductive activities and where private property developed early to put a premium on marriages and legitimacy.[10]

In responding to this very clear worldwide discrimination against the female of the species from pre-birth almost to post-death, international and national agencies including organisations of women have demanded redressal mechanisms such as laws, positive discrimination and special funding. For example, *HDR 1995* recommends a whole series of enabling mechanisms and legislations, especially positive discrimination through reservation of 25 per cent of places in all political and decision-making bodies for women. This recommendation was echoed both by the official document transacted at the World Conference on Women in Beijing in 1995, and also by the non-official women's movement.[11]

The premise of such intervention is that if women could be present in political forums, they could influence political and economic decisions in such a way that discrimination against them could be reduced or reversed, the presumption being that these political bodies have the power to redress injustice. Certainly such a presumption is not entirely off the mark—the basis of representative government is that by giving representation to all groups, through a process of electoral politics, debates and legislation, various groups would lobby for their own interests, and the end result would be closer to some form of justice than a system which is either autarchic or unrepresentative.

India has already achieved the first recommendation of *HDR 1995*. In 1993–94, the 73rd and 74th Amendments to the Indian Constitution instituted local self-government bodies elected through multi-party competitive politics and universal franchise.[12] A form of affirmative action or positive discrimination was introduced by reserving 33 1/3 per cent of the places on the councils for women. Further, over 15 per cent of the seats were reserved for dalits. Elections to these local bodies (panchayats at the rural level and municipalities at the urban level) have already been held.

However, the women's movement recognises that in spite of all these arrangements, the blatant disregard of women will continue because it arises out of various deeper sources associated with cultural and religious constructs. Today, the women's movement realises that the heart of the problem of women's subordination—the problem of discrimination against women worldwide, so dramatically laid out in the UNDP's *HDR* of 1995 and 1997—lies in gender relations.[13] Challenging the rigid hierarchies of gender relations is not easy, even though women have struggled against these hierarchies for centuries, across histories and cultures.[14]

Gandhi had a unique response to women who wished to resist such hierarchies based on gender stereotypes. He advocated a collective refusal by women to perform the obligations demanded of them by 'gender apartheid'—including marrying, having sex, wearing jewellery, cooking. Conversely, Gandhi sought to effect an inversion by persuading men to perform what are commonly regarded as 'women's jobs'. Gandhi's technique of role reversal reveals the constructedness of gender-related hierarchies. It suggests that the differences between the genders are not so much physiologically fixed, but rather emerge from the differences in women's life experience.

POLITICAL ECONOMY: DO WOMEN MAKE A DIFFERENCE?

A central issue for women is the increase in violence against them from childhood onwards, linked to macro, global forces and their perpetuation of disparities and natural resources depletion. The pivotal issue in the world today is the management of the global political economy. There is deep anxiety that the new millennium, while it brings with it the exciting levelling made possible by information technology and the affirmative spirit of rights movements, also brings with it planetary deterioration and conflict arising out of the persistence of poverty and the accentuation of disparities.[15] There is a noticeable vacuum in exemplary leadership, whether at the local, national or international level. It is here that Gandhi's ideas on political economy not only seem relevant but are being legitimised by experience, even if without attribution.

Gandhi's ideas on political economy are now returning as the new paradigm. For example, today's vanguard in development thought speaks of growing disparities as a threat to economic growth and political stability, and of the importance of restrained consumption for environmental sustainability. The theme of the UNDP's *Human Development Report 1998* is consumption,[16] following the focus of the previous *HDR* on eradicating poverty. Though Gandhi highlighted consumption as a key issue in fostering inequality or, conversely, in building equality, his practice and preaching on restrained consumption was also geared to the conservation of nature and resource sharing. Today's discourse on political economy talks of the importance of institutions and people in mediating justice both social and economic, and the necessity of community building and of morals.[17] Today's discourse admits that economics is about politics and the ideology and ethics of leadership.

In India, for all its push towards globalisation, the ghost of Gandhi's daridranarayani stalks the Indian conscience. She therefore manages to thwart every attempt to make a clean transit into the so-called 'fast track' of economic reform because of the built-in faultlines of such a course, namely, the neglect of poverty, inequality and social development. Thus the legacy left by Gandhi, India's Jiminy Cricket, the 'Conscience of India' as Sarojini Naidu called him, persists even if it is often overshadowed.

Let us now turn to an assessment of the presence of women in politics in India. Since the reservation of seats for them in local government bodies, women's presence in Indian political life has taken a quantum leap forward. The numbers are overwhelming—more than a million women have been elected to local bodies in rural and urban areas, a millionfold increase over the previous situation in which women constituted less than 1 per cent of the members of local government in some states.[18] Women's presence in the political arena and their participation in the expression of opinion has spurred more women in India to seek entry into politics. There is widespread concurrence not only that women should have a greater share in political power, but also that women can transform politics through their participation. Hence the solidarity around the issue of quota or reservation of seats for women in other representative bodies such as the state assemblies and the national Parliament.

Will women's entry through the quota, that is, the reservation of seats, come about without conscious effort to rearrange the electoral system, the rules and procedures, the ideological foundations of women's participation? Or will it only be a sex change and not a sea change? How and under what conditions can women's entry into politics create the transformation of politics and the use of power in consonance with the ideals to which the women's movement aspires? There has been much discussion on these issues in India for decades, particularly in the years 1995–97. The greater the vigour with which the women's movement works for the reservation of seats—the efforts to pass the 81st Amendment to the Indian Constitution—the greater will be the doubts and anxieties with regard to making women's entry into formal politics the occasion for a sea change in governance and the performance of the state.

Women are subject to the same structures of social stratification as the rest of society, and they manifest the same divides in conventional politics as expressed by political parties. So where does the notion of woman or gender come in as a source of cross-cutting identity? Women build their claim for space in political structures and in governance on two pillars:

- the broader issue of representation for a special category;
- and the more specific issue of giving expression to feminist leadership as a valuable contribution to governance and to the quality of management of the state.

The premises of both claims are challenged, not only by men but by women too. Once elected, do women really represent women's concerns, whatever that may mean? Leaders who happened to be female by sex, such as Margaret Thatcher or Golda Meir in the West, and Jayalalitha and Mayawati in India, have been held up as examples to devastate women's case/claim.

Ideologies of oppression and inequality, like those drawn from class, race, theology, the subordination of indigenous peoples such as in India or in Australia and of backward classes in India, are used to crush women's claim to an initial postulation of homogeneity as derived from the universal existence and oppression of patriarchy. However, poor women and their elite sisters affirm the identity of women, cross-cutting these barriers, like black consciousness which too is based on the idea of cross-cutting identities, as well as showing the difference in the quality and content of women's leadership.

A review I undertook of six experiences of spontaneous mass-based collective action by women—Chipko in the Himalayas against forest felling; the anti-arrack movement in Andhra against country liquor; the movement in Ahmedabad against the acquisition of vending space; the struggles in Manipur against alcoholism and in Assam against land settlement—show how women respond when there is a threat to livelihood or to social peace (see the Appendix at the end of chapter 3). The choice of issues and the methods used in these struggles is of significance. Women tend to mobilise around issues that have immediate bearing on their livelihoods or the security of their families. Their struggle relies on local idioms to generate solidarity, and they resist by putting their own bodies on the line.

A closer look at some of these struggles might be instructive. My first illustration is the anti-arrack struggle in Andhra. The anti-arrack agitation of Nellore district has been one of the most significant women's agitations in the last decade in India. What makes the agitation unique is that it was spontaneous, local, and spread like wildfire, convulsing the entire state of Andhra Pradesh for three years. It was historic in the sense that agrarian women confronted the state and emerged victorious in forcing it to make a definite policy change with the declaration of prohibition by the Telugu Desam government.

Liquor had emerged as a central issue that pushed household economies to the brink in the context of the deteriorating economic situation of the poor consequent upon the new economic reforms. Daily violence pushed women to the edge, and thereby spurred anti-arrack struggles in many parts of India. The Nellore experience has informed the discourse of political parties. Bans on arrack have become one of the common populist slogans during elections.

The struggle has instilled confidence among women and triggered off other changes in these villages. For example, the arrack struggle has been followed by an effective thrift programme which is self-managed. It has also been followed by effective social action by women's groups against social crimes, such as the use of female child labour, child marriage, rape and other forms of violence against women, revealing that women's collective struggle against arrack has had a greater value than just the elimination of liquor from households. It has removed or reduced violence, and also built self-confidence and strength among women to take collective action against those who inflict violence upon them.

It is always debatable as to what women's issues are, and how women's struggles direct policy. Women's struggles have tended to be against policy, sometimes against development; women have rarely been able to translate their struggles into a political platform, that is, into a government policy. The anti-arrack struggle proved that this can be done under certain conditions, but the recent setbacks women have faced (such as macro-level arguments showing the decline in tax revenue and therefore the crisis in the state's finance) also reveal the importance of wider support as well as more local mechanisms for safeguarding the objectives of the struggle.

Another illustration of women's collective action is from Uttarakhand—the Uttarakhand Mahila Manch. Women in the hilly Himalayan regions of Uttar Pradesh have been agitating against men's drinking habits for several decades. The hills district has been agitating for a separate state—Uttarakhand—through a separatist movement, and women have been at the forefront of the movement. This political movement has provided a strong new platform for women to press their point as they demand not only a free Uttarakhand, free from domination by plains people, but a liquor-free region. They use the slogan '*mukti* [freedom] from *sharab* [liquor]'.

In order to seek their inputs into the state-level plan of Uttarakhand, an official consultation was held with women of Almora district. The women revealed extraordinary clarity in defining the kinds of laws, economic policies and political arrangements they desired. Below is the plan they evolved over the day:

1. Laws: A total ban on the sale of liquor and a more severe criminal law to punish violence.
2. Rights: Women to have full rights over village land, trees and water. These resources were being misused for 'export' from the region, whereas they could use it for their livelihood.
3. Governance: That women must be given 50 per cent of the places in the agencies that control forest land (*van panchayats*) as well as forest corporations and development agencies. Women must be placed in charge of afforestation; they would choose to grow trees that were useful for their own economy, and not only for export, and they would also use the trees for their livelihoods.
4. Tourism industry: Women must be put in charge of developing the tourist industry, as tourism today threatens women's security by bringing with it the liquor trade and prostitution. So if women developed tourism, they would pay attention to enhancing natural resource beauty, local craft sales and so on—in other words, use it to enhance livelihoods and conservation (and not sex tourism).
5. Women must be given the plan funds to make five-year plans for their region. They would invest in providing piped water and cooking gas to households in the hills where women spend 8–10 hours fetching fuel and fodder.

Elsewhere, too, women have been far more sensitive to the ugly face of 'progress', with particular reference to the tourism industry. The Goan women's manifesto makes a strident demand for eliminating sex tourism, especially child prostitution. 'We decry all moves to make the economy dependent on tourism and to follow a tourism policy that is exploitative of women and children in particular and society at large.' The manifesto, apart from asking for greater participation of women at all levels, sets out a detailed agenda to enhance the status of women through a crackdown on pornography, indecent portrayal of women in the media, and on the constructive side through sanitation, crèches, and so on.

A fourth illustration is provided by the 73rd and 74th Amendments to the Constitution leading to the reservation of places for women in local self-government bodies—one of the most significant revolutions taking place in India. The quota has brought women into the political and decision-making arena in very large numbers, and women are showing a readiness to enter into governance. There will be much said on the need for training these women as they are entering such structures for the first time, apart from negative comments, for instance, that these newly elected women, such as corporators, are only proxies for their men, do not really know how to represent, do not know the rules, and would never have entered these councils if it was not for reservation. However, reviews of the performance of women both in rural and in urban local self-government bodies show a similarity of priorities and visions. In a survey of 'women-only' and women-led *zilla* (district-level) panchayats, it was found that women tended to attend first to domestic needs—water, schools, firewood patches, ration shops—twisting the direction of development away from liquor shops, roads and panchayat *ghars* (houses).

The work of women in governance may also be illustrated by the performance of women in city governance. A striking aspect of the interviews carried by *India Today*[19] of women engaged in city governance is that diverse and unlinked as these women are, they seem to converge in their opinions, as if they belonged to some cadre or political lobby, on the issues that they consider to be a priority and what they want to do with regard to these issues. Their principal focus and priority have been on providing a basic standard of life to citizens, for example, by improving drainage, drinking water supply, roads, and so on. The woman mayor of Bangalore recently sanctioned the imposition of fines on citizens who littered the city. While previous male mayors had merely eulogised the beauties of the garden city, this female mayor sat up and acted. Such consensus does seem to suggest that women's experience as women builds a common perspective.

WHAT IS NEEDED THEN?

Today, at the end of the 20th century, the worldwide women's movement is in an extremely fragmented state in its global political presence. 'Difference'—derived not only from class, geography, ethnicity and religion, but also from ideology, analysis, style of organisation, sectoral interest, educational history and a dozen other characteristics—divides its political stances or viewpoints. Grassroots, resource or advocacy centres, academicians or activists, membership or collectivity mode of organisation, Marxist or non-Marxist, political women's wing or neutral or local mobilisations, international, 'autonomous' or state-supported formations—we can go on endlessly producing a typology of difference. In large spaces like Beijing, or in small units like a district or a rural block, women and women's organisations claim their separate identity, and in a field of thought where value is placed on diversity and its affirmation for giving strength in identity, this accommodation of diversity within the boundary of a common gender is the mode.

There has been a political need for such affirmation of difference, but there is also a potential need for affirmation of unity, a common identity. Feminists would argue that while difference needs accommodation, unified action is possible when necessary on issues. But with all this accommodation of difference, there is also concern that the possibility of a unified stand, of unified action and of the notion of solidarity built around womanhood will dissipate.

In this context, adapting Gandhi's ideas to the women's movement as it enters the new millennium would not only reflect the convergence between currently held views of the worldwide women's movement and Gandhi's, but would also strengthen the former politically in the same way as the Indian freedom struggle was uplifted and made effective by Gandhi. Women, as they lay claim to transforming leadership and political behaviour, can stand on and fly from this platform that Gandhi created for them at the ideational level and at the practical level.

If this impending millennium has to be tamed, has to be dismantled from *The Exterminator*'s 'globe walk' and channelled into a determined march into a green and human world, an extremely powerful, single-minded, wide and deep typhoon needs to blow it off its current course. In today's highly stratified social scene, the one potential for unified idealistic action is the women's movement. Thus, it is not the achievement of education, health and livelihood parities that is the challenge before the women of India as they enter the new millennium, but political presence—and experience shows that this is a distinct possibility in India.

NOTES

1 Amartya K. Sen, 'Missing Women', *British Medical Journal*, vol. 304 (1992), pp. 586–87.

2 Devaki Jain, 'For Women to Lead—Ideas and Experiences from Asia: A Study on the Legal and Political Impediments to Gender Equality in Governance', paper presented at 'A Vision for the 21st Century', Asia Ministerial Conference on Governance for Sustainable Growth, Lahore, 1997.

3 Ibid.

4 UNDP, Human Development Report 1995.

5 Ibid., pp. 6, 88, 93.

6 Jain, *Indian Women*; see especially Bose, 'A Demographic Profile'.

7 Nirmala Banerjee and Devaki Jain, 'Indian Women's Experience of Development', ICSSR, New Delhi, 1990.

8 Ibid.

9 Data on the size of male and female populations, their age-specific distribution as well as occupation-wise breakdown of the workforce for different regions of India were drawn from census reports for various decades. These were supplemented by other official estimates of demographic as well as employment trends. Anthropological studies by several scholars as well as some literary sources provided many useful insights around which the paper was built.

The study, on the whole, fully supported the assertion that gender is an important variable in determining the distribution of well-being in Indian society, and that this is reflected to a significant degree in the demographic profile. For the girl child, the implications vary with class, caste, region and religion, but are not subsumed by any of these variables. *Rather, her experience of development is influenced by the combined effect of all of these variables, including gender. The persistently higher mortality rates of girl children in specific areas testify to this. Forces of development have succeeded in reducing overall rates of infant and child mortality in several of those areas. But this has not led to a corresponding cancellation of that bias to any noticeable degree.*

The paper argued that attempts to explain regional variations in the degree of bias against females in terms of variations in officially estimated levels of women's workforce participation rate (WFPR) for different regions have not been found satisfactory. There is considerable evidence to support the contention that, like the relative chances of survival of little girls, due recognition of women's work is also a fairly accurate indicator of women's relative social position in different parts of Indian society. Neither can explain or account for the other or determine women's position. The actual level of women's WFPR in a given region, in fact, appears to be closely and positively related to the level of men's WFPR in the same region. In general, these rates for both men and women would be relatively low or high depending on how far the region produced a surplus. See ibid.

10 Ibid.

11 UN, 'Action for Equality, Development and Peace', Fourth World Conference on Women, Beijing, 4–15 September 1995. The non-official women's forum held a press conference in Huairou on 3 September 1995.

12 For more on this, see the discussion in chapter 4.

13 UNDP, *Human Development Report 1995*; UNDP, *Human Development Report 1997*.

14 Feminist Review Collective, *Feminist Politics*.

15 Nelson Mandela, Inaugural Speech, Cape Town, South Africa, 9 May 1994.

16 UNDP, *Human Development Report 1998* (New York: Oxford University Press, 1998).

17 See, e.g., the work of the economist Frances Stewart.

18 George Mathew (ed.), *Status of Panchayati Raj in the States of India, 1994* (New Delhi: Concept Publishing, 1995), pp. 4–6.

19 *India Today*, 'From House Keeping to City Cleaning'. See chapter 4 for a more detailed discussion.

CHAPTER 7

Globalism and Localism

Negotiating Feminist Space

By 2002, since Beijing had flagged the importance of political reservation for women, many countries had introduced what was called the 'quota system'. India had introduced this system in local self-government, and the country became a showcase for women's political empowerment with one million women holding elected office. There was an idealism in the efforts to localise government, furthered by the idea that women would play a significant role in designing local development. It was in this context that the United Nations Development Fund for Women organised a global conference.

Simultaneously, however, there was a big push at the global level towards greater globalisation—basically through what we called 'neoliberal economics' involving free trade and the free movement of capital from government to financial institutions and MNCs. This made for a kind of confrontation between the call for localisation of government and the simultaneous entry of new global players with the capacity to determine the lives of 'local people'. I address these dilemmas in this paper, ending by arguing that it is only local power, especially in economic planning and led by women, that can heal the woes of inequality.

By one of those remarkable miracles of convergence, I am sharing the panel with Gigi Francesca, whom I frequently quote as having had the brilliance and the vision to have predicted, all of six years ago, that the two major actors or forces that will dominate the world in the 21st century would be the 'Globe' and 'Eurocentrism'. And indeed, a creature called *the globe* has arrived on the scene, and in many ways not only does it stride across nations, trampling over national sovereignty, but it has also replaced the earlier concept of internationalism or the *international*. Further, as we in India analyse the happenings in our state of Gujarat, which all of you would have seen and heard about, we also see the impact of Eurocentrism once removed. How, you may ask. There is a whole discourse which has now emerged on 'civilisations', dividing the world with notions like 'Western world' and 'Islamic world' and so on. I have quotations here from our brilliant writer and activist Arundhati Roy,[1] which say what I want to say but in her unique and passionate words:

> With each battle cry against Pakistan, we inflict a wound on ourselves, on our way of life, on our spectacularly diverse and ancient civilisation, on everything that makes India different from Pakistan. Increasingly, Indian Nationalism has come to mean Hindu Nationalism, which defines itself not through a respect or regard for itself, but through a hatred of the Other. And the Other, for the moment, is not just Pakistan, it's Muslim. It's disturbing to see how neatly nationalism dovetails into fascism....
>
> ... Can we not find it in ourselves to belong to an ancient civilisation instead of to just a recent nation? To love a *land* instead of just patrolling a territory? The Sangh Parivar understands nothing of what civilisation means.... In no time at all, the godsquadders from hell have colonised the public imagination. And we allowed them in.

To me, a shocking and vivid example of what has happened to the world's language of identification of 'the other' was an interview I saw on the BBC, on May 6th of this year, of the former Secretary General of the UN, Mr Boutros Boutros-Ghali, by Tim Sebastian of *HARDTalk*. Tim Sebastian had the archaic-ness to suggest to Mr Boutros-Ghali in the interview that 'what you [the "Arab world"] call freedom struggles and resistance, *we in the West would call Terrorism*.' He went on pressing Mr Boutros-Ghali on the practice of human bombing, suggesting that this was not only unthinkable in the West, but some kind of attribute of the 'other', constantly separating himself from the perceptions that Mr Boutros-Ghali was describing, saying 'this would not be *how we would see it in the West*' (read Anglo-Saxon world? Christian world?). And was it not the 'West' that had bred fascism? The Holocaust, the slave trade? And is there a 'West'?

Amartya Sen, in a lecture 'Exclusion and Inclusion' in 2001, said:

> This issue has become particularly important in the context of the present political crisis and confrontation, *with its ramifications becoming clearer since September 11*, though the roots of the problem go back much further.... By categorising the population of the world into those belonging to 'the Islamic world', 'the Christian world', 'the Hindu world', 'the Buddhist world', etc.,

the divisive power of classificatory priority is implicitly used to place people firmly inside a unique set of rigid boxes. Other divisions (say, between the rich and the poor, between members of different classes and occupations, between people of different politics, between distinct nationalities and residential locations, between language groups, etc.) are all submerged by this allegedly pre-eminent way of seeing the differences between people....

[Such boxing] is potentially a great ethical and political hazard, with far-reaching consequences for *human rights*.... I would argue that the main hope of harmony in the contemporary world lies in the *plurality of our identities*, which cut across each other and work against sharp divisions around one single hardened line of impenetrable division.[2]

I offer these quotations to emphasise the point that there is a back-slide to the Middle Ages, a 'return of the Dark Ages'. The intensity of the recent (post–September 11th) arrival of religious difference as a source of not only conflict but militant intolerance by arrogant power takes the world back to the days of the Crusaders of medieval times—to the Dark Ages, when bigotry defined the limits of the human imagination. Since then, not only the Enlightenment in the West, but the intellectual expression of societies in the 'South' and the 'East', had extended the boundaries of the imagination to other categories of stratification and division, such as class, ethnicity, caste, gender, occupation. Nations identified themselves not as Christian and pagan but as newly liberated or colonised. The place of religion as the conqueror was eroded in the 20th century, and there was a sharp fall in attendance in churches, temples and mosques worldwide. However, as many of us suggest, there has been a backslide.

Interestingly, the declaration of the NAM conference on 'Culture and Development' held in 1997,[3] to which I was a delegate from India, said that 'We, i.e., the peoples of the NAM countries' gathered in Colombia had similarity in culture even if we were different in language, race and location, political identity, economic strength, etc. Our culture could unite us, and divisions amongst us were created by our colonisers who tried to separate us by describing us as anthropologically different from each other. The *Report of the South Commission* also had a chapter on a cultural charter,[4] again making a case for unity through cultural homogeneity. Therefore, culture was an experience which superseded religion, and this is now getting eroded by the 'Dark Ages' type of intolerant Crusader—and that is Christianity and Anglo-Saxonism of the most archaic kind.[5] And Gigi I think saw this coming even as far back as 1995. It is an honour then for me to be sharing this platform with Gigi and I salute her brilliance.

I have begun with this larger picture because for those of us who are looking at gender, democracy and development, there is a great responsibility to work our way, during this significant conference with such an extraordinary representation of people from all corners of our world interested in the political element of economic transformation, to making this conference itself a tool for women's political voice to overpower, to push back, the attempts to reorganise social categories, moving them away from diversity, from multiple identities, which is so much a part of feminist expression, 'to one single hardened line of impenetrable division', to reinvoke Prof. Sen. We may look at best practices, at mechanisms of networking, and learn from each other, we may exercise our brilliant minds to do hair-splitting analysis, but Rome is burning. Our solidarity as a conference has to speak to this larger world, which is on the border of ruination not only due to environmental abuse, but due to the revival of the attitudes of the Dark Ages, or bigotry, and of course that bigotry includes anti-woman venom.

THE TERMINOLOGY

I have deliberately called my paper 'Globalism and Localism' as I think the 'ism' indicates what could be called an ideology, a philosophy, and not merely a phenomenon, a process or a practice. I use the 'ism' because to some extent the debate has moved into the 'ism' type of mindset—you are either a globalist or a localist. Reminds me of a remark by George Bush, which has been picked up by Arundhati Roy, which, however remote it might seem, I must share with you: 'Then President Bush's canon will come back to us: "Either you're with us or with the terrorists." Those words hang frozen in time like icicles. For years to come, butchers and genocidists will fit their grisly mouths around them ("lip-synch", filmmakers call it) in order to justify their butchery.'[6]

I do not want to appear polemical and make my paper purely a play on words. But it is also my belief or my view that unless terms and terminologies are disaggregated or deconstructed or decomposed, some of the issues that I am sure are implied in the theme and the question raised in this seminar cannot be addressed or clarified. Feminists who began with what looked like an acceptable construct of the 'ism' over the last two decades have moved to a recognition that the word escapes a universally acceptable meaning. I quote: 'An internationalist "we" has become unspeakable, the internationalist woman has been silenced before she was ever heard.'[7]

Similarly, globalism as well as some of the features associated with globalism need to be identified and given some meaning. For example, globalism could be benign, a philosophy which supports global endeavours, the concept of the world as one, the global village, the human race, the earth, looking at the globe as a whole, and supporting notions which strengthen the 'one world' concept. Globalism can also be virulent, made into a destructive force overpowering the local.

'Localisation' and 'globalisation' have become the two major words and concepts and processes being 'sold' by all concerned, whether it is the UN and its agencies such as the International Labour Organization (ILO), UNDP, etc., or the Bretton Woods Institutions, or governments and civil society. We cannot consider one without considering the other. However, both terms and the implied operations cannot be usefully assessed without further disaggregation or decomposition into their various forms.[8]

Decentralisation suggests reconstructing centralisation, giving more space to the periphery, to the lower levels of operations, be they of the government, of corporates, of any organisation or project/enterprise. While its interpretation is often linked with greater participation and community-driven enterprises, this does not necessarily follow. Terms like 'subsidiarity', bringing down to lower levels of organisation what does not need the higher level, appear in this discourse.

In India, we attempt not to use this term, but we name our attempts as 'building local self-government'. The connotation is to build *upwards*, build government and democracy from the local to the state (provincial) level and onwards to the national level. Thus, the excluding process implied in the term 'subsidiarity' is reversed. The local decides what the upper levels do.

I can give many more examples of such modes or modules of the concept of decentralisation. For example, the Pinochet model, the Ayub Khan model of basic democracies, the Ugandan model of a single-party structure which localises government, and so on. It is important to know what is the particular form before we judge its value.

A recent article by Dinoo Anna Mathew in one of our most eminent journals in India, the *Economic and Political Weekly*,[9] answers a criticism from another author, Poromesh Acharya, that the new system of governance introduced by two amendments to the Indian Constitution, the 73rd and 74th, has worsened the implementation of elementary education. Dinoo says all that needs to be said about the difference between 'decentralisation', seen as layering, and local self-government through electoral politics and its intent. He says: 'It is a well known fact that the 73rd and 74th Constitutional Amendment Acts have a wider purpose to be fulfilled.' In the first paragraph of Acharya's article,[10] he says that the 'panchayats have been conceived to be the third layer of government and are supposed to be entrusted with the responsibility of implementing universal and compulsory free education.' The fallacy, says Dinoo, is 'to perceive local bodies as implementing agencies of programmes of higher tiers of government. The constitutional amendments have clearly stated panchayats to be self-governing institutions. That a majority of the state governments are yet to enable their panchayats to be local self-governments is a matter of continuing concern.'[11] Dinoo concludes that 'political parties and state governments, instead of enabling panchayats to function as self-governing institutions, are making them mere tools in their hands.'[12]

A major concern raised by development activists is the existence of parallel structures which undermine the spirit of functioning of these elected councils. In India, donors and especially the World Bank in partnership with the state governments have set up alternative structures at the local level and call the scheme 'decentralisation', whereas it is mere 'subsidiarity'.

Taking on another criticism, Dinoo asks:

Isn't it utopian to assume that a process of decision-making at the village/panchayat level would be free of conflict and power play? Is a village community completely harmonised and sufficient in itself? Such an assumption would in effect negate the very basis of providing reservations for marginalised groups (women, dalits) in panchayats, which provides the entry point for such groups to participate in decision-making.[13]

Such views, that is, that politics is bad, wasteful and dirty, which are implied in the paper by Poromesh Acharya to which Dinoo Mathew is responding, are gaining prominence. I would like to argue that poverty and inequality are not economic issues—they are political issues. How political power is arranged determines the allocations and the access.[14] Giving expression to the politics of deprived groups can transform political platforms and the direction and substance of development to serve the interests of these groups. A critical base or foundation for citizens to reach for and claim equity or justice is provided by the *spaces* for them to exercise their rights, to differ, to deviate, to challenge, to protest—apart from to shape.[15]

Spaces and institutional mechanisms are needed, for example, for women's issues, women's concerns, women's opinions to enter the political fora where mobilisation and action, whether through law or economics, are decided. This is only possible in a highly democratic situation where there is freedom of expression, freedom to dissent, to protest, to challenge the traditions that are taken as givens.[16]

Proximity is a value to the poor and excluded. Women value proximity, whether it is to a drinking water source, a fuel source, a crèche, a health centre, a court of justice or an office of administration. Poor women have to walk to access these facilities, which is exhausting and consumes valuable time. Moreover, when there is an attack, a rape, a burning, a witch-hunt or other violence against a woman, seeking redress from councils, which are located far away, may not be feasible. But if these councils and the people in them are near, the chances of redress and effective action are greater.

A case in point is the experience of Mahila Samakhya, an innovative educational programme being supported by the central government.

It showed the capacity of women not only to nurture and stay in collectivities like the *sangha* or the *mahila panch* or the *nari adalat*,[17] but to dispense justice through dialogue and debate amongst women only—a remarkable innovation and practice in so-called 'backward states' like Uttar Pradesh.[18] This was a vivid example of the value of proximity for effective participation, for resolution of conflict and for holding state and society accountable. In assessing the outcomes, the presenters made remarkable conceptual innovations, affirming the feminist view that it is practice that is the teacher, not theory, and that practice can and should construct theory if it has to be efficient, that assessment indicators need to be fluid and move over time, depending on the phase of a process.

This experience/initiative illustrates how participation transforms a development input into a right if process is emphasised. These women were showing how the most important outcome, the solution, is not the end of the marital conflict. The solution is the woman recognising her agency, a concept that has been developed by Prof. Amartya Sen.[19] There has been a transformation in the family and in women's recognition of their own power. It is here that development is converted into a right, not in the *Human Development Reports*. Institutions like the Mahila Samakhya and, through them, the mahila panch and nari adalat, have enabled women to convert a development input in the form of a programme of education into a rights affirmation programme by skilfully using the collective, by being able to belong and nurture their collectives, something men cannot easily do.

I would also suggest that local self-government as mandated by the Indian Constitution through the 73rd and 74th amendments—now synonymous with decentralisation in India—is the best, if not the only, instrument available to the poor as well as other groups excluded from conventional power, such as women, minorities and Dalits in India, to participate in, direct and claim justice. I suggest that these amendments and the structures they have generated are democratising development, deepening democracy, and improving the quality of representation through the most well-established vehicles of democracy, namely, accountability affirmed by universal franchise and multi-party elections at regular intervals, and social justice enshrined by the reservation of seats for women and the excluded castes.

I further suggest that participation for excluded groups, for the poor, is most valuable when it involves participation in politics. The heart of the women's question lies in gender relations—the inequality in power and autonomy between men and women—and the redressal of this inequality/lack of autonomy for women is contingent on their political presence, their visibility in conventional politics. This was also strongly affirmed in Beijing in 1995 by the worldwide women's movement.[20]

I suggest that local self-government in India has for the first time generated participation; if we include participation in formal politics as a key aspect of participation, then we have massive participation. For the first time, we have more than one million elected women representatives amongst 3.5 million local political officials. What a massive force of politicians! I would argue that the PRI system has in fact ushered in participation in the most vital sphere, namely the power game, and while we mock at the women, they are transforming gender relations and their own perceptions of themselves as well as those of their crucial circle, the family.

This exposure to politics, of fighting elections even if they have been set up as dummies or proxies, this sitting in councils even if their hands and minds are being twisted by men, is politicising women in formal politics, and the scent of power, like the scent of honey, is not easily shed. Women are flexing their muscles and revealing their influence on local institutions. Women's strong presence in local self-government or in PRIs in India has influenced many dimensions of politics, both in theory and in practice. It has not only unpacked gender relations—the relations of power between men and women—but also transformed the quality and thrust of local self-government and the political landscape in India. Women are critiquing current ideologies of political economy, the notions of power and the methods of exercising it, and demonstrating how they can mould these into institutions that are gender-equitable, just and humane.

These institutional suggestions may appear to be well-trodden ground. However, it is interesting that in recent articles published in 2002,[21] both Prof. Joseph E. Stiglitz, Nobel Laureate and former

Economic Adviser to the World Bank, and Prof. Amartya Sen, also a Nobel Laureate, speak about the importance of institutions leading to regulatory mechanisms. In his essay, Stiglitz says: 'Globalisation has brought huge benefits to a few with few benefits to the many.'[22] Similarly, in a section of his paper headed 'Institutions and Inequality', Prof. Sen spells out what could be called necessary conditions for the safe landing of globalisation; the list is focused entirely around various types of institutional arrangements and provision of social services on the ground. Sen remarks: 'The market economy does not work by itself in global relations—indeed it cannot operate alone even within a given country. These enabling conditions themselves depend critically on economic, social and political institutions that operate nationally and globally.'[23]

In some sense, such proposals—from Stiglitz and Sen, and also articulated in the *Human Development in South Asia 2001* report,[24]—all underline the importance of regulatory mechanisms. What is common to all of them is the importance of international regulatory mechanisms to prevent abuse of liberalisation, globalisation and privatisation, and to ensure that there are safeguards against inequity and violation of human rights. Therefore, our assessment of this form of agency depends not only on how it is set up, but also on the broader picture or framework—the country's political setup, its political philosophy, form of democracy, experience of democracy and elections and, most of all, the presence of voice, especially the voice of dissent.

Thus, I would answer the question posed in the subtitle of the seminar, 'Is Decentralisation a Tool for Local Effective Political Voice?', by saying, 'It depends.' But as an activist, I cannot stop there. While I celebrate the diversity and multiplicity of local experiences, I would still say that if we wish to enable local power or the localisation of power, the localisation of development management, so as to enable 'voice', then the larger space must permit disagreement, protest, diversity and pluralism, that is, it must be democratic. Thus, it is important not to be inhibited and to find some core elements within the various forms of decentralisation which can restructure the organisation of society, which can shift gender relations and which can allow the upturning of the pyramid, in other words, the spreading of the local to the global.

Vindication for mobilising local resources through decentralisation has come and continues to come from ground experiences—the women's self-help groups which have taken up the developmental space almost as an all-India movement; positive and dynamic examples of elected women PRI members dealing with people's day-to-day problems; local water harvesting efforts that have solved water problems in chronically drought-affected Rajasthan—the examples are many and are steadily increasing in number. Still, in a country as vast as India, they appear sporadic and scattered.

So, this is not just about financing or raising resources, locally or otherwise, for local grassroots development. It is the entire philosophy and concept of local self-governance that has yet to be accepted (constitutional mandate notwithstanding) in toto. The discussions on this cannot still be limited to how much power or responsibility or capacity the PRIs should/can handle. Instead, the nitty-gritty has to come down to one specific area—how effectively to add this deeper dimension to our democracy.[25]

NUANCING GLOBALISATION

Globalisation is interpreted basically as a free flow of goods, services, knowledge, labour. It is built on the theory of free trade, which in turn is built on the economic model of perfect competition. These theories basically argue that the most efficient method of running the economy, maximising resources and maximising benefits is by allowing factors of production, in this case including services and knowledge, to move freely to take their positions within that maximising model.

I would like to argue that globalisation has not taken place, that globalisation does not exist and therefore we are tilting at a non-existent phenomenon. How do I say this? My argument is that while there may be free flow of capital, and while the knowledge-based industries on the internet are also globalised, not only is labour not globalised, but it is also the case that the push to deregulate, to liberalise, is asymmetrical.

Second, I would emphasise the importance of deconstructing, disaggregating or decomposing the term 'globalisation'. For example,

Prof. Jagdish Bhagwati of Columbia University, an influential free trade theorist, breaks the concept down into capital, investment and labour.[26] However, in a sense, Bhagwati leaves out the most important segment of globalisation. He omits the segment which has generated the most accessible globalisation, as well as triggered the intensity of interdependence of global economic forces, namely, information technology. Interestingly, however, the UNDP *Human Development Report* for 1999 has a diagram which demonstrates the digital divide. The US and other OECD countries make up 18.8 per cent of the world population, of whom 33.2 per cent are internet users. South Asia on the other hand makes up 23.5 per cent of the world population, but only 0.04 per cent of South Asians are internet users.[27]

Therefore, I suggest that since globalisation does not exist, we must take a more nuanced term such as 'regulation' and see the subtleties of where deregulation has taken place, where regulation exists, and where regulation can be improved.

A review of the literature[28] yields the striking observation that everyone in the system, be it the World Bank, academic economists, or NGOs, everyone is nuancing globalisation. By nuancing I mean drawing out the subtleties or the details. Thus, in the last five years the discourse has shifted from the 'mantra' stage (that is, sweeping statements about states and markets, and liberalisation and reform). The voices have now shifted to qualification, to a concern with *reforming the reform programme*.

This transformation from rigidity to humility is of course due to actual lived experience, but also due to new interventions in the discourse, such as those from the UNDP's *Human Development Reports*. This transformation also includes the effectiveness of groundswell movements such as the NGO movement, and the inclusion of women in larger numbers than before in the various consultative and decision-making processes at the local or international level. I suggest that the 'invisible hand' is at work from the notoriously invisible people of the world—women.

I suggest, further, that the leading players in global governance and the less visible ones are nuancing globalisation. They are creating spaces for negotiating and recasting the parameters of the discourse. The missing keys are unity, political ethics and moral purpose. These must be brought in by the women's movement. If that could be forged, then there are enough examples of leverage which are encouraging.

I argue that we must revise the language used and the measures introduced in the discourse on globalisation. We need to rethink the spaces that the global system provides and the direction in which we develop our energies and the purpose of movements dedicated to social justice. These are important elements in recasting the direction of development.

For example, some of the changes in terminology that suggest themselves as more powerful in stimulating change include replacing the term 'showcasing' with 'snowballing'. By this I mean that we should incorporate larger and larger spaces for public opinion and therefore public policy. These are small sparks that show promise of firing justice.

Like South Africa, I would substitute the word 'transformation' for 'development'.[29] I suggest that we the people have to teach the UN and the national governments how to develop their analytical and monitoring frameworks, rather than work into or with the ones they have created. Attention has to be shifted from the state to the achievements of civil society in transformation. These achievements need to be blown up into a storm to break down traditional structures of development.

Today, among those who are looking at globalisation, be it at the headquarters, that is, Washington, or in other economic forums, including academic forums or the UN Conference on Trade and Development, the interest is in developing regulatory institutions— institutions which bring justice, institutions which prevent unruly behaviour by financial markets, by information technology and so forth. There is a richer territory for agencies to engage in if we turn our attention to regulation and institutions. Over the last decade, even at the location from which this mantra was being preached, there has been strong revisionism. It is now understood that regulation is crucial even for liberalisation to function without the shocks that the system has received. Thus we hear of new financial architecture, we hear of the importance of some level of barriers in trade. It has been

recognised by everyone that the playing fields are not level, that liberalisation is asymmetrical both in its power and its practice, that world
organisations like the World Trade Organization (WTO) already have
in them the embedded power structures of international economic
governance. Thus there has been a sea change even in the thinking of
the very gods themselves.

REGIONALISATION: A POTENTIAL FOR CONVERGENCE

I suggest that regionalism (that is, geographically based continental
boundaries of integrated economic development) can perhaps provide the kind of institutional arrangements needed for coping with
globalisation successfully. It is now recognised that globalisation
needs regulation, it needs governance and preparedness. Individual
countries, like individual citizens, may not be able to manage the
globetrotting of MNCs and international finance. But if individual
countries link with others who are similar because of geography or
history, then their internal capacities can be strengthened before taking
on the global environment. This idea matches with the mainstream
point of view that the most effective way of handling globalisation is to
have it tethered to a national programme. The assumption is that the
procedures within national institutions would facilitate transparency
and the capacity to attempt to regulate financial markets. From there,
national institutions can move into regional alliances to broaden the
same procedures at that level.

If globalisation can treat the earth as one space untrammelled by
national boundaries, why shouldn't the South try *regionalisation* with
the same aim and have some roving regional economic giants—regional
MNCs that strengthen our own muscles with all the injunctions of
free trade theory? At the NAM Summit in Durban in 1998,[30] a policy
document also proposed greater attention to regionalism.[31] South Asia
is deeply engaged in deepening democracy through locally elected
councils of development administration. At the regional level, these
structures can be strengthened by enabling them to connect with each
other, strengthening their participation in national and international
governance.

Perhaps the UN should reclaim its original place as an intellectual spot which encourages and promotes public opinion and viewpoints and advocates for the luminous ideas. One of our suggestions was that the UN has a role in interconnecting countries within a region. In the stakeholders' meeting at UNDP India in 2002, the emphasis was also on networking, gender, as well as making micro–macro links. A role that the UN family can play is to support interconnectedness and regional perspectives.

GROUND-LEVEL PROJECTS IN PROGRESS

The Karnataka Women's Information and Resource Centre, located in Bangalore, is an organisation which pioneered interaction with those women who emerged into local self-government in India as far back as 1990, when Karnataka became the first state to promulgate an act by which power was to be devolved to locally elected councils, and 25 per cent of the seats were reserved for women. About 12,000 women were invited to Bangalore for the first convention of women elected to PRIs. It was an unbelievable sight to see these women who had emerged from actual electoral battles. It was almost like being in Mexico, where I found the presence of enormous numbers of women an inspiring experience, and also came to the understanding that this was where strength lay.

The centre now has three processes/projects which link the elected women. We call them elected women representatives, or local women politicians, just to flag the fact that they are political personae, even though there is plenty of literature which mocks at them as women who are puppets in the hands of their husbands, or as women who do not understand governance. One activity of the centre is to federate these women into an association, just like the Inter-Parliamentary Union, with a subset, the International Union of Women Parliamentarians. The federation is to traverse the four southern states of India, and the numbers that will emerge are mind-blowing. Already in one of the southern states, Tamil Nadu, 100,000 women have federated them-selves, and they invite the premier of the province apart from political leaders to their conventions for negotiations.

In Kerala, they have begun with small networks, but are beginning to reconstruct the methodology by which funds for women are utilised. In Karnataka, they are being exposed through the technique of participatory research to conversations on macro policy matters such as the population policy, health policy and so forth.

Another related project involves enabling these women to deconstruct the budgets for the areas where they govern, and then reconstruct them according to their sense of what the revenue collection and expenditure should be for their area. These projects have been on the ground only for the last two years, and it is our expectation that if they are further supported, at the end of five years they should become what we call the 'voice of women in the political firmament'.

Some of the interesting transformations that these women have already begun to effect, for example, relate to identity politics, representation, and the quota system. They are constantly building alternative ways of handling violence against women and alcoholism, and practices of data collection. Thus, they are teaching political theory and political practice.

The next step would be to create linkages between these women and processes of economic transformation. It is here that the larger international women's movement led by the UN Development Fund for Women and donors—the velvet triangle, as it is called—must recast the dialogue and conversation on globalisation, bringing to the table ideas such as institutional architecture that enables the voice of poorer women, financial architecture that enables the sovereignty of nations, and then the sovereignty of subnational groups, reviving UN principles. The latest blow to the UN has been the children's summit of 2002 and its outcome.[32] My friend Adrienne Germain, president of the International Women's Health Coalition, has gone on record saying that this is a disaster and the United States is to blame, and that 'it was shoved down the throats of the rest of the world by the United States.'[33] We cannot have the UN become a creature of the unipolar world. This requires us to be in partnership with those who come from local self-government.

Ultimately, the question of how we converge, or diverge, on these two processes, globalisation and localisation, knowing full well that they are basket terms, would be, in my view determined by our purpose. Long before the word 'globalisation' came into fashion, Mahatma Gandhi had thought of it. I quote:

> According to me the economic constitution of India and for the matter of that of the world, should be such that no one under it should suffer from want of food and clothing. In other words everybody should be able to get sufficient work to enable him to make the two ends meet. And this ideal can be universally realized only if the means of production of the elementary necessaries of life remain in the control of the masses. These should be freely available to all as God's air and water are or ought to be; they should not be made a vehicle of traffic for the exploitation of others. Their monopolization by any country, nation or group of persons would be unjust. The neglect of this simple principle is the cause of the destitution that we witness today not only in this unhappy land but in other parts of the world too.[34]

And here is another voice, one which to me represents a new Gandhi, Arundhati Roy:

> Independence itself came to us as what Gandhi famously called a 'wooden loaf'—a notional freedom tainted by the blood of the thousands who died during Partition.... Every political party has tilled the marrow of our secular parliamentary democracy, mining it for electoral advantage. Like termites excavating a mound, they've made tunnels and underground passages, undermining the meaning of 'secular', until it has just become an empty shell that's about to implode. Their tilling has weakened the foundations of the structure that connects the Constitution, Parliament and the courts of law—the configuration of checks and balances that forms the backbone of a parliamentary democracy. Under the circumstances, it's futile to go on blaming politicians and demanding from them a morality they're incapable of. There's something pitiable about a people that constantly bemoans its leaders. If they've let us down, it's only because we've allowed them to.[35]

I end with these words of hope and advice from Arundhati Roy:

> Unfortunately there's no quick fix. Fascism itself can only be turned away if all those who are outraged by it show a commitment to social justice that equals the intensity of their indignation.

Are we ready to get off our starting blocks? Are we ready, many millions of us, to rally not just on the streets, but at work and in schools and in our homes, in every decision we take, and every choice we make?

NOTES

1 Arundhati Roy, 'Democracy: Who's She When She's at Home?', *Outlook* (Mumbai), 6 May 2002.

2 Amartya Sen, 'Exclusion and Inclusion', paper presented at the conference on 'Including the Excluded', South Asians for Human Rights, New Delhi, 11–12 November 2001; emphases mine.

3 NAM Conference of Ministers of Culture, Medellin, Colombia, 3–5 September 1997.

4 South Commission, *The Challenge to the South: The Report of the South Commission* (New York: Oxford University Press, 1990).

5 Culture also is a problematique, as feminists know. And so is race or class, but culture is more fluid and malleable and flexible than religion, whose militant identity is always fundamentalist.

6 Roy, 'Democracy: Who's She When She's at Home?'

7 Elisabeth Prugl and Mary K. Meyer (eds), *Gender Politics in Global Governance* (Oxford: Rowman and Littlefield, 1999).

8 Nicholas Stern, *A Strategy for Development* (Washington, D.C.: World Bank, 2001).

9 Dinoo Anna Mathew, 'Panchayats Alone Are Not to Blame', *Economic and Political Weekly*, vol. 37, no. 18 (4–10 May 2002), pp. 1767–68.

10 Poromesh Acharya, 'Education: Panchayat and Decentralisation—Myths and Reality', *Economic and Political Weekly*, vol. 37, no. 8 (23 February 2002), pp. 788–96.

11 Mathew, 'Panchayats Alone Are Not to Blame', p. 1767.

12 Ibid., p. 1768.

13 Ibid.

14 Access has been identified as one of the most crucial rights for redressal of discriminatory practices in development by the Advisory Panel for the UNDP's 2002 HDR. See UNDP, *Human Development Report 2002: Deepening Democracy in a Fragmented World* (New York: Oxford University Press, 2002).

15 Devaki Jain, 'The Poverty Thing'.

16 DAWN, 'Challenging the Given: DAWN's Perspectives on Social Development', presented at the World Summit on Social Development, New York, August–September 1994.

17 Sangha (Sanskrit) refers to an association, community, assembly, or company. Mahila panch and nari adalat refer to women-headed arbitration courts.

18 International Centre for Research on Women, *Domestic Violence in India: A Summary Report of Three Studies* (Washington, D.C.: ICRW, September 1999); Devaki Jain, *The Vocabulary of Women's Politics* (New Delhi: Friedrich Ebert Stiftung, 2001).

19 Amartya Sen, who has provided the space to understand and draw the links between development, human rights and justice, has an interesting comment to make: 'We need a vision of mankind not as *patients*, whose interests have to be looked after, but as *agents* who can do effective things—both individually and jointly. We also have to go beyond the role of human beings specifically as "consumers" or as "people with needs", and consider, more broadly, their general role as agents of change who can—given the opportunity—think, assess, evaluate, resolve, inspire, agitate, and through these means, reshape the world.' Sen, 'The Ends and Means of Sustainability'.

20 Devaki Jain, 'Conference Journeys: What Have We Not Done? Where Have We Gone Wrong?', presentation at the Conference of Non-governmental Organizations, New York, June 2000. The Beijing conference, that is, the Fourth World Conference on Women in 1995, had drawn particular attention to the neglect of women in political structures all over the world and the importance of bringing women into political structures. The UNDP's *HDR 1995* has excellent data showing that women worldwide have had very little share in political processes in the form of political parties, parliaments, and so on. See UNDP, *Human Development Report 1995*.

On the other hand, women have always been very active in politics, if politics is taken to be the broader theatre of the struggle for rights. For example, women have been very prominent in freedom struggles. Therefore, it is not for lack of political consciousness that women are not in politics, but rather they have not been given the opportunity to translate this consciousness into what is called formal political expression.

21 Amartya Sen, 'How to Judge Globalism', *American Prospect*, Winter (2002); Joseph Stiglitz, 'Globalism's Discontent', *American Prospect*, Winter (2002), pp. A16–A21.

22 Stiglitz, 'Globalism's Discontent'.

23 Sen, 'How to Judge Globalism'.

24 Mahbub ul Haq Human Development Centre, *Human Development in South Asia 2001: Globalisation and Human Development* (Oxford: Oxford University Press, 2002).

25 'In Search of Equitable and Just Development', Round Table on Financing for District Level Development, Karnataka Women's Information and Resource Centre, Bangalore, and UN Development Fund for Women, New Delhi, 19 May 2001.

26 Jagdish Bhagwati, 'Globalization Has a Human Face', lecture at the India Habitat Centre, New Delhi, 18 October 1999.

27 UNDP, *Human Development Report 1999* (New York: Oxford University Press, 1999).

28 World Bank, *World Development Report 1999/2000: Entering the 21st Century* (New York: Oxford University Press, 1999); ILO, *World Employment Report 1998–99: Employability in the Global Economy—How Training Matters* (Geneva: ILO, 1998); United Nations Population Fund, *Population, Food Production and Nutrition in India* (New Delhi: UNPF, October 1999); Kirit S. Parikh (ed.), *India Development Report 1999–2000* (New Delhi: Oxford University Press, 1999); UN General Assembly, *1999 World Survey on the Role of Women in Development: Globalization, Gender and Work*, Report of the Secretary General, 18 August 1999; Bhagwati, 'Globalization Has a Human Face'.

29 Devaki Jain and Samia Ahmad, 'Towards Just Development: Identifying Meaningful Indicators', Working Paper, UNDP, South Africa, 1999.

30 The 12th NAM Summit Conference, Durban, South Africa, 2–3 September 1998.

31 Devaki Jain, 'Close Encounters of Another Kind: Building Regional Economic Cooperation on Women's Advice and Leadership', Asian Development Bank, Manila, 2 March 1998.

32 The final resolution of the summit watered down the provisions relating to sexual and reproductive health services under the pressure of US demands with regard to sex education, contraception and abortion.

33 See Edith M. Lederer, 'UN Summit Pledges to Help Children', Associated Press, New York, 12 May 2002.

34 M. K. Gandhi, 'Economic Constitution of India', *Young India*, 15 November 1928.

35 Roy, 'Democracy: Who's She When She's at Home?'

Women's Participation in the History of Ideas and the Reconstruction of Knowledge

Living in Bangalore, I was located close to one of the well-known national institu-
tions there—the National Institute of Advanced Studies (NIAS). There were many
distinguished scholars there, one of whom was interested in theories of knowledge
and the mind. In fact, consciousness was one of the themes that NIAS had engaged
in, starting from its founder Dr Raja Ramanna. I had once commented that 'given
knowledge', that is, knowledge created by some of the famous theorists in psychol-
ogy, sociology or even religion, was being challenged by feminists. The faculty at
NIAS asked whether I could give a lecture on this issue of the feminist challenge
to inherited knowledge usually created and argued for by men. The following
lecture, presented in 2004, was a result of that invitation. In it I referred to as
many sources that I could find of feminist scholars who had revealed errors in
the logic of some of the greatest theorists.

The problems of knowledge are central to feminist theorizing, which has
sought to destabilize androcentric, mainstream thinking in the humanities
and in the social and natural sciences.

—Helen E. Longino (1993)[1]

The feminist agenda raises questions on what constitutes knowledge and
how the disciplinary divisions are created. This questioning creates a
'politics of disturbance'.

—William Connolly (1993)[2]

It unsettles the given and starts to 'plough up inherited turfs without planting the same old seeds in the field'.

—Christine Sylvester (1998)[3]

The story of women's involvement in reasoning has been a story of unpeeling the various layers in which inequality is embedded. It speaks of the many faces of difference that need to be addressed, the strategies to be employed, and the structures needed for removing inequality from the local to the global level. It outlines the legal, political, social, cultural, economic and ethical elements that have come into play in the quest for equality. It points to the enemies of the idea of equality, just as indeed Mill pointed to the sources of the threats to liberty.

In this process of making the invisible visible, in peeling away the layers of the onion, other domains have also gained. In other words, the method or process of revealing that which had been excluded or rendered invisible has also thrown new light on other invisible facts or phenomena. This broader enlightenment has involved the flow of new knowledge into modernisation theories—obstructing, challenging, deconstructing and reconstructing them.[4] Another key aspect and purpose of women's struggle has been the challenge to the theorems of power and embedded hierarchies often legitimised through invoking culture in an archaic language.

Women's engagement with development has provided ideas for strategy and policy as well as pulling development out of its conventional paths. In the process of delivering a just development, there has been value added. Much of the contribution of the dialogue with women has been with regard to the 'how', in the form of strategies of using power, materialising effective transformation at the grassroots level, or measuring value: the exposition has been primarily on method. A whole range of issues that make up what is called 'measurement', both qualitative and quantitative, has been enriched. Distinctions between 'private' and 'public' space, 'formal' and 'informal' work, as well as the thinking regarding the traditional division of the labour force and the understanding of the location of 'inequality', have been challenged.

I hope in this paper to link two independent streams of work. One stream consists of some of the gleanings from what is called 'women's studies', but basically involves further investigations in the social sciences; the second stream includes the findings from the research for a book that I have written, titled *Women, Development and the UN: A*

Sixty-Year Quest for Equality and Justice,[5] which was part of a project recording the history of ideas that shaped the UN over a period of 60 years.[6]

Women, through the articulation of their lived experience, challenge the basis of given knowledge and the interpretation of phenomena in theory. They have expanded concepts, deconstructed and reconstructed the principles of various disciplines and offered new ways of doing things effectively. But their contribution to thought, and thereby to methodology or practice, is ignored both by academics and policy makers as well as by the UN and other agencies, as I discovered when I was writing the book.

One of the many values of women's reconstruction of knowledge is that what women are doing for themselves also enables others who have been subjected to similar exclusions or demeaning valuations due to poverty, race or religion. Thus, I argue that this intellection and the challenges it offers to various theories illuminate the road to truth through justice.[7]

While the body of literature is immense in this field of women's studies, what I would like to do is illustrate from a few of the disciplines how the interpretation of experience changes theoretical propositions, the language or nomenclature used, and thus the prescription too.

PSYCHOLOGY

In 1986, at a seminar at Leiden University on 'The Gender of Power',[8] a large number of scholars from the Netherlands, drawn from the fields of psychology, sociology and politics, not only challenged almost every theory from Freud to Foucault and beyond, critiquing their propositions in terms of both fact and analysis, but also offered reinterpretations from the feminist understanding of female experience. The scholars evocatively reinterpreted the illustrations usually offered of nervous diseases such as anorexia and hysteria. Anorexia was seen by presenters as covert and overt expressions of resistance by women, not as some form of depression to be treated with pills. It was interpreted as fasting rather than starving—fasting as a voluntary choice, which sends a threatening message, as different from starving, which is imposed by others, a victimisation by the outside.

Men, including many famous analysts, have historically tended to see women as hysterical and unreasonable. Robespierre, the leader of the French Revolution, and therefore one would imagine a champion of rights, nevertheless argued that women were like children. He called their voice 'the babble of women', and argued that they were not eligible for voting rights.[9] In other contexts, women have been regarded as mentally fragile or as mad witches. Fatima Mernissi[10] and Elizabeth Amoah[11] have argued with respect to Morocco and Ghana, respectively, that women who were strong within their communities and showed signs of leadership which threatened men's power were often labelled as hysterical or as dangerous witches. Joan of Arc comes to mind as a well-known historical example of such condemnation. Several strong women leaders of rural India are even now often labelled as witches and beaten or burnt. All through my childhood, I remember hearing of women who were said to suffer from hysteria or various forms of dementia and who were thereby marginalised.

We also find that in India, when a family wishes to access property that is a woman's—let us say a recent widow, or a mother—they have her declared as being out of her senses, not in control of her mind. So she is put away in a home, or sent to Brindavan to seek *moksha* (liberation from the cycle of birth and death). Then her property can be annexed without much litigation. This is possible because of the perception of women as mentally fragile, emotional, easily breaking down. Such stereotyping has been supported by the theories of behaviour put forward over time by male scientists.

In my paper,[12] I added another idea—that silence should be seen not as passivity, ignorance or dumbness, but as protest, as method. I drew this conclusion from watching my mother's responses to my father's wrath and dominance. As I recall it, my mother's silence did not arise merely from her diffidence, but was also the result of a conscious choice of method. There was a kind of stillness about her; she appeared to understand both the obvious and the hidden, but seemed to prefer watching in silence the resolution of human situations with her eyes and therefore with her mind wide open, without intervening. Whereas my father intervened and often scolded all the time. I am encouraged in taking this position by Rustom Bharucha, who says,

> Here it becomes necessary to question the cultural valences and resonances of silence, which more often than not are equated in monolithic terms with repression, cowardice, or fear.... Silence is unacceptable in dealing with any tragedy or atrocity, even if the absence of justice is tolerated. You have to speak out.... it could also be argued that the 'breaking of silence' should not be made into a dictum. Silence can be a political or cultural choice.... silence can be, in certain cases, for particular individuals, the only means of 'reconciling with reality'.[13]

ECONOMICS

The 'women's work' thread of discussion at the Leiden conference was perhaps the most interesting and influential in this interplay between prevailing systems of knowledge and the challenge offered by the feminist perspective. It will be used here to illustrate these intersections in economics. The feminist engagement with the issue of women and work has resulted in uncovering not just women's contribution to the economy, but also in raising questions regarding some of the basic tenets of neoclassical economics. For example, Diane Elson stresses the need for 'pluralism in thinking about economics',[14] and Nilufer Cagatay has shown how seemingly 'genderless' concepts like expenditure patterns and growth levels are influenced by the manner in which gender operates in any given society.[15]

The 'household' was considered the ultimate unit of classification not only for data collection but also for programmatic responses, especially those related to poverty, such as the counting of poverty numbers, provision of employment, the provisioning of services such as credit or food, and so on. Women's studies prised open the category of the household and found that women and children not only had different bread-earning activities, but also experienced differences in access to services such as health or education. They also had differential access to leisure. Further, households among the poor may not consist of homogeneous, bounded individuals collectively optimising their household operations. They are often fragmented and separated, and many among them are headed by women who fend for themselves and for their family's survival.[16] Within poverty households, especially the households of assetless labourers, women had higher labour force participation rates than men, as they were willing to accept harsh, badly paid work for the sake of the family's survival.[17]

This differentiation along gender lines within households in poverty, basically individualising the members of these households, changed the manner of collection of statistics, the nature of employment offers, the understanding of employment trends, efforts to unionise labour, and the nature of credit offers including the issue of collateral. The fact that women worked within the household, often as self-employed traders, drew attention to what is now known as the informal sector,[18] and to the importance of this sector in the economy. Concepts like household-level food security were replaced with the idea of individual food security within the household, as sequential feeding in several cultures meant that children, especially female children, and women often had smaller shares of household food and lower access to health services. This attention to intra-household inequality in all aspects—power, earnings, service utilisation, work and time load, leisure, morbidity and mortality rates—led to many transformations in the approach to 'development and freedom', to borrow from the title of Amartya Sen's book.[19]

For example, the importance of the concept of individual rights, and its impact on the perception of the family as an arena which is not 'fair' in its dealings with its members, matched the universality of the human rights approach. Women's situation revealed the importance of such universalisation. It also led to a focus on the importance of social inputs and social security as a public good to even out the inequality embedded in prevailing power structures. The facts that economic achievement measured in conventional terms hides the degree of progress in social protection, and that the two often do not go together, led to attention to social development going on to human development—these are not part of the standard meaning of economic growth. However, while many attempts have been made to valuate non-monetised and invisible transactions, these valuations are still compared against the 'standard' of money.

A study conducted in six villages of India used time and activity to record the activity patterns of men, women and children in a sample of households stratified by class (using land ownership as a proxy for class).[20] It found that women from assetless households were engaged in gainful economic activity for longer hours than men. Further, the work participation rate for women in West Bengal had been grossly under-enumerated, as their work of cooking meals for farm workers was not considered as labour, as economic activity. Thus, the data collected by the ISST survey challenged the official figures.

Using time as a measure of value, as against money as a measure of value, would reverse the values placed upon the work of men and women: women would always come out 'on top' as they spend more hours working than men. The UNDP's *Human Development Report 1995*, through a review of time-use studies worldwide, confirms this overturning of hierarchies.[21] Thus, the hierarchy in the assessment of male and female economic contribution would change dramatically, and therefore also the perception that a woman is less valuable as an economic agent than a man, if the valuating tool used is not money but time.

Further, apart from the increase in the numbers of poor women as well as in the proportion of women among all poor, women suffer from discrimination within discrimination, whether in armed conflict or in access to nutrition. Amartya Sen captures the phenomenon well when he says,

> The afflicted world in which we live is characterised by deeply unequal sharing of the burden of adversities between women and men. Gender inequality exists in most parts of the world, from Japan to Morocco, from Uzbekistan to the United States of America. However, inequality between women and men can take very many different forms. Indeed, gender inequality is not one homogeneous phenomenon, but a collection of disparate and interlinked problems. And within each community, nationality and class, the burden of hardship often falls disproportionately on women.[22]

THE DISTORTING POWER
OF VOCABULARIES

The nomenclature used can change interpretations, valuations, and hence the power relations and gender relations central to all issues of inequality, as well as important elements like inclusion in legal protection. In India there are 350 million workers engaged in the informal economy, which is predominantly home-based. Of this huge number, it is estimated that about 60 per cent are women and girls; in fact, 94 per cent of the female workforce is in the informal sector. If we rename 'home' as 'workplace', then those who work at home will be recognised as workers, and some of the invisibility of women's work, its undervaluation and exclusion from the legal protection of labour laws, will be overcome.

Another example of skewed nomenclature which affects the input of programmes and policies, and, as a result, their outcomes, is the characterisation of forest produce as major and minor forest produce. It is now well established that the value and volume of minor forest products, not only in India but the rest of the Third World, are greater than the volume and value of what is called 'major forest produce', yet the words 'minor' and 'major' are used inappropriately. To illustrate, in a study of forest-based industry undertaken for the Food and Agriculture Organization in Rome, it was found that a particular berry used as a souring agent, called *uppige* in Kannada, was being collected by women from a tribal community in one of North Karnataka's districts, one of the major sources of that product. However, there was no recognition of these workers, since collection of forest produce is considered 'free collection' as forest dwellers have rights over forest produce. Therefore, the product is not monetised, and so the collectors and the produce do not merit any recognition in economic calculations or in law. This meant that contractors could buy the produce at any price they wished and no protection could be provided to the workers; that women were not counted as workers and their employment or unemployment did not merit attention; and that the contribution of these women to the domestic product did not enter into the calculations.[23]

SOCIOLOGY

The notion of family and kinship organisation is an important part of Indian sociological studies. However, when this notion or observation is applied to the poor, an acute separateness of individuals is found, a competition for survival within the home, the family, the community; a Darwinian drive, making nonsense of the idea of community, even of caste, or the unity of family. Family as we know it does not exist among the poor. What I found from the time-use study that I conducted, as well as other studies of poverty households, was that these were fragmented non-families in which women 'battled' for life.[24] There is enormous dispersal which looks like indifference, but it is distance imposed by necessity. Women become adjusted to the pain of loss of child and husband as part of the survival drive. This made me ask: what were all these investigations of kinship organisations in India and their rules and regulations that were such an important aspect of Indian sociological studies?

Even when the family is viewed, not only among the poor, but from the perspective of women's experience, perceptions of the wholesomeness, supportiveness and bonding of the Indian family break down. R. K. Narayan illuminated women's place and loneliness in the family in his novel *The Dark Room*, a moving story of a woman who is assigned by her family to live in a dark room. A. K. Ramanujan wrote about the *mother's* tongue, as distinct from 'mother tongue' (the dialect). The mother's tongue was used for talking in the kitchen, telling stories and parables which spoke to children's moral sensibility and gave them their true education, while the father sat in the drawing room speaking the formal language in pompous platitudes. An amusing illustration is provided by the suggestion that if female seclusion were to be named 'female socialisation', as women do in fact enjoy their own company, then the odium cast on our cultures also could be reduced.

These examples are offered just to illustrate the transformation that occurs when we change the lens, or the corner of the prism, through which we look at reality and build our knowledge, analysis and therefore prescription. This shows the importance of valuation of any item, behavioural or otherwise, which places it in a hierarchy of value. The act of naming, the nomenclature used, also suggests a hierarchy. For example, is it fasting, or starving? Is it weakness to be silent, a proof of ignorance and incompetence, or is silence a proof of strength, the conscious decision to listen and think?[25]

WAR AND PEACE

As far back as in 1915, a group of women had met at The Hague, Netherlands, to protest against World War I and to suggest ways to end it and to prevent war in the future. They wanted an acknowledgement of women's role in peace and reconstruction, but they were not taken notice of. Today, war has returned in a certain form, as World War III, after September 11, 2000, and the events that have unfolded since have meant that attention has again been redirected to these concerns—of war, peace, security and the role of the UN. Once again, women's voices across nations have called for peaceful settlement of conflicts, for protection of civilians and the earth, and as before their voice has been ignored. The UN leadership again has men engaging in political negotiations while women work for humanitarian relief—the age-old stereotypical division of roles persists.

Women have also contributed to the conceptualisation of peace. For example, for years the UN and many other international bodies (as well as national governments) defined peace to mean the absence of war, with an almost exclusive military and statist focus. At the UN World Conference on Women in Nairobi in 1985, women chose to broaden this definition, stating that 'peace includes not only the absence of war, violence and hostilities at the national and international levels but also employment of economic and social justice, equality and the entire range of human rights and fundamental freedoms within society.'[26] For women, it is their daily experience of providing for day-to-day human security that guides their understanding of peace. Today even the mainstream has adopted a broadened concept of peace, but though this understanding was shaped by women, they are not at the forefront of contemporary debate.

Amongst other issues that demand attention is trafficking in women and children—an issue that tends to be neglected because sexual exploitation is often related to women, while drug trafficking gets far more attention. The trafficking of women and children received formal recognition in the 1949 Convention for the Suppression of the Traffic in Persons and of the Exploitation of the Prostitution of Others.[27] And yet the problem has not only persisted but has thrived and assumed newer forms. Today it is a $7 billion business, and INTERPOL has been called in to grapple with it on par with some of the major economic crimes.

Even in the area of economic equality, in 1919 the International Federation of Working Women had suggested, among other things, eight-hour working days, equal pay for equal work and minimum wages for housework. These proposals were politely 'accepted but put away as too radical'.[28] A US Congressional Study in 2000 found that the difference in managerial salaries for men and women in American industry had grown between 1995 and 2000.[29] In various international agencies and commissions, including the UN, women are still left knocking at the doors of clubs which continue to be dominated by the 'old boys'.

THE VALUATION OF WOMEN

The revaluation of women through shifting interest from the body to the mind is what is required. An earlier paper discussed the mind–body hierarchy and the parallel hierarchisation of intellectual work and activism, North and South.[30] The mind–body analogy has often been extended to suggest that women are bodies, and men the minds.[31]

The attitude of men towards women is similar to the biases embedded in the apartheid phenomenon in South Africa. Talking to citizens, especially white Christians, while in South Africa for a year in 1997, I found that they thought the black was not really a full human being. He/she, they felt, had no feelings, no moral fibre, and was a brute that could be handled as we handle inanimate things, as they do not feel. Hence, we have stories of white soldiers eating meat roasted on an open fire while the leg of a young black boy was being burnt on the same fire as punishment. Surely, this must be similar to how men feel about women if they can assault women and girls brutally, if cousins and uncles can rape girls in their families, if fellow students can throw acid at their female colleagues, and if women can be tortured sexually in armed conflicts. They must imagine that we cannot feel. We are regarded as merely holes.

This denial of recognition to women and their understanding of phenomena, their challenges to the bases of knowledge, seems to hinge essentially on how women are valuated. Hierarchies of value are embedded everywhere in the knowledge base. It seems that unless this valuation of woman is dismantled, the unequal and demeaning attitude towards woman cannot change. To break the hard rock of gender inequality, it is necessary to shift the attention to gender difference, from the body to the mind, to the differences in ideas and principles.

I have spoken earlier of Gandhiji's efforts at reversing gender roles in his ashrams in order to displace the hierarchies embedded in traditional roles. All the inhabitants of these ashrams had to perform both manual and 'meditational' work, so that the educated intellectual would not despise the manual worker. Gandhiji was responding to what he perceived as the terrible fact of female subordination in India's caste-ridden, hierarchical and diverse society. However, we are not today living in those ashrams, and the low valuation of women continues to haunt us. We hear for instance of atrocities against females in the form of the expansion and intensification of sex selective abortion (see the census reports of 2001 and 2011). I call this phenomenon India's hands being stained with the blood of its females. The practice of female infanticide has increased, as revealed by the infant sex ratios reported in the 2011 census, and moreover, this is now happening across all social and economic categories of the population. This is in spite of the strong advocacy by the women's movement and a Supreme Court order with regard to sex determination.[32] There are, of course, other exploitations too, such as the various ways in which women are treated in the political domain, with men manipulating the seats reserved for women.

Hence, the valuation of women is key. Prevailing perceptions have to change before law and policy can have an impact. For these perceptions to change, both women as well as men have to shift their focus from an emphasis on gender as bodily difference to seeing it as intellectual difference. Women and the policies geared to them are body-oriented, and this focus on the body is perpetuated by women too when they express their needs. Men also see women as bodies. However, it is the intellection of women that needs to be highlighted for this to change, along of course with the kind of activism and solidarity we saw in South Africa that worked to overthrow the white supremacist mindset.

I have undertaken this journey not only to reveal the value of women as thinkers, but also to show how the given hierarchies of mind over body, now totally challenged and dismissed by the latest findings in physics and mind research, blind us not only to justice but to truth, to knowledge created from lived experience. The valuation of the other is the basis of respect and of equality. This not only applies to women, but to Dalits and other socially oppressed groups. There is still a great deal left to be done in this regard by academics and others engaged in the knowledge-making and -disseminating industry.

FROM THE THREADS TO THE WEAVE

Almost all the diverse themes, events and debates over the last half century can be captured in just one issue, one notion, concept or aspiration—'equality'. The women's struggle provides a rich exposition of the complex, multidimensional idea termed 'equality'. The quest also seems to suggest that while one may seek to unravel and enrich this idea, it is difficult to actually achieve the outcome—equality is a will-o'-the-wisp that escapes all attempts to capture it. The many faces of inequality, their intertwined aspect, the universality of the condition as well as its particularity have been exposed. Legal attempts to address inequality, the struggles against it, the deep excavations of philosophy and politics, economics and sociology, culture and action, have enriched the topic even if not necessarily achieving the objective of equality.

But the exposition itself is worth the journey, as it has shed light on various forms of discrimination and attempts to redress them. There has been value added both through the reconceptualisation of ideas of equality and inequality as well as in the existence of a tangible awareness worldwide, even in the most remote, 'illiterate' spaces, that injustice needs to be redressed. Affirmative action has been accepted, as has inclusion, as crucial for justice.

Amina Mama's words, part of a speech at the Uganda World Congress on Women in 2002, offer us a perspective:

> Even our most radical political scientists have failed when it comes to addressing the intellectual and political challenge posed by the problematic nature of gendered identity. Postcolonial feminist theory has a great deal to teach our leading lights in contemporary political analysis. The complicated phenomena currently being grouped under the rubric of 'identity politics', for example, have not been adequately theorised, and ignores all the feminist theory on the gendered nature of identity. Yet it has been clear since the days of Freud that all identities are gendered, whether one is talking about identity at the level of individuality, sociality or politics. Feminist theory also has much to contribute to our understanding of statecraft and politics. At the very least it alerts us to the partial and limited manifestations of individuality, sociality and politics in patriarchal societies. It leads us to ask interesting questions, such as whether there is a link between male domination of social and political life and the prevalence of war and militarism?
>
> ... we women are in no position to deprive ourselves of the intellectual tools that can assist us in pursuit of gender justice. The arena of the intellect has been used to suppress us. We cannot afford to ignore the importance of intellectual work, especially in the 21st century when knowledge and information define power more than ever before.[33]

NOTES

1 Longino, 'Feminist Standpoint Theory and the Problems of Knowledge'.
2 William Connolly, 'Democracy and Territory', in M. Ringrose and A. J. Lerner (eds), *Reimagining the Nation* (Buckingham: Open University Press, 1993), p. 61.
3 Christine Sylvester, 'Homeless in International Relations? "Women's" Place in Canonical Texts and in Feminist Reimaginings', in Anne Phillips (ed.), *Feminism and Politics* (Oxford: Oxford University Press, 1998), pp. 44–66.

4 Hazel Henderson, *Paradigms in Progress: Life beyond Economics* (Indianapolis: Knowledge Systems, Inc., 1991); Marilyn Waring, *If Women Counted: A New Feminist Economics* (San Francisco: Harper & Row) (first published in New Zealand as *Counting for Nothing: What Men Value and What Women Are Worth* [Wellington: Allen & Unwin, 1988]).

5 Devaki Jain, *Women, Development, and the UN: A Sixty-Year Quest for Equality and Justice* (New York: Indiana University Press, 2005).

6 United Nations Intellectual History Project, 1999–2010, Ralph Bunche Institute for International Studies, City University of New York.

7 Jain, 'Are Women a Separate Issue?'

8 Jain, 'Power through the Looking Glass of Feminism'.

9 Emma Rothschild, 'An Infinity of Girls: The Political Rights of Children in Historical Perspective', mimeo, Centre for History and Economics, Cambridge University, 2000.

10 Mernissi, 'Femininity as Subversion'.

11 Amoah, 'Women, Witches and Social Change in Ghana'.

12 Jain, 'Power through the Looking Glass of Feminism'.

13 Rustom Bharucha, 'Between Truth and Reconciliation: Experiments in Theatre and Public Culture', *Economic and Political Weekly*, vol. 36, no. 39 (2001), pp. 3763–73.

14 Diane Elson, 'For an Emancipatory Socio-Economics', paper presented at the UN Research Institute for Social Development seminar, 'The Need to Rethink Development Economics', Cape Town, September 2001.

15 Nilufer Cagatay, Roundtable on 'Gendering Macro-Economic Policies: Concepts and Institutions', NGO Forum, Huairou, China, September 1995.

16 Devaki Jain, 'Through the Looking Glass of Poverty', paper presented at New Hall, Cambridge, 19 October 2001.

17 Devaki Jain, 'Valuing Work: Time as a Measure', *Economic and Political Weekly*, vol. 31, no. 43 (26 October 1996), pp. WS46–WS57; ISST, 'Impact on Women Workers: Maharashtra Employment Guarantee Scheme', mimeo, ILO, Geneva, December 1979.

18 Marilyn Carr and Marty Chen, *Globalization and the Informal Economy: How Global Trade and Investment Impact on the Working Poor* (Geneva: ILO, 2002).

19 Amartya Sen, *Development as Freedom* (Oxford: Oxford University Press, 1999).

20 Jain, 'Valuing Work: Time as a Measure'.

21 UNDP, *Human Development Report 1995*.

22 Amartya Sen, 'Many Faces of Gender Inequality', inaugural lecture at the New Radcliffe Institute, Harvard University, 24 April 2001.

23 Devaki Jain, 'Development Theory and Practice: Insights Emerging from Women's Experiences', *Economic and Political Weekly*, vol. 25, no. 27 (1990), pp. 1454–55.

24 Sen, 'Food Battles'.

25 Jain, 'Through the Looking Glass of Poverty'.

26 UN, 'The Nairobi Forward Looking Strategies', Third World Conference on Women, Nairobi, 1985, para. 13.

27 UN Office of the High Commissioner for Human Rights, General Assembly Resolution 317 (IV) of 2 December 1949, came into force on 25 July 1951.

28 Hilkka Pietilä, 'Women's Movement and Internationalisation', ECPR Workshop, Mannheim, 26–31 March 1999, https://ecpr.eu/Filestore/PaperProposal/81ecca4f-4dc8-4050-990c-c861489849f2.pdf (accessed 11 September 2017).

29 Elizabeth Becker, 'Study Finds a Growing Gap between Managerial Salaries for Men and Women', *New York Times*, 24 January 2002.

30 See Jain, 'Minds, Not Bodies: Expanding the Notion of Gender in Development', reproduced as chapter 4, this volume.

31 Ibid.

32 *Sabu Mathew George v. Union of India & Others*, 16 February 2017 (Supreme Court of India, Writ Petition [Civil] No. 341 of 2008).

33 Amina Mama, 'Talking about Feminism in Africa', Interview by Elaine Salo, *African Feminisms*, vol. 1, no. 50 (2001), pp. 58–63, http://www.wworld.org/programs/regions/africa/amina_mama.htm (accessed 8 June 2017).

CHAPTER 9

Feminist Networks, People's Movements and Alliances

Learning from the Ground

The World Congress of Women, a conference of feminist scholars, held its 2004 congress in Uganda. There was a session on how alliances could build up the strength of the international as well as the national women's movements without the mediation of the UN. The idea of having regular UN-driven World Congresses on Women had dried up, largely due to the anxiety that the progress made at the Beijing Conference, where government and civil society were able to come together to initiate many progressive policies, might get corrupted.

As someone who had engaged with networks as well as with UN conferences, I argued that women had to shift the emphasis of their effort from mobilising to consolidating women's opinion at the macro level, for instance, with reference to economic globalisation. That was where they would get the power to effect transformation at the local level.

Networking has been a special feature of the feminist movement and reflects in many ways the ideals of the feminist method—flexible and non-hierarchical arrangements to bring collective perspectives to issues and to give collective voice to them. However, networks and newsletters, alliances and coalitions seem to have reached the stage, to use corporate language, of flooding the market. Given the flood of these 'informal' connectivities, and given that there is a deep concern about the unipolarity of the current political landscape, about the march of the new 'empire'[1] across the globe, there is need for these networks and coalitions to hammer out some philosophical if not ideological basis, some minimal purpose, to respond to the current environment.

Women's networks need to mobilise at the global level around a few issues which legitimise 'women' and 'women's identity' and simultaneously call attention to women's influence as a lobby. They need to identify one or two poles around which to politicise the women's movement so that their power as a global force is asserted significantly. There are many local struggles, such as the powerful 'sit-ins' of women in Nigeria against oil pipelines, and in Columbia against the narcotics mafia, to mention only a very few. These appear on the global screen and are applauded by vibrant networks, but they cannot be sustained or enlarged in space so as to overpower Empire. It is necessary to build ideological solidarity and institutional mechanisms to support such local efforts more effectively, to sustain and enlarge the space women have occupied in many 'local' places so that they encompass the public and political sphere to the full. Networks thus are a necessary but not a sufficient condition by themselves of bringing women's collective strength to bear on society and on the state. They need a political premise and purpose, even a mass base, to be able to effect transformation.

Between 1975 and 1990, many feminist networks were born which enabled women to build international alliances as well as develop a deeper knowledge base for their struggle for rights.[2] However, this is not enough. As knowledge becomes more broad-based and diverse due to the increasing availability of internet technology around the world, there is a fragmentation of the space earlier used by the networks for their advocacy work. This seems to have diluted their actions and weakened their impact compared to earlier decades when they were first formed.

This paper touches on some significant achievements involving women's networks while pointing to the slow meltdown of the early participatory and solidarity-building movements. It suggests that the central role of these networks is being lost to people's movements, which nevertheless need the support of the networks to mobilise at the global level.

NETWORK VALUES

Networking as a conscious form of organising has emerged for many reasons, both pragmatic and value-based. The pragmatic consider-ations have been a recognition that the global problems of today have to be countered on a global scale, and that networking improves the effect, visibility and efficacy of the people involved in advancing a cause.

Networks are powerful instruments for working for social change. Their strength lies in their exceptional ability to enhance and deepen critical thinking and creativity through dialogue and exchange; to address global problems by joining forces to take global action; to transcend isolation and strengthen local action; to link local organis-ing efforts and structures to international ones; to facilitate participa-tion; and to be flexible and respond quickly to new and changing situations.

Feminist networks are based on and validate the belief that the exercise of coming together and sharing experience, knowledge and information is by itself useful. Networks tend to avoid the traditional pyramidal structures that do not allow expression on the part of those who are 'lower down'; they strive to be inclusive and bring people together for common causes while respecting diversity. Networks also imply a reciprocity. They are a coming together of allies, an achieving of 'social synergy'. They have managed to sustain processes which allow space for evolution, for accommodating difference, for converging and dispersing, for engaging in dialogue and collective decision making. Platforms are built on issues that cut across dif-ferences and on viewpoints or quests that seem to echo widespread anxiety or inspiration. Sally Baden and Anne Marie Goetz,[3] in their assessment of the 1995 Fourth World Women's Conference in Beijing, state: 'The creation of coalitions between groups with very different interests certainly seemed to be taking place in Beijing, with for example a broad alliance on reproductive rights between north and south women, which allowed for rather different interpretations of these rights.'

WOMEN'S NETWORKS

In the last 25 years, hundreds of women's networks have mushroomed—some on specific issues such as health, for example, the International Women's Health Coalition;[4] some region-based, for example AAWORD; some inter-regional and focused on gender and development like DAWN;[5] some based on class or occupation (peasant women's groups, Homeworkers' Network or HOMENET), religion (Islamic Women's Association), race (black women's groups), and so on. There are networks for law, for economy, for women's studies, for peace, and these operate on the ground formulating policies and engaging in advocacy at the regional and international levels.

There are international networks to protect the rights of people who live along the banks of rivers, there are committees to protect rivers from the assault of development. These networks not only mutually reinforce each other, but have been able to hold back some of the most powerful world agencies. For example, during the three-year process (1997–2000) of the World Commission on Dams,[6] it was the international networks of river peoples, indigenous people and natural resource rights groups that 'encircled' the commission and ensured that the end product was just and grounded in principles of human development. Other examples include Isis International's former Geneva campaign on baby food products, which finally led to the placement of a warning label on all baby food products that 'breast milk is best' for the health of an infant; and the mobilisation by the International Women's Tribune Center[7] to gather signatures to present to the Chinese government protesting against the issue of selective visas for the Fourth World Women's Conference in Beijing in 1995.

In India, for example, in different parts of the country, women's organisations network at the local and national levels, taking up a variety of activities and campaigns. They also collaborate with women in the community and with elected women in the panchayats. For example, two groups of women in a district in Kerala managed by networking to link their production with demand in the district, thus overcoming the problem local women's groups usually have of finding customers for their products.

CHALLENGES

What needs to be recognised though is that none of these considerable successes of women's networks has reduced the misery or redressed the exclusions and oppressions endured by women. In fact, data worldwide show that there is an increase in domestic violence against women.[8] In India, for example, there are higher and more virulent dowry demands and, of course, higher incidences of sex-selective abortions.[9] The improvements in women's lives referred to in the *World's Women 2000* publication are segmented and highly sectional and minimal.[10] Masses of girls, women and female children worldwide are under assault. A number of studies and surveys by UN organisations as well as other sources emerging at the end of the last millennium reveal this downslide.

Rural women are primary victims of hunger and poverty despite being crucial partners in combating these problems and achieving global food security, says a Food and Agriculture Organization review:[11]

> the most disadvantaged population in the world today comprises rural women in developing countries, who have been the last to benefit—or negatively affected—by prevailing economic growth and development processes. Gender bias and blindness persist; farmers are still generally perceived as 'male' by policy-makers, development planners and agricultural service deliverers.

The *World Culture Report 2000* by the UN Educational, Scientific and Cultural Organization (UNESCO)[12] also emphasises inequality, in this case the importance of inequality of access to resources, political power, information and the media for people's capacity to make choices, which is the true capability of exercising rights. The report underscores the fact that women often experience this unequal access due to inhibitors linked or attributed to cultural practices.

The World Health Organization's A-Z of ailments, the International Classification of Diseases, gives a code to 'extreme poverty' and calls it the 'world's most ruthless killer'.[13] Nikki van der Gaag writes:

The 'world's most ruthless killer' is coded as Z59.5. It has meant 'widening gaps between rich and poor, between one population group and another, between age groups and *between the sexes*'. It has caused more suffering to more people than anything else on earth. And it has got worse over the last ten years. Despite improvements in education and health, for hundreds of millions of women, Z59.5 has meant lives lived closer to the edge than before. Beneath the rhetoric of 'post-feminism' and 'equality between the sexes' lies another, more sinister, phenomenon.

... In a study carried out over 20 years up to 1990, 'the number of rural women in poverty has increased by 50 percent, reaching an awesome 565 million, while that of men has grown by 30 per cent to about 400 million.' The poverty problem is not confined to the Majority World. In the US, almost half of all poor families are supported by women with no spouse present, and their average income is 23 percent below the official poverty line.[14]

In a special study, the International Food Policy of the Statistical Division of the UN Secretariat states that there are 110 women per 100 men in households in the poorest expenditure/income quintile. Difference decreases as income increases. These results indicate that in general there are more women than men in poor households. In half of the data sets from Africa and two-thirds of the data sets from South and Southeast Asia, women are overrepresented among the poor. Data from 41 countries which account for 84 per cent of the total rural population in developing countries indicate both growing numbers and proportions of women among the rural poor since the mid-1960s. Table 9.1 further reveals the disparity between men and women in poverty.

Table 9.1 *Total Number of Rural People Living below the Poverty Line by Sex (in millions), 1965–1970 to 1988*

	1965–70	1988	Percentage Change
Women	383,673	564,000	47.0
Men	288,832	375,481	30.0
Total	672,505	939,481	39.7

Source: ILO, *Gender, Poverty and Employment: Turning Capabilities into Entitlements* (Geneva: ILO, 1995), p. 9.

The understanding of women's networks as 'enabling' women has to shift to an emphasis on their role as mobilising, generating and consolidating women's opinion on national and global issues, such that women's struggle towards macro-level transformation will ultimately protect them at the micro level. In the 21st century, there is a need to build up women as an opinion lobby with some transactional power, either through numbers via votes or through ideas, money or moral power. Networking to keep in touch, by itself, is not enough. Opinion building, and translating this into a political force, are beginning to emerge as the most critical elements informing and generating change. But the challenge is to build up greater solidarity politically. The need, therefore, is to turn the networks into transnational political actors with sustained input into the political process and the ability to keep cross-national interests alive.

The very flexibility which is so much a factor in women's networking success can also be a weakness in achieving focused action. As Catherine Hoskyns has noted with respect to the European Women's Lobby's ability to influence the European lobby, 'On one hand the women's lobby has provided focus and articulate spokeswomen, and good sources of information; on the other it has experienced difficult problems with internal democracy, representation and efficiency. The danger is that fluidity and diversity are traded for structure and coherence.'[15]

Another challenge for feminists is that it has often been strategic combines of women that have opened up spaces for women. For example, women in government delegations can collude with women officials within the secretariats and women in NGOs to engineer a desirable outcome. This has been called the 'velvet triangle', a metaphor to capture the three major actors/groups typically involved in gender/women's politics—first, femocrats and feminist politicians; second, academics and experts; and third, NGOs. However, the same three partners can also be the cause of failure. Women who are officials in delegations often do what their governments want and so can become impediments.[16]

Some argue that the greater diffusion of information across national and state boundaries produced by information technology actually makes the state visibly accountable, especially in international forums, for growing and persisting inequalities.[17] Feminist arguments have gone further to analyse the role of the state as an actor in the enforcement of human rights, and to question early attempts to use male standards to define violations of human rights.[18] However, feminists have faced contradictory pulls. For example, governments and institutions in the North are, on the one hand, criticised as intrusive and manipulative when they stipulate that aid to the poorer states of the South be granted on conditions of harsh financial reform, which often negatively impacts women much more than men. On the other hand, these same governments and institutions in the North are urged to interfere in the policies of aid-recipient states to ensure that women have equal access with men to the benefits of their loans, and to enact sweeping legal reforms to regulate people's activities in the 'private sphere', within families or households, as fully as activities in the public sphere. This is to ensure that women have rights as individuals, related to the universalisation of rights.

SHORTCOMINGS

One of the shortcomings of the current global women's movement is that it has begun to function often in a conventional mode. It has become a 'response' to governments and intergovernmental institutions. Government is seen as the main player in transformation and in drawing up national and international initiatives for change; the women's movement becomes a monitor, a reporter of progress. This is a conventional relationship; it also diminishes responsibility.

It is often said that there is no women's movement, no united social flow towards a purpose, only a large, scattered, diverse set of women-focused organisations. Far from the earlier 1970s when national initiatives for women were in the hands of women, as at the First World Women's Conference in Mexico City in 1975, where the broad-based women's movement gave birth to itself, today national initiatives are in the hands of government. This is a major backslide.

Strong alliances between mass-based struggles for justice and the women's agenda are not easily seen. In India, for example, mass-based struggles, like that against arrack (native alcohol) in Andhra Pradesh,[19] have not always been adopted by what can be called a national women's movement.

Today, economic reform programmes, as the structural adjustment policies are euphemistically called, are attacking workers' movements worldwide. In India, the trade union movement was and is one of the strong institutions of democracy. However full of warts and patriarchy, it is one of the bulwarks against state and corporate sector domination. Yet the national or worldwide women's movement does not appear to be taking a global stand against the deconstruction of this institution. There are many examples of such isolation from mass-based struggles, often led by women but dealing with natural resources. For example, Medha Patkar spearheads the movement against big dams and for the conservation of natural resources.[20] Aruna Roy spearheads the right to information movement in India, a movement for political transparency.[21] Ela Bhatt works for the rights of home-based workers to legal protection.[22] Vandana Shiva advocates for rights over seed.[23] Yet the visible feminist movement does not either collaborate with these movements or voice these demands.

The struggle against racism has much to teach us, as we have to teach those struggling against racism.[24] The myths are in the mind, and politics works to sustain those myths. A highly political, broad-based feminist movement with alliances with other oppressed classes is necessary for the revolution that is needed to stop the careless crimes against women.

Changing the condition of women—the hardships they face through poverty or basic discrimination—requires monumental change in social perceptions of 'woman' across caste, class, ethnicity and other differences. Studies show that owning assets, bringing in income, being educated, even being equal to men according to social indicators like the gender development index or the gender empowerment measure, as in Kerala in India,[25] does not reduce rates of violence against women or dowry deaths, nor the basic disregard which makes an adult or adolescent male rape a girl child even if she is a relative or a neighbour.

For this long march to begin, what is needed is political mobilisation of women, united even if temporarily by their sex. We then have to move out of the conventional grip of the 'arrival hall'. Most movements, when they gain self-confidence and shape, think that merely being the subject of governments' consideration is itself an achievement, and the process of lobbying at conferences then consumes all their energy.

OPPORTUNITIES

Yesterday's workers' movements and their collective voice are today's people's movements. Workers' movements have had to take a back seat partly because, in economies like India, trade-unionised labour represents less than 10 per cent of the labour force, as the changing structure of production and trade systems worldwide have blurred as well as dampened working-class culture. As trade unions and co-operatives are weakened as a source of strength and voice for large masses of the less privileged, people's movements must be seen as the institutional vehicles for carrying the voices of the masses into public debate and policy making. The left movements have also been marginalised by world events, as well as being weakened by injustice within, and have been criticised by women, blacks and coloured people, Dalits and minorities.

The space for voices of the oppressed, once occupied by the left and the unions, is then available, and in the last decade or two has been filled by people's movements all over the world, North and South. But people's movements by definition do not have the institutional structure that political parties and trade unions have. They do not have a space in states' institutional frameworks, nor do they come under any legal framework. They are fluid, and this enables them to be inclusive as well as broad-based and massive in numbers. But it also demands from them unity of purpose, which in turn requires shared knowledge and clarity—attributes of efficiency. These movements need to be taken seriously by agencies of the state and society as the most vital safeguards of democracy and the best means for sustaining democratic spaces outside of the often suffocating conventional structures. It is only extensive, ideologically driven networking through collaboration with people's movements, and, more importantly, the coalescing of diverse and dispersed efforts, that can channelise the flow of resources towards the marginalised, the masses, the poor.

The institutional frameworks that develop at intermediary levels will be the ultimate test of networking and advocacy skills. Success at this level will determine whether the dispersed initiatives can come together and coalesce over a period of time to effect structural transformation, or whether they will die in the wilderness.

FOR THE FUTURE

Experience reveals that poverty is a political issue.[26] Poverty eradication cannot take place unless political institutions are built which represent the voices of the poor, and those institutions in turn become vote banks which transform the political leadership and make it representative of the poor. The women's movement is the most effective, possibly the least tarnished and the most united across the divides of political and social forces in the world today. Hence, it is the ideal vehicle to spearhead transformation and poverty eradication. Not surprisingly, women today lead many significant mass-based social and economic rights movements in India. For women, democratic spaces are even more crucial, as their resistance to oppression from family, culture and patriarchy in general requires open spaces with firmly embedded laws that safeguard individual rights.[27] At the state and national levels, women are engaged in drafting modifications to the People's Representation Act[28] and other details of electoral reform. Electoral politics has found vibrant support in India, as evidenced by the million-strong force of local women politicians, historically subordinated castes and minorities. The populace has benefited from the freedoms and inbuilt checks of democracy.

Treatises have been written, by Nobel Laureate Amartya Kumar Sen among others, showing that unless the voices and strength of collective public action are included as a shaping element in our economic models, there is no way of generating equity with development. This is the political element in economics—the space for negotiation in making choices at the macro level. Thus, it is time to move beyond the 'report card approach', which focuses on measuring government performance, such as following up on the Platform for Action adopted at the UN's Fourth World Women's Conference in Beijing or the Millennium Development Goals (MDGs) proposed in Geneva in 2004. Instead, a platform of ideas and practices emerging from large-scale women's actions in the world can be built to teach and move the UN and the Bretton Woods Institutions towards a revised, reconstructed agenda.

It would be useful to identify one or at most two issues especially affecting poor women around which the international women's movement could rally. The idea is to move from mobilising as a negotiating agency, to mobilising as a social force which commands attention by its very presence and ethics. Unified action always has a better chance of winning than twenty scattered activities. A one-point programme of full employment, using that lens to critique everything under the sun, might make a dent. Networks need a goal, a single-minded purpose, a lens that they can use at all levels.

When Gandhiji picked up a fistful of salt from the beaches of Gujarat,[29] he was not trying to give free salt to the people of India. It was a symbol, an idiom of political assertion, but in a language, a vocabulary, which represented the masses of people, not the elites. When President Mandela asked in his inaugural speech for bread, water and salt for all, it was not that he wanted to limit the lifestyle of his people to bread with salt and water; it was to signal the aspirations of the masses and to use a vocabulary which was representative of both political assertion and identification with the deprived. Imagine if these actions and words had been interpreted in their literal sense? That Gandhiji wanted to give people free salt, or that Mandela only wanted bread with salt and water for his people? How absurd it would have been. Imagine if Gandhiji's salt satyagraha had not fired the imagination of Indians and opened the floodgates of the movement for freedom. What a loss to the grammar and method of politics, and most of all to democratic processes which attempt to move the state towards justice.

What the international NGO movement needs is a fistful of salt, a symbolic unifying gesture to roll back the overwhelming force of the current paradigm of development, not through essays and articles but through international solidarity on one public action.

APPENDIX: LIST OF NETWORKS

1. African Women's Development and Communication Network (FEMNET)
2. Asia Pacific Forum on Women, Law and Development (APWLD)
3. Asian Women's Human Rights Council (AWHRC)
4. Association of African Women for Research and Development (AAWORD)
5. Center for Women's Global Leadership (CWGL)
6. Committee for the Defense of Women's Rights (CLADEM)
7. Development Alternatives with Women for a New Era (DAWN)
8. Gender and Science and Technology Association (GASAT)
9. Global Campaign for Women's Human Rights
10. International Women's Health Coalition (IWHC)
11. International Women's Rights Action Watch (IWRAW)
12. International Women's Tribune Centre (IWTC)
13. Isis International
14. KARAT Coalition (regional network of Central and Eastern European countries)
15. TWAEMAE
16. Women in Law and Development in Africa (WiLDAF)
17. Women Living under Muslim Laws (WLUML)
18. Women's Environment and Development Organization (WEDO)
19. Women's Global Network for Reproductive Rights (WGNRR)

NOTES

1 Devaki Jain, 'The Empire Strikes Back: A Report on the Asian Social Forum', *Economic and Political Weekly*, vol. 38, no. 2 (11 January 2003); Arundhati Roy, 'The New American Century', *Nation*, 9 February 2004, https://www.thenation.com/article/new-american-century/ (accessed 28 May 2017).

2 See the partial list of networks provided in the Appendix at the end of this chapter.

3 Sally Baden and Anne Marie Goetz, 'Who Needs [Sex] When You Can Have [Gender]? Conflicting Discourses on Gender at Beijing', in Cecile Jackson and Ruth Pearson (eds), *Feminist Visions of Development: Gender Analysis and Policy* (New York: Routledge, 1998).

4 http://www.iwhc.org/ (accessed 28 May 2017).

5 http://www.dawn.org (accessed 11 September 2017).

6 World Commission on Dams, *Dams and Development: A New Framework for Decision-Making* (London: Earthscan Publications, 2001).

7 Maud Hand, 'Patience Is the Key at This Golden Opportunity That Is Prepcom 2', Internet and ICT for Social Justice.

8 Devaki Jain, 'Need of the Hour: Political Response to Violence against Women—Perspective from India', SADC Conference on the Prevention of Violence against Women, Durban, 5 March 1998.

9 Gautam Bhan, *India Gender Profile: Report Commissioned for Sida*, no. 62, BRIDGE, Institute of Development Studies, Brighton, August 2001; *Census of India* 2001.

10 UN, *The World's Women 2000: Trends and Statistics* (New York: United Nations Statistics Division, 2000).

11 Food and Agriculture Organization, 'FAO Plan of Action for Women in Development', FAO Conference, 28th Session, 20 October–2 November 1995.

12 UNESCO, *World Culture Report 2000: Cultural Diversity, Conflict and Pluralism* (UNESCO, 2000).

13 ICD List, 'ICD-10 Diagnosis Code Z59.5: Extreme Poverty', http://icdlist.com/icd-10/Z59.5 (accessed 11 September 2017).

14 Nikki van der Gaag, 'Women: Still Something to Shout About', *New Internationalist Magazine*, no. 270 (August 1995).

15 Catherine Hoskyns and Michael Newman (eds), *Democratizing the European Union: Issues for the Twenty-First Century* (Manchester: Manchester University Press, 2000).

16 Alison Woodward, 'Building Velvet Triangles: Gender in EU Policy Making', Paper in Revision from the European Consortium for Political Research, 28th Joint Session, Copenhagen, April 2000.

17 Margaret E. Keck and Kathryn Sikkink, *Activists beyond Borders: Advocacy Networks in International Politics* (Ithaca, NY: Cornell University Press, 1998).

18 Donna J. Sullivan, 'Women's Human Rights and the 1993 World Conference on Human Rights', *American Journal of International Law*, vol. 88 (1994), pp. 152–67; Donna Sullivan, 'The Public/Private Distinction in International Human Rights Law', in *Women's Rights, Human Rights: International Feminist Perspectives* (New York: Routledge, 1995); Alda Facio, 'What Will You Do? Women's Human Rights: Excerpts, Statement by the Center for Women's Global Leadership, 13 September 1995', *Women's Studies Quarterly*, vol. 24, nos 1–2 (1996), pp. 66–68.

19 Anveshi, 'Reworking Gender Relations, Redefining Politics'.

20 Dilip D'Souza, *The Narmada Dammed: An Inquiry into the Politics of Development* (New Delhi: Penguin, 2002).

21 K. Srivastava, N. Dey and N. Mishra, 'Taking Democracy Forward: The Right to Information Movement in Rajasthan', paper presented at the technical workshop on 'Indigenizing Human Rights Education in Indian Universities', Karnataka Women's Information and Resource Centre, Bangalore, December 2001.

22 Renana Jhabvala, 'SEWA and Home-Based Workers in India: Their Struggle and Emerging Role', paper presented at the technical workshop on 'Indigenizing Human Rights Education in Indian Universities', Karnataka Women's Information and Resource Centre, Bangalore, December 2001.

23 Vandana Shiva, international conference organised by Navdanya, India International Centre, New Delhi, 29 September–1 October 2001.

24 Devaki Jain, 'Gender Inequity as Racism', *Hindu*, 23 September 2000.

25 Planning Commission, *National Human Development Report 2001* (New Delhi: Government of India, March 2002).

26 Jain, 'The Poverty Thing'; Mark Malloch Brown, 'Foreword', *Human Development Report 2002*.

27 Devaki Jain, *For Women to Lead—Ideas and Experience from Asia* (New York: UNDP, 1997).

28 Madhu Kishwar, 'An Alternative Women's Reservation Bill', *Indian Express*, 18 March 2003.

29 Narayan Desai, *The Fire and the Rose* (Ahmedabad: Navajivan Publishing House, 1995), pp. 445–76.

To Be or Not To Be

Problems in Locating Women in Public Policy

In June 2005, academics from Cornell University, in collaboration with the Institute of Social and Economic Change in Bangalore, held a conference on public policy and how it needed to be inclusive of various social categories. This conference gave me an opportunity to share my deep pessimism with regard to all the strategies that had been used by women and the women's movement to influence public policy. Inclusion had been stereotyped, and the movement continued to work to educate the state on women's condition and seek inclusion in its programmes. My argument was that this did not actually enable what was crucial, that is, for women to have the power to determine public policy, rather than merely ask for inclusion and contribute the 'gender dimension' to public policy.

Women face three problems in incorporating their concerns in public policy. First, how can we have 'woman' as an exclusive category given the heterogeneity among women? Women belong to all the classes, castes, religions, political ideologies and cultures in society. Thus, to project an identity of 'woman' as defined by feminine experience to represent a collective point of view or opinion is a challenge. Yet a case can and has been made for taking 'woman' as a specific category (or imaginary) on the basis that across these conventional divides, various forms of discrimination converge. Indeed, it was this recognition, namely, the experience of discrimination against women across all social groups, that led the pioneers of women's rights, the founding mothers of the UN conventions, to craft the Convention on the Elimination of All Forms of Discrimination against Women. The universality of discrimination against women gives them an identity across differences. But such an identity based on discrimination alone cannot overcome the other problems of gendering, as discussed below.[1]

The second problem with gendering arises from the flawed nature of inherited knowledge. Women's studies have demonstrated how knowledge of society and knowledge about women are constructed by patriarchal biases—that all knowledge is gendered.[2] A very typical example relates to women's work. What kind of work is called 'work', how work is valued, the measures used to determine the value of work are all determined by the perception of women's work by society, official agencies and men. As a result, women's work is undercounted, underestimated and often is invisible. There are dichotomies such as public and private space, and hierarchies embedded in language and practice.[3] For example, the large space occupied by the majority of women workers is called 'informal', implying its secondary status to the so-called 'formal sector'. The non-monetised sector is either accorded a lower value or no value compared to the monetised[4]—an approach totally invalid for a largely subsistence economy where the non-monetised sector is substantial. Thus, if a policy arises out of such inherited 'flawed' knowledge, women advocates would not want to participate in it. They would not like to engender it. They would like to deconstruct it or challenge or reject it.

INTEGRATION AS SURRENDER

Thus, integrating into an existing framework has problems. If the formulation of public policy that arises out of the accepted theories and frameworks and out of given data and analysis is unacceptable to, say, a group like women or Dalits,[5] then their integration into that setup and sitting on committees or at negotiating tables is surrender. Insofar as we start from a premise that is inaccurate and flawed, it can lead to undesirable results. But staying away also has its negative effects, in other words, exclusion. This is one of the dilemmas. In the language of the feminists, this problem is often posed as the question: 'Do we want a piece of the poisoned cake?'[6] Another way of raising the same question is, 'Do we want to swim in the polluted stream?' Hence, ideas like integrating, gendering, mainstreaming, used in current discussions on the inclusion of women in policy-making efforts, do not achieve the desired results.

The third problem arises out of women's unhappiness over constructing 'boxes' to contain phenomena within strict boundaries. To women, such boundaries are invalid, especially where boundaries are fluid. They do not easily accept attempts at imputing a false identity and deriving judgements on that basis. If one defines the boundary of identity by women's ways of doing things, it is rejected as 'essentialism'. If one suggests that wage work for women empowers them, it is called 'instrumentalism'. There is a tendency among women advocates themselves to question every notion or concept which attempts to arrive at a boundary for identity fixing. I call this the *neti neti* (not this, not that) syndrome, borrowing from the Upanishads. It is definition by negation.

But such an overcritical view of identity that negates any boundary fixing impedes the participation of women in policy as a political presence drawn from a collective identity. An identity tag (based on some markings, either bodily or through the experience of subordination and exclusion) is crucial for claiming rights and special attention.[7] Such a clear identity tag, which is more easily available to, say, Dalits, or to blacks in Africa or in white nations, is difficult to forge for the female identity due to women's presence in all these other categories with all their separate politics. The issue of gendering public policy is intimately related to our answers to these questions.

In *Women, Development, and the UN: A Sixty-Year Quest for Equality and Justice*,[8] I have reviewed the historical struggle of women to be understood and included and given space and citizenship on an equal basis in the international arena of justice. I found that whenever women did achieve some 'success' in breaking through the male bastions of knowledge and power, it was through strategising on their collective identity as women, as well as by the inclusion of even one woman on a drafting committee. I call this strategising space a 'place of one's own',[9] or 'the women's tent'.[10] While a place of one's own is needed to develop the self-confidence to face the bigger world, it also makes the 'outside' see the 'tent' as a separate entity. This perception perpetuates the 'of women for women by women to women' syndrome, a syndrome which not only excludes women from recasting and reordering development, but also prevents the course of development from reflecting the lived experience of women. Policy issues are not only about women's issues. Women need a say in all issues as partners in the development of society. Thus, a place of one's own can be a powerhouse or a ghetto, or both.

AN ORGANISED VOICE

The 60-year review just referred to[11] does point to some useful directions for women's participation in social change. First, there is value and usefulness in bonding across differences on the identity of woman, and strategising in meaningful ways for inclusion in public affairs. Hence, an organised voice represented by the 'women's tent' is a crucial brick in this effort. Such inclusion is necessary, for instance, if we want to stem militarisation. Then the 'women's tent' can also be a 'peace tent'.

Second, we need knowledge that delineates concealed details regarding differences within households and families, between the sexes, and in the various processes of reproduction, production, exchange. We may call this a process of mapping the social and economic location of women in these landscapes. Knowing can be a first step.

Third, power can be claimed through some semblance of a collective identity, a 'USP' or flag. There has been much discussion on this issue of building a maintainable unity, a united stand.[12] This continues to be a quest. However, it is increasingly being argued that participation in leadership, in formal politics,[13] can provide the turning point. Bonding across differences on the identity of woman, and strategising for inclusion as a collective voice, can redress all aspects of gender-derived discrimination, be it in the form of the demeaning gaze or mindset, the stereotypical perceptions of women's roles and capabilities, or embedded discriminatory practices—all these are linked elements of gender relations. The recent conference in New York called Beijing +10[14] revealed again the continuing disjunction between the reality on the ground and the sense of progress created by the 'visibility' level achieved by gendered analysis.[15]

This disjunction can be seen in two opposite trajectories relating to women and development. The first trajectory is the emergence of a strong political presence on the national and international scene of the women's movement. There is now a widespread consciousness of the necessity of engaging in gendered analysis that recognises both difference and inequality and their implications for development design. The other trajectory reveals that the situation on the ground for many women, especially those living in poverty and in conflict-ridden situations, seems to have worsened, despite the fact that it has been addressed specifically by both the state and in development thought.

The question that arises then is, why does this disjunction exist after decades of what appears to have been a vibrant and ostensibly effective partnership between policy makers and the women's movement? How much of these oppositional trajectories can be attributed to the external atmospherics of global power politics and its attendant economics? How much can be attributed to other factors, such as the style of functioning and priorities of the women's movement or its experience of the gendered institutional architecture of governance?

INTERVENTIONS IN POLICY

Two examples from Karnataka of gendering policy will be discussed to illustrate these problems. The problem of differences between women need not be a hindrance; one can address the common experience of discrimination and inequality as a group. We can build adequate knowledge of the social embeddedness of gender roles, then intervene in policy by studying the impact of gender-insensitive formulations and identifying areas where interventions are possible.

The first example is drawn from an attempt made in Karnataka to integrate women's interests into a state five-year plan in 1983.[16] Before we discuss the actual study, it is pertinent to recall the tremendous advances made in understanding women's work. Without this background knowledge, one would not be able to evaluate any policy or programme.

The field of women's work had become a major research domain both nationally and internationally. It was one of the most creative pursuits, influencing international organisations like the ILO. This focus helped to underline the ground realities in developing countries. The women's movement then began to address the core issue of survival security for the principal defender of the family—the woman. This generated discussion on issues such as measurement and inclusion of invisible unpaid work, rural women's work, discrimination in wages, job security, and revaluing what was called the 'informal' sector.

This new research about women as workers entered the development discourse. It led to scrutiny of practices of national data collecting agencies that listed women engaged in domestic work as unemployed, and concern about and analysis of unequal wages, discrimination against women in the workplace, women's double burden of work for wages and work at home, the role that women performed to make possible other members' involvement in marketable production or service, and the absence of social security for women who performed unpaid labour at home. From a narrower and more focused approach to women's status vis-à-vis men, this research broadened the scope of investigation to look at the implications of global and national economic, political and social changes and their impact on women's lives in their entirety.

The study under review was initiated in the 1980s by the ISST partly because of the impetus of the overall 'ideology' that had developed in international fora of bringing women into development; and partly due to our interest in finding ways to enable women to move out of poverty. It should be recalled that it was around the 1970s and 1980s that women's studies and women's advocacy were emerging as major players in the struggle for women's equality. There was increasing recognition that the 'household' needed to be broken open as it was not, as believed, a 'benign' shelter for all its inhabitants.[17]

DISPARATE IMPACTS

Individuals within households had highly disparate locations in power, apart from inequalities in occupation, health and education. This disparity among individuals seemed to become the more enlarged the lower one went on the asset/income scale. Inspired by the international efforts at documenting the disparate impact of development on men and women, the study focused on examining the reach of the anti-poverty programmes vis-à-vis women. What emerged was that the household was not benign and definitely not a level playing field for men and women. In poor households, women had a different source of income from men. The study came up with the idea that women within poverty households should be independently identified and targeted with anti-poverty programmes such as the Integrated Rural Development Programme. We found that the setting of targets for women within such programmes was flawed on many counts, not least by inappropriate development offers and false reporting by functionaries.

This was further corroborated during the process of preparing a report for the Karnataka State Planning Board, titled 'District Level Planning for Social Development'.[18] District-level studies were commissioned for the report from one backward district, Gulbarga, and one advanced district, Dakshina Kannada. The target of covering couples of reproductive age with contraceptive services was irrelevant in Dakshina Kannada (a district on Karnataka's west coast, known for its advanced social indicators), where the fertility rate had already reached two births per woman in the reproductive age group (replacement-level fertility), and in some villages less than two. Yet the fund allocated to the district continued to be allocated only for that purpose, and when its irrelevance was brought out, nothing could be done to shift the funds from contraception to more advanced healthcare.[19]

Planned development appeared, as it does even now, as the blind rubber-stamping of schemes. An even more significant lesson was that the methodology being used did not reach poor men either. The process was completely flawed for men and women among the poor or deprived. It transpired that the method adopted for stimulating development was critical, and even superseded the task of gendering or integrating women into development.

The second example is a project undertaken in Karnataka by the World Bank to improve the quality of the cocoons in the sericulture industry.[20] The project did not use the available knowledge about women's work. Sericulture was one of the dominant land-based activities in Karnataka. The perception of the policy designers was that women were not relevant in this project. It was thought that women were merely using discarded cocoons which had holes in them to make garlands. They were seen as not engaged in the basic chain of production and sale of cocoons.

An actual investigation that sought to break down tasks in the chain of production revealed that while mulberry was grown by the (male) farmers, it was women who not only picked the leaves but looked after the trays in which the silkworms were nursed or nurtured. Silkworms are usually kept in trays called *chandrikes* in shelves inside the home, and have to be fed mulberry leaves every three hours, like infants. The offal has to be removed as frequently so that they do not get diseased. Women in areas with a strong sericulture practice complained that not only were their houses completely cramped with silkworms, leaving hardly any place for the kitchen or their children, but the silkworm was more demanding than a child as it had a compulsive demand for leaves every three hours. Thus, they were awake most of the night, and most of them had chronic illnesses due to the suffocating atmosphere in the hut and the unremitting labour of cocoon rearing.

Despite their being the main rearers of worms, the women were not brought into the project at all. They were not given training on better rearing, on the special characteristics of feeding and care for the new worms that had been introduced; they did not receive information about the new fodder; they were not shown how to upgrade the quality of the yarn. Thus, women's contribution to the process of silk manufacture was unrecognised, with consequences for policy. It appears that Ester Boserup's[21] old complaint of the 1970s where she bemoans the non-recognition of women as farmers continues to be valid.[22]

CLASSICAL INVISIBILITY

As a result of lobbying with the government both in Washington and in Karnataka, a task force on sericulture was set up by the Government of Karnataka with the principal secretary, agriculture, as its chair. All the relevant agencies were gathered around the table at a meeting held to show that there needed to be greater inclusion of women as workers in sericulture development programmes. It was found that this classical invisibility of women workers, especially when the productive work took place within the home, had deprived them of access to training for improved rearing practices as well as marketing.

There was no hostel accommodation for women at the Sericulture Training Institute, a state government institution. A proposal was put forward by the task force to build a women's hostel using another government scheme called Hostels for Working Women. However, the task force neither sustained itself, nor did it effect any transformation in the lives and concerns of women in the sericulture project.

A similar experience is recorded in the matching study that ISST took up with the tasar[23] industry in Maharashtra. Again, women were major workers in this industry, but unrecognised, and nothing was done. The report, funded by the Swiss Agency for Development and Cooperation, tried to change this perception but it had no impact. The studies undertaken by ISST in various parts of India and in Karnataka presented information on women's productive roles, and argued that the projects were losing out on success by not recognising this.[24] While this resulted in gendered analysis, it did not change the project.

Some new opportunities are emerging in India, and more strongly in Karnataka. These may help us incorporate the lessons learnt from history, mentioned earlier in this essay. To reiterate: we had talked of: (a) the usefulness and value of bonding across differences with respect to the identity of 'woman' and strategising for inclusion; (b) the need for knowledge about women's various productive and other roles and their location within the household, family and community; and (c) power claimed through a collective identity.

An aspect of the Karnataka landscape of governance and development, which offers some niches, some conduits for affirming these views, is the long-standing and politically well-supported decentralised management of development, especially the economic and social justice agendas. For example, as far back as in 1994, Karnataka's State Planning Board (earlier called the Economic Planning Council) set up two subgroups, one for district-level planning for employment, and the other for district-level planning for social development. The main task of the subgroups was to provide effective social and economic security to the poor and improve the quality of administration of these services, all at the district and subdistrict levels of accountability. Interestingly, in 2005, the Planning Commission has set up an expert group to draw up guidelines for the states on what they call grassroots planning for development. The thrust is on reducing if not eliminating state-dictated schemes, the pre-packaged development bundles that are handed out, and leaving local communities to plan and design the use of untied funds.

CONSOLIDATING MULTIPLE SCHEMES

The subgroup, working with secretaries to the government for each sector and some CEOs, or chief secretaries of districts as they were called at the time, was able to rationalise the 75 schemes into 15 bundles. It suggested that instead of having 15 schemes coming out of 15 departments, even these could be bundled into a social development service as one sector, and the fund could be used for 'provisioning of social development services to the poor'. The functionaries attached to the service would come under the single nomenclature of 'social development services providers'. Thus, departmental boundaries would be liquidated, and the multiple schemes would be consolidated without losing the overall intention.

One of the suggestions made by the subgroup, that there should be social mapping of the state to show variations in human development indices between districts in order to identify gaps in performance and to spot interdistrict variations, was not implemented. However, this compliance came later. During 1995–97, Karnataka developed a human development report that put together district-level indicators and indices—a first in state-level human development reports in India.[25]

In neither of the illustrations from Karnataka presented above did this opportunity for intervention yield a clear 'tool' to tell us what to do and how to intervene. However, there is now, as I write this article, an opportunity to engage with political power due to the clearer, legally firmer and politically ordained devolution of economic planning power and funds to locally elected bodies in Karnataka. Significant changes have been brought about in the state in the fiscal year 2005–06 (as embodied in the state budget). State sector schemes pertaining to the 29 subjects in Schedule XI of the 73rd Amendment have been merged in the district sector schemes to be implemented by the panchayat institutions. From 1 April 2005, about ₹3,500 crore (35 billion) has been thus devolved to panchayat institutions at the *gram* (village), *taluk* (subdistrict) and *zilla* (district) levels. The departments have been asked to amend and issue afresh all government orders, notifications, circulars and so on in accordance with these charges.

Most importantly, some of the negative features in administration have also been removed. Departments have been directed not to establish parallel bodies which were scuttling devolution as intended by the 73rd Amendment. Existing parallel bodies are to be now reconstituted under the chairmanship of the *adhyaksha* (president) of the *zilla parishad* (district council). Besides, World Bank or externally aided projects are to be implemented through PRIs only.

Right from the beginning, when the Ramakrishna Hegde government in Karnataka in collaboration with Abdul Nazeer Saab, the minister for rural development, brought in legislation to set up elected local councils, the legislation also included reservation for women. Women elected to councils have been invited to meetings held by women's organisations, and attempts have been made to give them a collective identity and a sense of knowledge-based confidence. As the panchayati raj movement grew and broadened with the introduction of the 73rd and 74th Amendments under the then prime minister Rajiv Gandhi, the Singamma Sreenivasan Foundation, for example, got even more deeply engaged in strengthening women who had been elected to serve on these councils.

UNITING ACROSS PARTY LINES

One of the first initiatives that the foundation took was to bring these women under one organisation, described as 'an association of elected women representatives'. While this may seem baffling since the representatives came from different parties, in Karnataka it was found that women were willing to join an association that cut across party lines. They seemed to need that collective strength in order to generate the self-confidence to bring their voice into the meetings. The women's collectives and collectivities also have an additional feature: they are united across class, whereby poor and non-poor women engage in issues which impact all women, like domestic violence, water, or reproductive health, especially in urban slums and rural areas.

Using the collectives, especially at the level of gram panchayats, the foundation built three other programmes on the basis of these groups. The foundation then initiated similar projects in the three other southern states—Kerala, Andhra Pradesh and Tamil Nadu—and is now coordinating a network of agencies in these four states, all of which are engaged in creating collectivities of elected women and enabling them to strengthen their technical skills as well as their political presence in local self-government institutions. Rather than 'training' them, the women have been formed into groups which engage among themselves to create their own space; they debate among themselves and devise programmes instead of being in mixed councils. Women's capability for collective action and for forming collectivities is transforming many programmes, processes and outcomes.

Currently, many women's organisations are partnering with state governments to strengthen the capability of women elected to local self-government institutions to participate in if not lead development in their areas. For example, the Singamma Sreenivasan Foundation has made a novel endeavour to enable elected women representatives to construct budgets such that the interests of women and other subordinated groups are safeguarded. It is not just a programme to raise awareness about budgets among local women politicians, but one that aims to enable women to direct the economy from a space available to them. This helps them to understand, participate in and transform local budgets.

The design of effective participation has been enabled by collaboration with Janaagraha, an urban NGO which uses three-cornered stakeholders' meetings, including the civil servant who is the commissioner of the municipality, the ward committee and the elected corporators, to build a transparent process of understanding and influencing revenue collection and expenditures and monitoring outcomes. This method has been tried in two municipalities—Mysore and Tumkur. The municipalities have changed their budget allocations as a result of collective lobbying by elected women corporators across party lines. A similar experience was observed in two other pockets of Karnataka—Bijapur and Bellary.

Another project to which women were exposed was to use their kitchen gardens for growing medicinal plants. This has now caught the imagination of the gram panchayats, and at least four districts will be engaged in a movement for environment security, health security and livelihood security through the growing of medicinal plants. One outcome of these exercises has been that in the Mysore City Corporation, women's issues are not only included, but allocations to certain women's schemes have been increased in the budget for 2005–06.

DRAMATIC SHIFTS

Today, the situation and character of the various actors in governance have shifted quite dramatically and in significant ways. The state is receding from its earlier role of being responsible to its citizens for their well-being, especially through the provisioning of basic securities. Civil society, including the women's movement, is becoming stronger on the one hand, but also paradoxically more fragmented. The international configuration of power is changing, with the UN's influence receding and other world organisations like the World Bank and multilaterals like the WTO occupying centre stage. The market economy, signified by corporates, is playing a larger role in national and international governance than before, including the provisioning of public goods. There is also a return to conservative politics and various forms of fundamentalism across the globe.

Simultaneously, there are the usual paradoxes in the women's domain. There is an increase in the political participation of women in governance, especially at the local level. There is an increase in the capabilities and power of the women's movement, in its knowledge base, its organisational capacities in the informal economy as workers and traders, and in contesting violence against women. There is a shift in the nature of employment opportunities. There is increasing absorption of female labour into the new opportunities for earning income, like export processing, and simultaneously a decline in opportunities for men. This has arisen because of the nature of the growth poles, i.e., the sectors/lines of production where the rate of growth is rapid, and the organisation of production and trade. Women are on the move, selling either their bodies or their time to earn income for their families. The UN report on women and development for the year 2004[26] shows how the largest group or proportion of workers uncovered by any protection are women, especially women migrants. The demand for women as workers in the flesh trade has increased the flow of women across borders by leaps and bounds. The value of the flesh trade is now greater than the value of the trade in narcotics.

At the very beginning, women's quest was for equality, or for overpowering if not eradicating inequality. The strategy of levelling the playing field by bringing in laws, introducing the power of rights, and finding ways to move women out of what looked like disadvantaged positions seemed all right for several decades. But it was clearly not enough. There was deep, widespread, unimaginable and invisible discrimination. The women's movement responded to this by making inequality visible. But that did not take care of the ignorance and non-recognition of women's value as citizens, workers and providers. Their contribution to society is equal to if not even richer in value than men's. So the movement generated new knowledge to show the role of women in development—again with the expectation that revealing the truth would lead to women's equality with men. But that strategy still disabled them, because they had no voice in the determination of their lives and their roadmaps. Thus, the notion of equal participation, of equal power, of leadership was worked into the approaches to redress inequality.

THE OLD METHOD CONTINUES

What we have seen is that while knowledge has increased and been funnelled into policy spaces, the advice of women has not been taken, their leadership in directing public policy has not evolved to a corresponding extent. The old method of 'integrating' them through women-only packages, mainly in the form of social development package schemes for women, continues.

The revelatory aspect of this story can be summarised in the importance of space not only in terms of funds, but at the level of the intellect, for the excluded to claim their rights. Decentralisation, with a quota of one-third seats for women, has opened a new gateway in India and especially in Karnataka. But it is not enough.

The first need is to reconsider the paradigm of development itself, the identification of the engines of growth. Instead of seeing the poor as a target group who need special ladders within a framework of economic development, enabling them to become economic and political agents could itself become the engine of growth. Thus, turning away from a 'trickle-down' or social safety net approach, it would be useful to look at what can be called the 'bubbling up' theory of growth.[27] This alternative theory argues that putting incomes and political power in the hands of the poor could generate the demand and the voice that would direct development. The purchasing power and the choices of the poor could direct the economy to a pro-poor or poverty-reducing economy. The review of past experience seems to suggest the need for some dramatic reversal of current theories of where the engine of growth lies if the interest is in poverty eradication.[28]

Mahatma Gandhi in fact had designed such a theory and a proposal for its practice. To some extent, it could even be said that such a theory is close to, though not the same as, Keynes's theory of stimulating an economy by generating effective demand. Here the further question is, whose effective demand? Whose purchasing power? Gandhi's talisman, his test for action, was this:

> Whenever you are in doubt, or when the self becomes too much with you, apply the following test: recall the face of the poorest and the weakest

man/woman whom you may have seen and ask yourself if the step you contemplate is going to be of any use to him.[29]

A major faultline that runs through narrations of history and through the knowledge base, be it political, economic or social, is the failure to take note of, to understand and respect and absorb, women's ideational and intellectual skills and outputs in the area of theoretical and analytical knowledge. While some of the values emerging from the new understanding of poverty, inequality, discrimination, conflict resolution, participatory methods and politics generated by this interaction or partnership with women have been applied or pursued belatedly, recognition of the intellectual and leadership powers of women has lagged behind. The minds of men have not changed.

For that to happen, it seems necessary to recast the development framework, to come out with a treatise, a stand-alone theoretical model of development which satisfies the changes in the external world and yet represents women's quest. The women's movement did some of this 20 years ago, at Nairobi, through DAWN, the third world network.[30] But another such framework is needed now, and it can be done if women put their minds together. Women's brilliant struggles need to be treated as a body of knowledge, chiselled into theory, into an intellectual challenge to what 'is', that is, the currently dominant ideas for national and international advancement. The importance of a theoretical construct forged out of ground experience, which can claim space in the world of intellectual discourse, must not be minimised. A new *Das Kapital* or *Wealth of Nations* is the only bomb that can explode the patriarchal mindset and end the exclusion of the real agency of women in public policy.

NOTES

1 C. Morrisson and J. P. Jutting, 'Women's Discrimination in Developing Countries: A New Data Set for Better Policies', *World Development*, vol. 33, no. 7 (July 2005), pp. 1065–81.
2 Jain, 'Power through the Looking Glass of Feminism'; Devaki Jain, 'Women's Participation in the History of Ideas: The Importance of Reconstructing

Knowledge', National Institute for Advanced Studies, Indian Institute of Science, Bangalore, 6 February 2004. See chapter 8, this volume.

3 Devaki Jain, 'PRI Impact on Private Structure (Domestic Sphere): How Important Is the Private–Public Dichotomy—The Case of the EWRS', Seminar on 'Women in Panchayat Raj', New Delhi, 27–28 April 2000; Devaki Jain, 'Valuing Women: Signals from the Ground', paper presented at the conference on 'Cultural Diversity and Universal Norms', University of Maryland, 1 June 2001.

4 Luisella Goldschmidt-Clermont, 'Unpaid Work in the Household: A Review of Economic Evaluation Methods', ILO, Geneva, 1981.

5 Gopal Guru, 'How Egalitarian Are the Social Sciences in India?', *Economic and Political Weekly*, vol. 37, no. 51 (14 December 2002), pp. 5003–9.

6 Devaki Jain, 'The Role of People's Movement in Economic and Social Transformation', paper presented at 'The Role of NGOs in the 21st Century: Inspire, Empower, Act', Seoul International Conference of NGOs, Seoul, 10–16 October 1999.

7 Devaki Jain, 'Globalism and Localism: Negotiating Feminist Space', paper presented at the seminar 'Rethinking Gender, Democracy and Development: Is Decentralisation a Tool for Local Effective Political Voice?', Ferrara University and Modena University, Italy, 20–22 May 2002.

8 Jain, *Women, Development, and the UN*.

9 Virginia Woolf, *A Room of One's Own* (Toronto: Granada, 1977 [1929]).

10 At various international conferences, women organised a separate 'tent' where many activities were carried out with an autonomy not available in the general conference schedules.

11 Jain, *Women, Development, and the UN*.

12 Longino, 'Feminist Standpoint Theory and the Problems of Knowledge'.

13 UN Economic and Social Council, 'Assessment of the Implementation of the System-wide Medium-Term Plan for the Advancement of Women 1996–2001', Resolution 1996/34, 25 July 1996; UN Economic and Social Council, Commission on the Status of Women, 44th Session, 28 February–2 March 2000; UN, 'Report of the Fourth World Conference on Women, Beijing, 4–15 September 1995, including the Agenda, the Beijing Declaration and the Platform for Action (Extract)', in *The United Nations and the Advancement of Women, 1945–1996* (Department of Public Information, UN, 1996), pp. 649–735.

14 Commission on the Status of Women, 49th Session, New York, 28 February–11 March 2005.

15 Devaki Jain, 'Spaces and Hopes', *Hindu*, 3 April 2005.

16 ISST, 'Integrating Women's Interests into State Five-Year Plan'. See also K. S. Krishnaswamy and Shashi Rajagopal, 'Women in Employment: A Micro Study in Karnataka' (based on the ISST Bangalore Report), in Devaki Jain and Nirmala Banerjee (eds), *Tyranny of the Household: Investigative Essays on*

Women's Work, Workshop on Women in Poverty (New Delhi: Shakti Books, 1985). See also the discussion in chapter 1, this volume.

17 Devaki Jain, 'The Household Trap: Report on a Field Survey of Female Activity Patterns', in Jain and Banerjee, *Tyranny of the Household*, pp. 215–46; Nancy Folbre, *Who Pays for the Kids? Gender and the Structures of Constraint* (New York: Routledge, 1994).

18 Devaki Jain (Chairperson of Subcommittee), 'District Level Planning for Social Development', Karnataka State Planning Board, Government of Karnataka, 1994.

19 Shalini Rajaneesh, report from Dakshina Kannada.

20 ISST, 'An Assessment of Women's Roles: The Karnataka Sericulture Development Project'. See also the discussion in chapter 1, this volume.

21 Ester Boserup, *My Professional Life and Publications 1929–1998* (Copenhagen: Museum Tusculanum Press, 1999). Another instance is provided by Maithreyi Krishnaraj's study which she had titled 'Women Farmers of India'; on publication it was retitled *Women in Agriculture*, vol. 25 of *State of the Indian Farmer: A Millennium Study* (New Delhi: Department of Agriculture and Cooperation, Ministry of Agriculture, Government of India, 2004).

22 Devaki Jain, 'Are We Knowledge Proof? Development as Waste', Lovraj Kumar Memorial Lecture, New Delhi, 26 September 2003 (reprinted in *Wastelands News*, vol. 19, no. 1 [August–October 2003], pp. 19–30).

23 ISST, 'Interstate Tasar Project', report on a field survey in Chandrapur district of Maharashtra, 1982. *Tasar* is a form of silk that is extracted from worms that grow on the leaves of a species of tree that grows in Maharashtra and Madhya Pradesh. It is different from the silk from worms reared in cottages, common in the rest of the silk manufacturing industry.

24 ISST, 'Impact of Sericulture Pilot Project in Karnataka: An Evaluation', Bangalore, 1989.

25 Government of Karnataka, *Human Development in Karnataka 1999* (Bangalore: Planning Department, Government of Karnataka, 1999).

26 UN, *2004 World Survey on the Role of Women in Development: Women and International Migration*, Department of Economic and Social Affairs, Division for the Advancement of Women (New York: UN, 2005).

27 See also chapter 4, this volume.

28 Devaki Jain, 'Enabling Reduction of Poverty and Inequality in South Asia', in *Population and Poverty: Achieving Equity, Equality and Sustainability* (New York: United Nations Population Fund, 2003), pp. 99–100.

29 Jain, *Minds, Bodies and Exemplars*, p. 8.

30 ISST, 'The Bangalore Report: A Process for Nairobi at Development Alternatives with Women for a New Era', New Delhi, 1984.

CHAPTER 11

What Is Wrong with Economics?

Can the Aam Aurat Redefine Economic Reasoning?

The Council for Social Development, one of the well-known centres of research and policy located in Delhi, was founded by a remarkable social worker who had been part of India's freedom movement in the 1940s. This woman, Durgabai Deshmukh, not only pioneered the idea of setting up social development centres as an NGO activity to be supported by government, but was also associated with the movement emphasising the provision of social inputs as a way of actually enabling a country to move forward—in other words, strengthening the people as one of the best ways of approaching the goals of economic development. Asked to give a lecture in her honour, I recalled the angry question she once posed to me: 'What is wrong with economics?' Her husband was the finance minister at the time, and when she asked for more budget allocations for social welfare programmes, he had argued that they were not productive ways of spending funds. Taking off from Gandhiji, who had also always held that the poorest of the poor need to define 'development', I argue here that poor women's struggles, strategies as well as needs should inform development strategy.

This might look like a mouse taking up a mountain of a topic—*what is wrong with economics?*—but you would not be surprised if I shared with you the fact that this is the question that Durgabai Deshmukh posed to me at our first meeting in the late 1960s in Delhi. And thereupon hang many tales....

This lecture, in honour of our marvellous foremother Durgabai Deshmukh, will be a string of narratives, tales of another kind, woven together to support or buttress my main argument or proposition: that the measures and values in use in applied economics and policy making need revisioning. They need to be revisited and revised to understand and thereby include the value of the economic spaces occupied by women from the masses.

I will unfold this argument or proposition as follows. First, I will narrate the tale of my own journey of understanding women's roles and value in poverty households and spaces, a journey which led to my being questioned by Durgabai. Then I will present tales revealing the relevance of her question, and how it has resonated with economists in different ways, from Joan Robinson who wanted it grounded in empirical signals, data or information gathered from the ground, to economists like Mahbub ul Haq and Amartya Sen who have espoused the human development approach, going on to the more recent challenges since the financial crisis.

I move on to illustrating, with more tales, the point that existing measures of value and of economic progress, in their very conceptualisation or content, deny or exclude the value invisibly embedded in the lives of the *aam aurat* (the 'common woman', the female counterpart of the 'common man'). Thus, the signals they give to the design of economic policies and practices are flawed. I then illustrate how understanding and including the life situation of the aam aurat, and then building an economic programme and policy framework which follows her footprint and incorporates ideas for moving her forward and upward, could usher in a really inclusive and sustainable growth path. Finally, I try to induce all of you here to engage in developing a consciousness of this neglected genome, the aam aurat who can, in building herself up, rebuild a just India.

LEARNING FROM DOING

My first tale concerns how I happened to be asked the question regarding women's roles and value in spaces of poverty. The learning, the knowledge I gained while composing my first book *Indian Women*,[1] pushed me straight into what, for the sake of brevity, I would like to call the 'women's question'—in this case, questioning so many of the then current propositions about women in India. I focused on one such issue, namely, the official figure for female labour force participation at the time,[2] which was given as 64 per cent for men and 31 per cent for women. It just did not seem accurate. I saw women everywhere, working away in the fields, on the roads, in the markets, so how come the figure was so low? So I undertook an investigative study, using a registered society which had been set up by the late Prof. Raj Krishna specifically to engage in policy-directed research on work and employment—the ISST.

Thanks to my beloved Lakshmi Jain, ever loving and generous, ISST was established in the third bedroom of our three-bedroom flat in Jor Bagh.[3] And from there, our research team, which was just one person plus two in the field, visited and started living in three villages in Bharatpur district in Rajasthan and three villages in Bolpur district in West Bengal for a whole year, recording the activities of every individual including children at half-hour intervals in a sample of households.[4] The sites were deliberately chosen to represent very different agro-climatic zones, dry farming in Rajasthan and wet rice cultivation in West Bengal.

I wish I could just go on talking about that study! It revealed such strong variations across class, caste and, interestingly, culture, not just economic zones, in the work life of women and children. A shocker as well as a wake-up call to data collectors and employment planners. Women from landless households had a formal labour force participation rate which was higher than that of men. So I challenged the perception that women were supplementary breadwinners, which is the way the formal statistical system sees women. The aam aurats were actually the main support of their households. In West Bengal, the culture of respect for women had a cruel twist when it came to those living in assetless households, that is, the poorest rural households. Women were not allowed to work for a wage in the fields, but they could beg, that is, go around seeking alms, or work as domestic help and be paid with food! It was considered to be more dignified!

Naini and Khartoum, two 11-year-old girls from landless households living miles apart—one in Bharatpur district of Rajasthan and the other in Birbhum district of West Bengal—could have been conjoined twins. Their daily schedule seems as if they both went to the same school and class: get up at 5 a.m., clean the house, bring water, fire the stove, then go out to clean the outside, help their mothers with preparing lunch, clean the utensils, go to the field to help with weeding, come back, fetch water and start all over again, till bedtime—14–16 hours of work. Their brothers go to school or play *gilli danda* in the yard.[5] We will find many such Nainis and Khartoums in India.

I tried to capture some of this in the Padmaja Naidu Memorial Lecture I was invited to give at the Nehru Memorial Museum in 1982.[6] Since Prof. André Béteille, not only a distinguished sociologist/anthropologist but a very dear friend, was chairing the lecture, I asked what were all these explorations of kinship organisations in India and the proposition that the family was a strong shelter, a centrepiece in understanding India? What I found from the time-use study as well as other studies of poverty households was that these were fragmented *non-families* in which women and little girls not only had very unequal positions but often battled for life.[7] Amartya Sen has captured this struggle in his famous essay 'Food Battles',[8] where he highlights the phenomenon of unequal food distribution within a family. The sociological family is different from the economic family, and I suggest that the economic family, especially amongst the poor, has not been studied sufficiently.

MY FIRST ENCOUNTER WITH DURGABAI

Around those years, that is, in the late 1960s, Kamala Devi Chattopadhyay, Lakshmi Jain's mentor and, if I may say so, my 'third mother' (my mother and Lakshmi's mother being the other two), used to visit us regularly, and one time she brought Durgabai with her who, of course, straight away asked me what I did. Those of you who have met Durgabai can I am sure picture this. She was direct—no frills, formidable to contend with, and clearly trying to ensure that I was not idle and was using my life for service to humanity. I replied that I was teaching economics at Delhi University and doing what was called rural studies. To which she responded, visibly upset, 'What is wrong with economics?'

She elaborated, arguing that the discipline did not seem to value social welfare services. She said she had not been able to get enough funds sanctioned from finance ministers' budgets, initially for her work with the Central Social Welfare Board,[9] and later for her efforts to set up educational and other societies in various cities, such as the Andhra Mahila Sabhas,[10] on the grounds that in economics, social welfare expenditure was not 'investment'—something that yielded returns—but 'consumption', something that ended with itself and was destroyed.

So begins the story, and just to finish that anecdote, Durgabai wanted to know if I could write a note that justified such expenditure as economically valuable. Amartya Sen was at that time at the Delhi School of Economics,[11] and was capturing attention and excitement by talking about welfare economics and teaching social choice theory. I suggested that Durgabai recruit him for this task. I was making a connection between Sen's language and her concern for welfare. I told Amartya that I had mentioned his name to Durgabai.

Luckily for me, I met Professor Sen recently in London,[12] and he confirmed that Durgabai had invited him for breakfast and served him idlis, as he recalled with pleasure. (This was around 1967, and I guess Dr C. D. Deshmukh was then the vice-chancellor of Delhi University.) He added that he had not only immensely enjoyed listening to her, but that it had added to his knowledge. Amartya had agreed to write the note. He said that he had co-authored it with the late Professor K. A. Naqvi, who was then at the Delhi School of Economics. He thinks it was even published, but does not remember when and where; alas, we were not able to trace it. I think Durgabai did get the additional funds for the social welfare sector that she was fighting for, but I cannot claim that there was a cause and effect relation to this episode.

This is the problem in economics that I will be further elaborating on and exploring in this lecture on 'what is wrong with economics'. The issue on which I want to build this narrative, to continue this story, is measurement, or valuation—one of the many branches of economics. I would also argue that this error in conceptualising both value as well as its measuring tools particularly affects the understanding of the location of the aam aurat, the 'daridranarayani' (I am here taking liberties with Gandhiji's term 'daridranarayana', as the true bottom-of-the-pile person is the woman). Yet, as I will show, the aam aurat is the real genome, the nucleus which holds not half the sky but all of it. Building economic reasoning drawn from a more inclusive measurement of her life—not only her needs but her engagement with political and economic forces, her social networks—could rebuild justice apart from stimulating the engine of growth.

THE BASIC FLAW: EVALUATION AND MEASUREMENT OF PROGRESS

However, before I go any further, I would like to clarify that in my view economics as a discipline, as a science, or as a vocabulary of identifying phenomena, exploring and offering theories of their relationships, has not lost legitimacy. It is particular aspects, such as valuation and measurement of what constitutes economic progress and the reasoning on how to achieve that progress, that I am dealing with as the problem of 'what is wrong'.

And for support on this mode of questioning, I can do no better than to call upon Joan Robinson. Titan of economics, someone with whose name I am sure all of you here are familiar. She brings in openness to economics, but with a firm belief in the fundamental arguments and vocabularies of the discipline. I cannot help quoting from her essay on teaching economics in India, as it will relieve us to know that we, Durgabai and people like us who want to reconstruct the measures and reasoning employed in economics, are not philistines. Writing on teaching economics, Joan Robinson says:

> For many years, I have been employed as a teacher of theoretical economics. I would like to believe that I earn my living honestly, but I often have doubts. I am concerned particularly for India and other developing countries whose economic doctrines come to them mainly from England and in English. Is what we are giving them, Indian students who come to Cambridge for studying, helpful to their development?...
>
> ... But even at the gloomiest, I do not think of giving up. The subject does exist. For better or worse it has become the basis of a flourishing profession. There is no stopping it now. We must keep on pegging away and try to make the best of it.[13]

She continues:

> Welfare I should treat in human terms and teach the students to look, not for 'preference surfaces', but for objective tests of standards of nutrition and health.
>
> In all this, I should emphasize that economic theory, in itself, preaches no doctrines and cannot establish any universally valid laws. It is a method of ordering ideas and formulating questions. For this reason, I should pay a good deal of attention to method.... To find causal relations we must know how individuals behave and how the behaviour of various groups reacts on each other. I should try to break down the awe that students feel for formulae, not so as to induce a sceptical drift into intellectual nihilism, but so as to form the habit of picking them to pieces and putting them together again with the ambiguities cleaned off, and keeping them firmly in their place as useful adjuncts to common sense, not as substitutes for it.[14]

Another tale which I cannot resist telling is this: Joan Robinson is one of my goddesses, among whom I count Durgabai, Kamala Devi Chattopadhyay, Rukmini Devi, Aruna Asaf Ali and others. Joan, as some of you might know, was a regular visitor to India. She would go straight to K. N. Raj's flat on Probyn Road. She admired Raj for his empiricism and yet rigorous analysis of the Indian economy. She would stay for a month or more during winter in the UK, when the weather in India was nice.

I was fortunate to have caught her attention for doing fieldwork as also for engaging in case studies of women's work.[15] She applauded me for applying my education to good purpose, as I had been at Oxford (and had had the benefit of spending Christmas at her home, thanks to another of her Indian friends, Sita Narasimhan). So when the Rajs were not in New Delhi during one of her visits, she stayed with us, a great thrill for me, in our very awkward few rooms at Jawahar Nagar at the corner of Malka Ganj! She slept on charpoys, ate our food, read my work, and encouraged me to keep going with empirical work to formulate my theoretical propositions—an amazing gift for me.

A FEMINIST ASIDE

While many of her male students and admirers in India may not agree with this interpretation, Joan to me exemplified the difference between men and women in reasoning, in understanding and building theory but also finding its fountainhead in practice. She might not have wanted to be seen as a feminist or believe in any form of essentialism, or she might not have minded, but her millions of worshippers would feel that it is demeaning to associate her with the characteristics of being 'woman' that we feminists see as a positive trait.

There is another layer here, which I call the stigma of identity. That is, if you are identified with a cause, like myself as the voice of an identity called 'woman', then you are stamped with that tag so deeply that you cannot also be seen as a scholar, a political leader, a commentator on issues apart from women. Therefore, many women who are leading struggles on issues such as land or other rights would not like to be named as feminists, as it straight away boxes them out of other domains. Just to caricature myself, when I am invited to or am present at a conference or meeting on other issues such as the Lokpal Bill, for example, it is assumed that I will speak about women's exclusion, etc., and my views on the broader issues are not in demand. This narrowing of identity can be demeaning.

BEGINNINGS OF THE CONCEPT OF 'HUMAN DEVELOPMENT'

Durgabai's pioneering, perspicacious question, 'What is wrong with economics?', and her interrogation of the inadequate way the discipline defines value, were translated to the world by Mahbub ul Haq in the form: 'What is wrong with measuring progress only through the gross domestic product [GDP]?' This led to a better understanding of the building of human capabilities, as Amartya Sen described it, and the value of investment by the state in education and health. So, from Durgabai's days when social welfare or social sector expenditures were considered as consumption, that is, as not generating spin-offs, there has been a movement towards ideas such as human capital, human resources development and of course, the *Human Development Reports* and indices.

This is where the work of both Haq and Sen, as well as the knowledge that all of us have, as indeed Durgabai had, of what is required to lift those at the bottom of the pile out of their condition—to level up the bottom—become valuable and need to be brought back. It requires an economics that addresses the whole package. This proposition could not be better addressed than in the way Mahbub ul Haq described it in the *Human Development Report* released in 1995:[16]

> For too long, it was assumed that development was the process that lifts all boats, that its benefits trickled down to all the income classes—and that it was gender-neutral in its impact. Experience teaches otherwise. Wide income disparities and gender gaps stare us in the face in all societies.... it requires a new way of thinking—in which the stereotyping of women and men gives way to a new philosophy that regards all people, irrespective of gender, as essential agents of change.[17]

At another place, he says:

> People must be at the centre of our development debate—what really counts is how they participate in economic growth and how they benefit from it. Production processes are indispensable but they cannot be allowed to obscure human lives. The focus of our reports is on those human lives— how they change over time, how they contribute to national and global economic opportunities, how they share these opportunities, how the range of people's choices can be measured—whether economic or political, whether individual or national....
>
> Our 1990 Report demonstrated that it is not only the income level of a society that matters but how well that income has been translated into human lives.[18]

But Durgabai's question did not stop there. Since the 2008–9 global financial crisis, further questioning, which goes somewhat deeper into challenging the very basis of economic reasoning, has come into vogue. The financial crisis thus led to a big shake-up of economics. Apart from downsizing the value of market-led, capital-led, trade-led growth, it provided space for the entry of other ideas on how to build the GDP—less peaked, less capital driven, more employment generating. It brought back the value of regulatory mechanisms, the importance of a welfare state, old ideas like nurturing the domestic economy, providing employment and so on.

D. Subbarao, the governor of the Reserve Bank of India, says,

> What the crisis has done is to cause a massive break down of trust: trust in the financial system, trust in bankers, trust in business, trust in business leaders, trust in investment advisers, and trust in credit rating agencies, in politicians, in the media and in the process of globalization. When you break down the complex gamut of the causes of the crisis, several skeletons tumble out of the cupboard. Were professionals in the financial sector legally right, but only legally right and morally wrong?[19]

He continues:

> People often forget that the godfather of modern capitalism, and often called the first economist—Adam Smith—was not an economist, but rather a professor of moral philosophy. Smith had a profound understanding of the ethical foundations of markets and was deeply suspicious of the 'merchant class' and their tendency to arrange affairs to suit their private interests at public expense. In short, Smith emphasized the ethical content of economics, something that got eroded over the centuries as economics tried to move from being *a value based social science* to *a value free exact science*.[20]

Similar but not the same sentiments have been expressed by many, but I quote the Nobel Laureate Joseph Stiglitz, as he is a known name here in India apart from Amartya Sen:

> If we have poor measures, what we strive to do (say, increase GDP) may actually contribute to a worsening of living standards.... Statistical frameworks are intended to summarize what is going on in our complex society in a few easily interpretable numbers. It should have been obvious that one couldn't reduce everything to a single number, GDP.[21]

So those of us who are arguing for another way of helping India prosper are in good company.

In India and some other places, Gandhiji is being invoked again as having developed an economic package which satisfies the various elements of a just economy, building prosperity from the bottom, an approach which most of all is relevant to the situation in India. Joan Robinson would have been happy to have had him as a student, I suggest, as he did both—he rejected the model of the imperial masters of the time on how they became rich and powerful, as well as designing an economic growth path suited to the location of the aam aurat. When asked by a British journalist, soon after the British left, whether he would like India to have the same standard of living as Britain, Gandhiji replied, with his usual sardonic sense of humour, that considering that a small island like Britain had to exploit half the globe to have this living standard, there were not enough globes for a big country like India. Interestingly, the great J. R. D. Tata, a patriotic industrialist who built one of the greatest industrial houses in India, said: 'I do not want India to be an economic superpower. I want India to be a happy country.'[22]

Coming back to my questions in economics with regard to valuation, measuring what constitutes economic progress, how to build on the economic struggles and roles of the poorest of women, and the reasoning on how to achieve that progress, I can relate many tales on the fights we put up in the 1970s, whether during the designing of household survey questionnaires by the UN, where we were again put in that terrible basket of the 'useless', a section which bundles together the physically challenged, called in those days the 'handicapped', widows, the destitute and women, or similar struggles later with national data collection systems. This struggle to notify the particular economic profile of women amongst the poor continues. In trying to understand the poverty of the aam aurat, it is not enough to look at household income or consumption. She lives in a community, and so her social income needs to be understood, and that is where her security lies and that has to be enhanced.

This new concept or measure, 'social income', is drawn from a field-based survey conducted in Gujarat in 2007–8.[23] It is fundamentally a perspective, a means of forcing us to think of income as an integrated process of building entitlements and security, and offers a framework that enables the analyst to weave a story that is richer than could be conveyed by simple measures of money income alone. The expanded concept fits into the feminist understanding that neighbourhood, family and community play significant roles in enabling individuals.

Recently, during the finalising of the 11th Plan, a committee was formed of women economists to enable the identification of women's roles and requirements in the economic sectors of the plan. Through the exercise, the committee members were able to locate with statistics the depth of engagement of women in agricultural production apart from allied industries, as well as in export industries, infrastructure, and every productive economic sector.[24] The group, after scanning data, found that women were key to India's GDP growth rate in most sectors, including savings and exports, and argued that women were India's 'growth agents' and needed to be called that, rather than seen as objects or subjects of social welfare services. The group provided data on women's location in the various economic sectors, and it is heartening that the final version of the 11th Plan has taken note of this knowledge.

For example, adopting the basic premise of women as economic agents of change, the 11th Plan includes data like the differential wage earnings of men and women to reflect on the discrimination faced by women. There are data inclusions on female workforce participation in India and other countries, emphasising the double burden of women in India. The 11th Plan also for the first time includes an entire section on the unorganised sector and home-based workers, and female concentrations in both spheres. The data provided in both these sections are drawn from feminist economists' work in the field.

A further stark illustration is from the unorganised sector. According to the report of the expert group on the informal sector, '118 million women workers are engaged in the unorganised sector in India.'[25] Another case study by Patil and Nuzrat states:

> According to the National Accounts Statistics, the workers in the unorganized sector contribute over 62% to the NDP. The sector also contributes over 50% of the total household savings thus dispelling the myth that poor do not save. A substantial 39.3 percent (Rs. 46 thousand crore) is the contribution of the informal sector to India's total exports (NHRC, 2006).[26]

Moving on to export-oriented production of goods and services, women are predominant if not the major value adders, whether it is in business process outsourcing, special economic zones, or in some of the sunrise industries like garment export firms, processed foods, and even services like the burgeoning hospitality industry.

VISIBLE INVISIBILITY

What this review of knowledge is pointing to is that women amongst the poor, the aam aurats, are the warriors who with their bodies and their intelligence and sense of responsibility fuel the engines of production. This needs to be accounted for and their work needs to be valued and enhanced in quality, in remuneration, and through the reduction of hardship.

The aam aurat crowds the spaces of the poor, and is usually among the first to lose her livelihood in a crisis. Her daughters are either surrogate mothers or sold for survival. She is alive to issues and participates in public protests and struggles, and she votes diligently. She fights for her rights, even if she is often killed in the process. But this aam aurat, while she is used in all the publicity campaigns—for example, hers is the face used to publicise social welfare programmes like the National Rural Employment Guarantee Scheme or the Sarva Shiksha Abhiyan, or the latest National Rural Health Mission, or water conservation—her face is also used to show the opposite picture by the media or critics. The gaunt faces of women dying of hunger, or weeping over the death of a farmer driven to suicide, are not identified as the genome, the energy that spans the spectrum of economic, social and political action.

The aam aurat should be recognised as the key factor, the nucleus, the genome, the oil that keeps the Indian economic engine running. For this, she needs to be recognised as a worker, however non-monetised, however invisible. For her, there is no difference between social services and economic support; it has to be a socio-economic package, a bundle of securities, but beginning with securing her earning capacity.

When we build an economic growth model starting with the aam aurat, we are really safe: there are no exclusions, there is no rise in gross inequality, there is no death due to starvation, and most important of all, there is maximum use of resources as she is a thrifty, non-wasteful person. Her zest for building her family up would drive her to send her children to school, but only if she has an adequate wage. Her capacity to socialise in work groups enables collective and cooperative development, as we see in the self-help groups or in the Lijjat cooperatives,[27] or SEWA, the first association of self-employed women workers to have ensured social security for its women, and other such efforts.

So, dear friends, we come back to our foremother Durgabai, who challenged the logic of policy which could not see the value of social welfare as a major foundation for economic progress, and see how the world has followed her first call. All of you here, deeply involved in public action, can, I hope, like Durgabai, challenge the kind of economic growth path that generates gross and increasing inequality, slowly effaces the vibrant crafts and handloom industries, moves small farm and small enterprise systems into plantation agriculture and multi-brand retail trade, and perpetuates corruption due to the deeply unequal distribution of economic power. I hope that you will enable India to foreground the aam aurat and feel driven to reorder the economic growth path so as to start with her needs, her life's messages on what comes first.

NOTES

1 Jain, *Indian Women*, official publication of the Government of India for the first UN Women's Conference held in Mexico in 1975. The book contains essays by women leaders of that era, such as Lakshmi Menon and Kamala Devi Chattopadhyay, eminent historians such as Romila Thapar and Kapila Vatsyayan, social anthropologists such as André Béteille and Veena Das and Morris Carstairs, demographers like Ashish Bose, and so on.

2 Rural India Statistics for 1977–78, NSSO Report 32nd Round (July 1977–June 1978).

3 www.isst-india.org/ (accessed 20 June 2017).

4 Jain, 'The Household Trap'; Jain, 'Valuing Work'.

5 Gilli danda is a traditional Indian game for children played with two wooden pieces: one is a large stick called *danda*, and the other a smaller one, called *gilli*.

6 Jain, 'Indian Women Today and Tomorrow'.

7 Devaki Jain, 'Questioning Economic Success through the Lens of Hunger', in Devaki Jain and Diane Elson (eds), *Harvesting Feminist Knowledge for Public Policy: Rebuilding Progress* (New Delhi: SAGE, 2011).

8 Amartya Sen, 'Food Battles: Conflicts in the Access to Food', *Food and Nutrition*, vol. 10, no. 1 (1984), pp. 81–89.

9 Durgabai Deshmukh was the founder chairperson of the Central Social Welfare Board during the first years of its existence from 1953 to 1962.

10 A charitable and service-oriented organisation founded by Durgabai in 1948 with the noble vision of providing services to the needy.

11 Amartya Sen taught at the Delhi School of Economics from 1963 to 1971.

12 I was in London for the Commonwealth Secretariat Conference, 20 June 2011.

13 Joan Robinson, 'Teaching Economics', in Joan Robinson, *Collected Economic Papers*, vol. 3 (Oxford: Basil Blackwell, 1965), pp. 1–6, originally published as 'Teaching Economics: A Passage to India', *Economic Weekly* (Bombay, 1960s).

14 Ibid.

15 Jain, 'The Household Trap'; Jain et al., *Women's Quest for Power*; ISST, 'Impact on Women Workers: Maharashtra Employment Guarantee Scheme'.

16 Mahbub ul Haq was the principal co-ordinator of the UNDP *HDR* released in 1995.

17 Mahbub ul Haq, 'Overview: The Revolution for Gender Equality', *HDR 1995*.

18 Mahbub ul Haq, 'Human Development in a Changing World', Occasional Paper 1, Topical Background Research for *HDR 1992*, UNDP, http://hdr.undp. org/sites/default/files/mahbub_ul_haq.pdf (accessed 21 June 2017).

19 Duvvuri Subbarao, Governor, Reserve Bank of India, 'Ethics and the World of Finance', Keynote Address at the conference organised by Sri Sathya Sai University, Prasanthi Nilayam, Andhra Pradesh, 28 August 2009, https://www. rbi.org.in/scripts/BS_SpeechesView.aspx?id=434 (accessed 12 September 2017).

20 Ibid.

21 Joseph Stiglitz, 'The Great GDP Swindle', *Guardian*, 13 September 2009, https://www.theguardian.com/commentisfree/2009/sep/13/economics-economic-growth-and-recession-global-economy (accessed 12 September 2017).

22 J. R. D. Tata (1904–1993), after receiving the Bharat Ratna in 1992.

23 Guy Standing, Jeemol Unni, Renana Jhabvala and Uma Rani, *Social Income and Insecurity: A Study in Gujarat* (New Delhi: Routledge, 2010).

24 Working Group of Feminist Economists, *Engendering Public Policy: A Report on the Work of the Working Group of Feminist Economist during the preparation of Eleventh Five Year Plan 2007–12* (New Delhi: Planning Commission, Government of India, May 2010).

25 National Commission for Enterprises in the Unorganised Sector (NCEUS), *Report on Conditions of Work and Promotion of Livelihood in the Unorganized Sector* (New Delhi: Government of India, August 2007).

26 Parveen Nuzhat and N. H. Patil, 'Women in Informal Sector: A Case Study of Construction Industry', *International Research Journal*, vol. 1, no. 11 (August 2010).

27 Sonia Gandhi, 'Women as Agents of Change', Commonwealth Lecture, London, 17 March 2011.

CHAPTER 12

The First Challengers

The Feminists of the South

The editor of the quarterly discussion magazine of the United Nations Industrial Development Organization (UNIDO), Making It: Industry for Development, invited me to contribute an article for an issue of the magazine which was to focus on South–South cooperation, to tie in with the UNIDO/UNDP Global South–South Development Expo 2012 in Vienna. Many champions of the economic South were to contribute to this issue. The editor wanted a short article of around 1,000 words on a feminist perspective on South–South solutions. I illustrated how women and their networks in the South were revealing errors in the description of the economies of the South as well offering ideas for rethinking development itself.

[A] third intellectual trend [is] the emergence of a new virulent strain of economic imperialism based on market, especially informational failure. Whilst mainstream economics has become absolutely intolerant of dissent within its own discipline, it has increasingly sought to colonise other disciplines, understanding both market and non-market phenomena as the rational, historically evolved response to market failures.... this approach has been applied to development, alongside more or less everything else, and underpins the shifting rhetoric and scholarship of the World Bank in its move from Washington to post-Washington consensus.

—Ben Fine, 2002[1]

The original theory of socioeconomic development that accompanied the post-1945 decolonization of Asia and Africa rested on the idea of modern society as the goal of development. Modern society supposedly had typical social patterns of demography, urbanization and literacy; typical economic patterns of production and consumption, investment, trade and government finance; and typical psychological attributes of rationality, ascriptive identity and achievement motivation. The process of development consisted, on this theory, of moving from traditional society, which was taken as the polar opposite of the modern type, through a series of stages of development—derived essentially from the history of Europe, North America and Japan.

—John Toye, 1993[2]

In the 1980s, while there was much critique and challenging of the development paradigm and what was called the 'modernisation project',[3] it was feminists of the South who first established both an intellectual identity of the South, pinned on the understanding as well as removal of women's poverty; and then challenged the development transfers derived from the characterisation of women of the South in the image of their Northern sisters.

> What is amazing when it comes to development thinking by and within the United Nations system, is the dominance of Western ideas in an Organization that is now composed of almost 200 nations and even more cultures. Starting with modernization theory, all the development approaches are 'Western' and are dominated by economists. This remains true even with strategies conceived by thinkers from the South or the East.[4]

It was feminist scholars and advocates who revealed how the characterisations of Southern women's economic roles were dramatically different from the roles being played by their sisters in the North. At the same time, there was great similarity across the Southern continents. For example, women vendors were a part of the market scenario in most of these continents: the higglers of the Caribbean islands, the market women of Ghana and Liberia, and the street vendors of South and Southeast Asia. In many of these regions, for example, in Manipur, a north-eastern state of India, women are the principal wholesale and retail traders.[5] They are also the informal banks.[6] Home-based production was another critical economic characteristic of women in the Southern continents. Women in these continents were engaged in cultivation of food and cash crops, often owning land too, very different from their Northern sisters.[7] This characterisation, apart from the identity it established, generated both organised voice and theoretical intrusions into the concept of development.[8]

For example, DAWN, a feminist network of the South,[9] identified the 'crises' in these regions—Africa's food crisis, Latin America's debt, South Asia's poverty, and the militarisation of the Pacific Islands—as the frameworks within which the efforts to enable women to move out of poverty needed to be located. Poor women in these regions were not only totally engaged in the economies of their countries, but were suffering from and also responding creatively to these onslaughts. A new framework began to emerge.[10]

The analysis by DAWN noted that only a few countries that had pursued export-led strategies for growth had gained systematic results. In fact, countries that had experienced economic booms were the same as those that had a record of growing inequality. The analysis located the structural roots of poverty not in insufficient economic growth, but in 'unequal access to resources, control over production, trade, finance, and money and across nations, genders, regions, and classes'.[11]

The next challenge to what could be called 'the given gospel' of macro-economic reasoning, even when it was designed to 'develop the underdeveloped South', came from the South Commission (1987–90), initiated by the NAM countries under their then chairman Robert Mugabe. The commission was chaired by the former president of Tanzania, the visionary Dr Julius Nyerere. At the very first meeting, the members, all economists from the Southern continents,[12] proposed that the very language, the whole package of 'progress' as generated by Eurocentric thought needed to be challenged. This involved a redefinition of what could be called 'advancement' and, therefore, a great thrust on or prioritisation of measures/indicators.[13]

As the world economy ran into trouble with the crisis that started in 2007,[14] feminists of the South, in partnership with scholars from the North, analysed the sources as well as offered ideas for reconstructing the very basis of economic reasoning as well as measures of progress.[15] In India, for example, the potential for generating sustainable growth of output along with jobs and livelihoods is tangible. Data from official sources on the output of small and medium enterprises (SME) as well as hand-driven sectors reveal a steady contribution to the output of the industrial sector, even without the support of strong public policy initiatives.[16] Women are the predominant labour force in these forms of production and exchange, as shown in Table 12.1.

According to the Arjun Sengupta Commission Report, of the total workers in the unorganised sector, 148 million (32.3 per cent) are women. More than half of them, nearly 80 million women, do home-based work.[17] Even though the household industry is undervalued

Table 12.1: *Employment Creation by Handicraft, Handloom, and Khadi and Village Industries Sectors in India*

Sector	Total Employment/ Livelihood Creation	% of Women Employed
Handloom	4 million	78%
Handicraft	7 million	48%
Khadi and village industries	11.4 million	More than 80%

Source: Syeda Hameed, **Report of the Steering Committee on Handlooms and Handicrafts Constituted for the Twelfth Five-Year Plan (2012–17)** (New Delhi: Planning Commission, 2012).

and not supported either, it is household savings that contribute to domestic savings. As Y. V. Reddy has pointed out, 'domestic savers… in any case, finance over ninety percent of investments.'[18]

The South then has the potential to redesign and relocate its engines of growth. By firing these engines, it is possible to generate what can be called wage-led growth (as opposed to capital-led growth), as a paradigm shift from the current system of 'market-led growth'—a misnomer, as traditional local markets have been a lifeline for the poor in developing countries.

One of the most inspiring economic programmes for building inclusive growth and progress has come from Gandhiji himself. I call his ideas for economic progress the 'bubbling-up theory of growth',[19] as a way of challenging the current 'trickle-down theory of growth'. The 'bubbling-up' theory argues that the process of removal of poverty can itself be an engine of growth, that the incomes and capabilities of those who are currently poor have the potential to generate demand, which in turn will fuel production, but of goods that are immediately needed by the poor which are currently peripheral in production. The oiling of this engine, then, will allow the economy to grow in a much more broad-based manner. Unlike export-led growth, it will not skew production and trade into the elite trap which is accentuating disparities and creating discontent.

South countries and women in them are a fertile field right now for generating industrial growth which is 'inclusive', in other words, which generates employment, as opposed to industrial growth which is jobless and tends to create corporate empires and gross inequality. Feminists of the South have revealed that women are the principal actors, but are underpaid and unrecognised in the so-called emerging economies whose success is built on their providing cheap, unprotected labour. If this phenomenon is converted into value through recognition as well as through building another theory of growth such as the 'bubbling-up' theory of growth, UNIDO then can fly a flag for 'industrial development for economic justice'.

NOTES

1 Ben Fine, 'Globalisation and Development: The Imperative of Political Economy', paper presented at the conference 'Towards a New Political Economy of Development: Globalisation and Governance', Sheffield, July 2002.

2 John Toye, *Dilemmas of Development* (Oxford: Blackwell, 1993).

3 With the birth of the UN, coinciding with both the end of World War II and the devastation of Germany, development as designed for the 'newly liberated' countries was modelled on the Marshall Plan. Because the colonial masters saw their former colonies as backward, the development paradigm of this era is described as the 'modernisation' project.

4 Louis Emmerij, 'Development Thinking, Globalization and Cultural Diversity', paper prepared for the North–South Roundtable, 'Imperative of Tolerance and Justice in a Globalised World', Cairo, 27–28 November 2002.

5 Devaki Jain, 'Night Patrollers of Manipur', in Jain et al., *Women's Quest for Power*.

6 Devaki Jain and Seromena Asem, 'A Feminist Mart: Women's Empowerment', *Deccan Herald*, 26 October 2007, http://archive.deccanherald.com/DeccanHerald.com/Content/Oct262007/editpage2007102532303.asp (accessed 26 June 2017).

7 Ester Boserup, *Women's Role in Economic Development* (New York: St Martin's Press, 1970).

8 Devaki Jain, 'Women's Economic Reasoning and Development Economics: A Discussion on Some Intersections', SCA Joint Project Workshop, Sixth Conference of the Science Council of Asia, New Delhi, 17 April 2006.

9 DAWN official website, http://www.dawnnet.org/ (accessed 26 June 2017).

10 Devaki Jain, 'A View from the South: A Story of Intersections', in Arvonne S. Fraser and Irene Tinker (eds), *Developing Power: How Women Transformed International Development* (New York: Feminist Press, 2004), pp. 128–37.

11 Jain, *Women, Development, and the UN*, p. 96.

12 V. Prashad, *The Darker Nations: A People's History of the Third World* (New York: The New Press, 2007).

13 The South Centre, http://www.southcentre.org/index.php (accessed 26 June 2017).

14 Kristopher S. Gerardi, Andreas Lehnert, Shane M. Sherland and Paul S. Willen, 'Making Sense of the Subprime Crisis', *Brookings Papers on Economic Activity*, vol. 39, no. 2 (Fall 2008), pp. 69–159.

15 Devaki Jain and Diane Elson, *Harvesting Feminist Knowledge for Public Policy* (New Delhi: SAGE, 2012); Devaki Jain, 'Using the Turbulence to the Advantage of the Less Privileged', paper presented at 'Turning the Global Economic Crisis into Opportunity: Women's Ideas', Commission on the Status of Women, UNDP, 53rd Session, New York, March 2009.

16 The output of the SME sector has not only been steady but growing in India; it currently occupies 40 per cent of the output of the manufacturing sector. The SME sector also generates jobs (second only to agriculture) and is an employment-oriented substructure of manufacturing. It contributed 40 per cent of total exports directly and a significant amount of exports indirectly through large trading houses or third parties. The handicrafts industry contributed about 25 per cent of the GDP of the unregistered manufacturing sector in the country, about 7.5 per cent of the total manufacturing sector. The crafts sector accounts for 15–20 per cent of the country's manufacturing workforce, and contributes 8 per cent of GDP in manufacturing. See India Brand Equity Foundation, 'SMEs Role in India's Manufacturing Sector', www.ibef.org, p. 6.

17 NCEUS, *Report on the Conditions of Work and Promotion of Livelihoods in the Unorganised Sector* (the Arjun Sengupta Report).

18 Y. V. Reddy, 'Global Economic Developments and India', 17th Prem Bhatia Memorial Lecture, 2012, http://www.prembhatiatrust.com/lecture17.htm (accessed 12 September 2017).

19 Devaki Jain, 'Enabling Poverty and Inequality Reduction in South Asia', paper presented at the UN Population Fund Consultation on Population, Reproductive Health, Gender and Poverty Reduction, New York, 30 September–2 October 2002.

CHAPTER 13

The Evolution of Ideas

A Feminist's Reflections on the Partnership with the UN System

There was much activity preceding the Millennium Summit in 2010, not only in the UN but also in international research organisations, around reviewing progress towards achievement of the MDGs and making suggestions to be considered at the summit. The Roosevelt Institute in New York was eager to produce a book to coincide with the Millennium Summit conference, which would review how women saw the whole process as well as its purpose. My own experience of the UN, its ideas and its programmes had become extremely negative. I felt that while the UN asked for ideas, its mandate was to have agreement across all the countries of the world; since it could not sanction anything without international acceptance, it was a dead end for ideas. This paper argues that to give opportunity to their ideas, women should stay away from the UN and generate political power for themselves through alternative global, regional and national structures.

In its early years, the United Nations struggled valiantly to craft workable international covenants to protect nations and peoples from wars and injustices.[1] It also served as a marketplace for the exchange of knowledge and the building up of transformative ideas, and as such became a critical space for women to form collectives and build strength outside of the state. In collaboration with women's movements, the UN brought about several international covenants to protect and advance women's rights and nurtured various feminist networks organised geographically or around specific subjective identities. These entities have since acted as important voices for change on the global stage and within states and other power clubs.

But with the advent of globalisation in recent years, and the growing power of the private sector including international capital and MNCs, governments and multilaterals like the UN have increasingly been pushed aside and have lost their power to negotiate justice. In the troubling conditions of the world around us today, the UN's mandates are not working, whether in the context of regional conflicts or economic crises, or even the fulfilment of its own goals, as in the case of the MDGs. I am especially disheartened by the lack of change in the condition of women and girls in our countries. Yes, there is more awareness of gender and many commitments to rights and equality in high places, but, as I will demonstrate, the ground remains largely still.

The UN's role as an effective designer and monitor of development has receded and, therefore, these brief reflections argue that the institution should return to its original role as a marketplace for ideas. It should dismantle its unwieldy development bureaucracy—or at least that aspect of it which is focused on women—and provide a space for us to rethink basic assumptions, strategies and goals instead.

I am, of course, aware of and understand the value of the UN in certain spaces, such as the Security Council, however powerless it may also sometimes be. And I applaud its humanitarian efforts. However, on questions of economic and social development, the institutional need to build consensus among so many disparate and often conflicting constituencies no longer serves the bests interests of any one of them well. For women, especially, I argue that regional or national affiliations may be more productive. The UN as a whole is just not as effective as it used to be.

Further, I suggest that there is a faultline in the content of the feminist movement, where the main, headlined argument is for gender equality. As feminists have long maintained,[2] understandings of and responses to gender inequality must be situated in the context of other forms of inequality. Efforts to advance women's status should not be divorced from those promoting a more equal world for all. It is not enough to call for the participation of women in existing patterns of market-based production, or for gender mainstreaming within existing configurations of institutional power. It is these paradigms—the forms of production, the institutions themselves—that need to be questioned and transformed through social mobilisation around new ways of thinking about political economy.

We must begin by redefining and re-evaluating all the terms we use to assess progress, such as GDP or MDGs, or even 'gender equality' itself. In the old days, we used to argue picturesquely, 'Do we want a piece of the poisoned cake? Do we want to swim in a polluted river? Do we want equality within the confines of existing political and economic spaces?'

Experience can have value in planning for the future, but it can also be a dampener. I have walked alongside the UN system for 40 years and have also written a history of its efforts on behalf of women. I have been part of many feminist networks and of more expert groups and panels of eminent persons than I can count. But, in the end, I wonder what all this effort has wrought.

UNDERSTANDING THE POLITICS OF PLACE AND THE DIFFERENT VIBRATIONS OF NORTH AND SOUTH

The UN came of age from the 1940s through the 1960s—heady times, especially for the former colonies. 'Emancipation' and 'liberation' were the guiding words of the moment. And out of the struggles for freedom and for affirmation of political rights in so many countries of the global South, many prominent women leaders emerged. The spirit of struggle and the self-confidence that it brought led to the beginning of the articulation of differences between women from the colonies and those from the Northern countries.

Hansa Mehta (1897–1995), a freedom fighter who was part of Gandhi's famous Quit India movement, is a good example. As retold by Kamala Devi, here is a description of Mehta's courage in defying British rule:

> The Congress decided to hold a mammoth procession.... As all activities had come to be banned at the time, every move had to be in defiance of the law.... very quietly without a murmur, the processionist, Hansa Mehta, sat down on the road. All traffic on the main road of this vast metropolis was stopped.... New history was made that night on a weary road under the dark purple canopy of the heavens. In the early hours of the morning the spell was broken, the siege was raised, the police bowed and passed

out. The procession rose and moved on to meet a new dawn, a new life, as silent in its victory as in its adversity.[3]

Later, Hansa Mehta represented India at the UN Commission on the Status of Women and as a delegate to the UN Human Rights Commission, where she was responsible for changing the language of the Universal Declaration of Human Rights, 1948. The draft formulation of its first article, proposed by Mrs Eleanor Roosevelt, stated that 'all men are created equal.' Ms Mehta protested this gender-opaque language, insisting 'that would never do'—that 'all men' might be interpreted to exclude women.

My book *Women, Development, and the UN*[4] uncovers many such tensions in intellectual perceptions between North and South in these years, tensions far transcending gender. As the North followed a development trajectory defined by such driving forces as the Keynesian economics exemplified in the Marshall Plan, the South marched along to a different rhythm of state socialism and new experiments in democratic governance. Economic plunder and the effacing of cultural and intellectual identities by the imperial powers were the strong legacies that shaped the history of developing nations like India in these years.

ENABLING A GLOBAL WOMEN'S MOVEMENT

Still, as I have said, the UN at this time served as what another volume on its history[5] calls 'a marketplace for ideas', a particularly apt description of the role it played for women's movements. Again, I repeat, these were heady times overall, and especially for women: the experience of learning from sisters all around the world; the excitement of finding extraordinary similarities of gendered living and identity; the forging of bonds that never broke; arguing, negotiating, merging differences into a collective agenda; and recognition of a common claim of power.[6] Women's participation influenced both the politics of the UN and the understanding of development within the institution in these early years.

The institution continued to provide women an especially critical space in the two decades between 1975 and 1995. New national, regional and global networks emerged from the cluster of conferences the UN sponsored on women, helping to mobilise women's groups and connecting them to private foundations with financial resources. These networks, in turn, had a palpable impact on the world's broader conversation about development. Some years ago, my colleague Shubha Chacko and I argued:

> Over these decades, women's engagement with the UN's work in development... has been to challenge the terms of reference, open the door to reveal other contours even of the industrial typology, of the hierarchies in values given to various aspects of social and economic organization, to spaces—the public and private—to the basis of knowledge creation, to the very notions of theory or bounded ideas. Their engagement revealed the variety of interpretations and appearances of what can be called difference and the prismatic quality of the concept of equality and its accommodation by even the basic mandate of the UN, as envisioned in its charter. The dilemmas these concepts pose are summed up as the equal but different debates and also permeate into ideas such as giving of quotas to redress inequality.[7]

Unfortunately, the thinking on women and their engagement with development, as it was perceived in the North, became embedded. The equity principle became enshrined and linked with the utility principle. 'Women in Development' became the Decade of Women's overnight catchphrase, a seductive one, which for a time at least could evade the question of what kind of development women were to be drawn into.[8] And equally important, what kind of development women could design.[9]

At the second UN World Conference on Women in Copenhagen in 1980, women also began to see the *differences* that characterised the North and the South. In non-official spaces, women from the South expressed their discomfort with the patronage of their Northern sisters, expressed in the latter's research, analyses and conclusions regarding them.

BUT WHERE DO WE FIND OURSELVES TODAY?

All this effort aside, I am sorry to say that reports on the progress of women in recent years, including those prepared by the UN itself, make for disappointing reading. I offer just a few highlights.

Women continue to be absent from key decision-making forums, which further perpetuates gender inequality. Constraints faced by women include their disproportionate concentration in vulnerable forms of work, occupational segregation, wage gaps, and the unequal division of unpaid domestic work. Women are more likely to be unemployed than men. They dominate the unprotected informal sector, are more likely than men to be in part-time formal employment in most high-income regions, spend more time than men in unpaid care work globally, have lower levels of productivity and earn less than men for work of equal value, and are poorly represented in public and corporate economic decision making.[10]

Women in many parts of the world continue to face discrimination in access to land, housing, property and other productive resources, and have limited access to technologies and services that could alleviate their work burdens. Unequal access to resources limits women's capacity to ensure agricultural productivity, security of livelihoods and food security, and is increasingly linked to poverty, migration, urbanisation and increased risk of violence.[11] Existing statutory and customary laws still restrict women's access to land and other types of property in most countries in Africa and about half the countries in Asia.[12]

Despite gains in gender parity in education, women account for two-thirds of the world's 774 million adult illiterates—a proportion unchanged over the past two decades. Gender disparities in adult literacy rates remain wide in most regions of the world.

While rates of women exposed to violence vary from one region to the other, statistics indicate that violence against women is a universal phenomenon, and women are subjected to different forms of violence—physical, sexual, psychological and economic—both within and outside their homes.[13]

Time-use studies in 30 developed and developing countries show that despite women's increasing labour force participation, they devote more time than men to housework and childcare, with differences ranging from about 50 per cent more in Cambodia and Sweden to about three times more in Italy and six times more in Iraq. But in no country do women spend as much time as men in market work.[14] Evidence collected by the ILO from 83 developed and developing countries shows that women earn between 10 and 30 per cent less than men.[15]

Thus, a quick scan of the progress of women on almost all indicators shows little or no change over the last 40 years, especially in the condition, entitlements and capabilities of women.[16] Papers written by economic statisticians as well as feminist groups reveal that while on certain fronts like education there has been some improvement, other areas like work, violence and survival leave a lot to be desired.

HOW DID WE LOSE OUR WAY?

Let me suggest two major structural problems with the UN that may account for the lack of results—for why, as I have said, the ground is still.

First, over the course of time—in attempting to fulfil its multiple roles as development activist, human rights champion and negotiator of peace and security—the UN has converted itself into an unwieldy bureaucracy intent on developing goals and frameworks for member countries to adhere to and on monitoring their implementation. By its very nature as a multilateral institution, the UN must incorporate into this process the many differences in viewpoints of its member states. Building coherence out of so many differences has wound up having a negative impact on larger goals of peace and justice, to which women's movements are also dedicated.

I would argue that since 1995, the UN's need to build consensus and its reliance on private/public partnerships has actually impeded the progress of feminist efforts and thinking. The UN fosters private investment, but there is often a lack of transparency and accountability of such investment, and it is impossible to have consensus around women's and girls' rights with conservative member states in the mix. Therefore, the time has come for the international feminist movement to reconsider its desire to be involved in the post-2015 UN agenda.[17] In my view, it would be more useful to put our energy elsewhere.

Second, the rights framework, incorporating the Universal Declaration of Human Rights and the Convention on the Elimination of all Forms of Discrimination Against Women, has been a strong component of and an enabling tool for uprisings and demands by subordinated or excluded groups, and has been especially valued by women. The language of rights cannot be questioned for its power and relevance in the fight for justice. It gives access to the legal system, to courts and laws, and that is, in fact, the only and best protection for citizens, especially those who are discriminated against and who are unjustly treated. However, much as I appreciate the value of these tools to promote civil justice and equality, I say again that more advanced and just economic frameworks are a necessary condition for rights to be an effective enabling tool.

Those civil rights that do not require financial outlay or economic change to advance a more just society—the right to vote, or to expose corruption and other violations,[18] for example, may be working. But social and economic rights, like the right to education,[19] which require vast outlays of state resources for schools and teachers and supplies,[20] or the right to food, which also necessitates public investment, have been reduced to rhetoric. This is precisely what has happened to so much of the women's rights agenda. It has foundered for lack of resources to back it up.

LINKING THE EBB OF THE UN TO GLOBALISATION AND INEQUALITY

Since the 1990s, moreover, a new ogre has arrived in the form of the neoliberal economic programme. Many countries that have accepted the terms of economic restructuring and so-called 'advancement' put forth by international financial institutions now find their societies crippled by deep inequalities and the loss of basic livelihoods. Fact-focused arguments are appearing from a whole range of places, UN-led as well as elsewhere,[21] showing that a dramatic increase in national and international inequality of wealth and income has occurred and is responsible for the economic convulsions that began in 2008 and are still shaking the world.

A review of current academic books, papers and reports from the major economic institutions offers significant lessons for necessary course corrections to prevailing theories of growth and macroeconomic policies. Thomas Piketty's book, *Capital in the Twenty-First Century*,[22] has been a powerful addition to these arguments. His basic reasoning is that capital-led modes of engineering economic growth have neglected the other crucial factor of production—labour. He also points out that as developing countries become industrialised, inequalities grow worse, not better. In the developed capitalist world, he warns that 'the prospect of slower economic growth in the years ahead, combined with the political domination of the super-rich in our political systems, threatens to make these extreme inequalities even more grotesque.'[23]

The contribution of the UN's own ILO to these domains is most pertinent. Unintentionally, the ILO echoes Piketty in arguing: 'It is time to reconsider the validity of these pro-capital distributional policies and to examine the possibility of an alternative path, one based on pro-labour distributional policies, accompanied by legislative changes and structural policies.'[24] The ILO puts forth a case for wage-led growth, a platform which I believe needs to be moved forward by the feminist movements of the North and South. It resonates with what feminists have been arguing over many years. We need livelihoods secured by social protection.

Other reports from NGOs, such as 'Working for the Few: Political Capture and Economic Inequality' by Oxfam,[25] argue that such deep inequalities place a very few elites in control and will as a result lead to policies that naturally support their narrow interests. Feminists had flagged these links between poverty and inequality earlier,[26] but until the big agencies made this connection, and Piketty blew the whistle, this was not always noted.

FINDING OUR WAY AGAIN

The Indian economic landscape and many of the other economies of the South offer fertile soil for reversing the current reform process and putting on the ground broad-based growth that does not exacerbate inequality. The Indian economy, despite the prominence given to the corporate sector in public policy, is still tethered in a deeply embedded landscape of small agriculture and entrepreneurship.[27]

Also, there is now a 'rising up' of the nations of the South. Groups such as the G-77[28] are talking about separating themselves from the UN and defining their own futures. At the recently held African Summit in Washington, D.C.,[29] moreover, Paul Kagame, Uhurru Kenyata and Yoweri Museveni, presidents of Rwanda, Kenya and Uganda, said:

> While conflict and poverty remain serious problems in many African regions, our continent is not only more stable than ever before; it is also experiencing some of the highest economic growth rates anywhere on the planet. Over the past decade, tens of millions of people across Africa have joined the middle class; our cities are expanding rapidly; and our population is the most youthful in the world.[30]

These countries now request a more 'normal' relationship with the US, focused on reciprocity in relationships between business sectors rather than on what Americans can do for them through foreign aid. The countries in the new economic club made up of Brazil, Russia, India, China and South Africa (BRICS) also 'are telling a different tale: one of agency and power',[31] says an article in *Time* magazine from 2011. In 2013, the BRICS countries formed the New Development Bank as an alternative to the existing US-dominated World Bank and IMF to foster greater financial and development cooperation among their emerging markets.[32] With $50 billion in initial capital, the bank will primarily finance infrastructure and 'sustainable development' projects in the BRICS countries, but other low- and middle-income countries will be able to buy in and apply for funding.[33]

THE POTENTIAL OF RENEWED FEMINIST VITALITY THROUGH REGIONAL OR TRANSNATIONAL NETWORKS

I have acknowledged that a large number of regional and international women's networks have emerged in recent years on a multitude of issues ranging from trafficking and legal protections to globally connected trade unions based on occupation. Some of these efforts indeed came directly out of UN gatherings, while others were created only as a result of local or regional mobilisation.[34] Moving forward, I would argue that putting more effort closer to home makes more sense.

The NGO Women in Informal Employment: Globalizing and Organizing (WIEGO) is an example of a network that grew out of regional mobilisation rather than being UN-led, and is now a worldwide coalition of institutions and individuals concerned with improving the status of women in the economy's informal sector, including a branch for home-based workers in South Asia and a waste pickers' network in Latin American and the Caribbean. There are also many other instances of women taking control of resources and managing economic entities in developing countries. A key example in India is SEWA,[35] a trade union of self-employed and home-based workers that owns a bank and provides health insurance and retirement benefits to working women in rural India.

Founded in 1984, DAWN is a feminist network of women, researchers and activists from the global South. The intervention by DAWN in the discourse on women and development not only transformed the intellectual underpinnings of this discourse, but also shifted creativity and intellectual leadership from the 'patrons' in the North to the 'clients' in the South.

Another network, called the Casablanca Dreamers, founded in 2006 and composed of leaders from UN agencies as well as feminist scholars, authors and activists from across the world, critiqued the development framework used by the UN, including the goal of gender equality. It came up with a new message—'Getting the Fundamentals Right: Women, Water and Wealth'. These networks support and reinforce each other and provide a formidable defence against powerful agencies. There is increasing regional networking as it is less fund-demanding and also emphasises the common bonds of geography. Inter-regional networking and advocacy may be more effective than global resolutions. For example, in 2010 a campaign by WIEGO and HomeNet, a group in Thailand, resulted in the ratification of the Homeworkers' Protection Act.[36]

AN IDEA FOR THE FUTURE: TRANSACTING FEMINIST KNOWLEDGE WITH THE OTHER

Amartya Sen, who has given feminists so much potent language about agency,[37] brings forth another powerful concept in his extraordinary book, *The Idea of Justice*.[38] 'Open-minded engagement in public reasoning is quite central to the pursuit of justice,' Sen writes. His deviation from the old discourse of participatory decision making lies in his use of the term 'reasoning'. Reasoning leads to the mind, and to Sen the mind is the most important element for establishing and affirming human agency. All of Sen's contributions to vocabulary are embedded in his basic belief that argument, reasoning and the application of thought are critical in building a just world. Another shift he makes—though in this case not a linguistic or even a hierarchical one, but one of focus—is to use injustice as the fulcrum of his argument, and not justice. Eliminating injustice should take precedence over striving for that perfect goal of justice. He argues that there is so much tangible injustice around us and that focusing on reducing it is itself just.

Taking off from Sen, I would suggest that this is the time for the feminist movement to build on the many ideas born out of our lived experience—our many action-oriented illustrations of engineering change, our work on knowledge and on our own experience-driven reasoning. Feminist theorists have given us valuable descriptions of how this should work. Helen Longino has this to say: 'The problems of knowledge are central to feminist theorizing, which has sought to destabilize androcentric, mainstream thinking in the humanities and in the social and natural sciences.'[39] Christine Sylvester suggests: 'The feminist agenda raises questions on what constitutes knowledge and how the disciplinary divisions are created. This questioning creates a politics of disturbance.' It unsettles the given and starts to 'plough up inherited turfs without planting the same old seeds in the field.'[40]

In *Harvesting Feminist Knowledge for Public Policy: Rebuilding Progress*,[41] a book published by the Casablanca Dreamers, Diane Elson and I argue that combating poverty can itself be an engine of growth. This growth is driven by empowering women at the poorest level by guaranteeing employment, in turn powering production and moving the economy in a broad-based, socially equitable direction. We ask for economic democracy and social and economic transformation that 'bubbles up' rather than 'trickles down'. The book points out that we feminists have 'ghettoed' ourselves and that feminist knowledge has not been able to cross the barriers into mainstream economic thought. How then can we better transform feminist knowledge into feminist policy?

After almost four decades of research related to public policy and feminist movements in India and around the world[42]—including many forays with the UN—I agree with this assessment. Our knowledge of lived experience, as well as our research, has not crossed the barriers into the mainstream. I have also come to the view that we have spent too much time emphasising demands arising out of our bodily differences—biologically and socially defined. Another faultline, perhaps, has been that our engagement with activism has been so intense and wearying that it has sidelined intellectual work. Women who are true public intellectuals must be more visible and influential.

CONCLUSION

Seen from the perspective of many years, I cannot help feeling that the UN system needs a very revolutionary overhaul. The roles it is now able to play do not justify the kind of high levels of expenditure that the structure and its employees absorb. It needs thinning down to reflect contraction elsewhere in the economy. A sharpening and a selective reassembling are crucial.

The feminist movement should convince the UN to take up the challenge of the overall increase in inequalities—not limit ourselves to gender equality—and we should take note of the 'rising' in the

South and of new ideas of wage-led growth, instead of only batting for gender equality. This could be a great leap forward. We need new macro-economic theories built and transacted by women. Mild modifications will not suffice—as Joseph Stiglitz says in his latest paper, the financial meltdown after September 2008 was not just a crisis for economic policy, but also for economic theory.[43]

I end by emphasising that our struggle and our fact-based arguments should be directed towards reconstructing growth theories and developing broad-based growth measures. The UN could return to its valuable role as a marketplace for ideas and as a builder of the strength of social and economic movements against injustice, and move away from attempting to put together development agendas and frameworks to monitor countries' progress. Then indeed women and girls—all of us together—will rise. As the feminist theorist Amina Mama has said:

> We women are in no position to deprive ourselves of the intellectual tools that can assist us in pursuit of gender justice. The arena of the intellect has been used to suppress us. We cannot afford to ignore the importance of intellectual work, especially in the 21st century when knowledge and information define power more than ever before.[44]

NOTES

1 The author gratefully acknowledges the research assistance of Divya Alexander and Smriti Sharma, and the editorial support of Ellen Chesler and Terry McGovern.

2 Sakiki Fukuda-Parr, James Heinz and Stephanie Seguino, 'Critical Perspectives on Financial and Economic Crises: Heterodox Macroeconomics Meets Feminist Economics', *Feminist Economics*, vol. 19, no. 13 (2013), pp. 4–31.

3 Kamaladevi Chattopadhyay, *Inner Recesses Outer Spaces* (New Delhi: Niyogi Books, 2014).

4 Jain, *Women, Development, and the UN*.

5 Louis Emmerij, Richard Jolly and Thomas Weiss, *Ahead of the Curve? UN Ideas and Global Challenges*, 1st edn (Bloomington: Indiana University Press, 2001), p. 10.

6 Devaki Jain and Shubha Chacko, 'Unfolding Women's Engagement with Development and the UN: Pointers for the Future', *Forum for Development Studies*, vol. 35, no. 1 (June 2008), pp. 5–36.

7 Ibid.

8 Lucille Mathurin Mair, 'International Women's Decade: A Balance Sheet', Third J. P. Naik Memorial Lecture, Centre for Women's Development Studies, New Delhi, 15 December 1984.

9 Jain, *Women, Development, and the UN*.

10 UN Women and ILO, 'Decent Work and Women's Economic Empowerment: Good Policy and Practice', Policy Brief, 2012, http://www.ilo.org/wcmsp5/groups/public/—ed_emp/—emp_ent/—ifp_seed/documents/genericdocument/wcms_184878.pdf (accessed 2 July 2017).

11 UN, *2009 World Survey on the Role of Women in Development: Women's Control over Economic Resources and Access to Financial Resources, including Microfinance*, Department of Economic and Social Affairs, Division for the Advancement of Women (New York: UN, 2009).

12 UN, *The World's Women 2010: Trends and Statistics* (New York: United Nations Statistics Division, 2010).

13 Ibid.

14 UN Women and ILO, 'Decent Work and Women's Economic Empowerment'.

15 Ibid.

16 Devaki Jain and C. P. Sujaya (eds), *Indian Women Revisited* (New Delhi: Publications Division, Government of India, 2014).

17 UNDP, *Post-2015 Development Agenda*, http://www.undp.org/content/brussels/en/home/mdgoverview/mdg_goals/post-2015-development-agenda.html (accessed 3 July 2017).

18 Aruna Roy, 'Time to Move Ahead of RTI', *New Indian Express*, 10 November 2013, http://www.newindianexpress.com/states/odisha/2013/nov/10/Time-to-move-ahead-of-RTI-Aruna-Roy-535878.html (accessed 3 July 2017).

19 Vimala Ramachandran, 'Gendered Inequality and Education', Advocacy Brief, UNESCO Bangkok Asia-Pacific Programme of Education for All, 2010, http://unesdoc.unesco.org/images/0018/001898/189825e.pdf (accessed 3 July 2017).

20 Vimala Ramachandran, 'Right to Education Act: A Comment', *Economic and Political Weekly*, vol. 40, no. 28 (July 2009), pp. 155–57.

21 UNDP, *Humanity Divided: Confronting Inequality in Developing Countries* (New York: UNDP Bureau for Development Policy, November 2013); UN, *Inequality Matters: Report on the World Social Situation 2013* (New York: UN Department of Economic and Social Affairs, 2013); World Economic Forum, 'The Reshaping of the World: Consequences for Society, Politics and Business', World Economic Forum Annual Meeting 2014, Davos-Klosters, Switzerland, 22–25 January 2014; ILO, *Wage-Led Growth: An Equitable Strategy for Economic Recovery* (eds Marc Lavoie and Engelbert Stockhammer) (Basingstoke: Palgrave Macmillan, 2013); Oxfam, 'Working for the Few: Political Capture and Economic Inequality', Oxfam Briefing Paper 178, 20 January 2014; World Bank, *Inequality in Focus*, http://www.worldbank.org/en/topic/isp/publication/inequality-in-focus (accessed 3 July 2017).

22 Thomas Piketty, *Capital in the Twenty-First Century* (Cambridge, MA: Harvard University Press, 2014).

23 John Palmer, 'Book Review: Capital in the Twenty-First Century by Thomas Piketty', *Red Pepper*, April 2014, http://www.redpepper.org.uk/book-review-capital-in-the-twenty-first-century-by-thomas-piketty/ (accessed 3 July 2017).

24 ILO, *Wage-Led Growth*, p. 13.

25 Oxfam, 'Working for the Few'.

26 Devaki Jain, 'Growth, Poverty and Inequality: The Linkages and Relevance of Macroeconomic Policies', UNDP Gender Equality, Economic Growth and Poverty Reduction Expert Group Meeting, Essex University, UK, 21–22 June 2007; Jain, 'The Poverty Thing'.

27 Devaki Jain and Deepshikha Batheja, 'Using Inequality to Engineer Growth', *LiveMint*, 13 June 2014, http://www.livemint.com/Opinion/HC2XT2gQSdtck73VsP6e7H/Using-inequality-to-engineer-growth.html (accessed 3 July 2017).

28 *South-South News*, 'Algiers Ministerial Conference of the Non-Aligned Movement (NAM) Reviews Existing, New and Emerging Challenges to the Developing World', 16 June 2014.

29 US-Africa Leaders' Summit, Washington, D.C., 4–6 August 2014.

30 Paul Kagame, Uhurru Kenyata and Yoweri Museveni, 'The Dream of an African Century', *LiveMint*, 8 August 2014, http://www.livemint.com/Opinion/fsvyGkHNItOMSFmm4koVgL/The-dream-of-an-African-century.html (accessed 12 September 2017).

31 Sylvia Ann Hewlett, 'Is a Woman in Brazil Better Off than a Woman in the U.S.?', *Time*, 24 October 2011, http://ideas.time.com/2011/10/24/is-a-woman-in-brazil-better-off-than-a-woman-in-the-u-s/ (accessed 4 July 2017).

32 *Economist*, 'The BRICS Bank: An Acronym with Capital', 19 July 2014, http://www.economist.com/news/finance-and-economics/21607851-setting-up-rivals-imf-and-world-bank-easier-running-them-acronym (accessed 4 July 2017).

33 Raj M. Desai and James Raymond Vreeland, 'What the New Bank of BRICS Is All About', *Washington Post*, 17 July 2014, http://www.washingtonpost.com/blogs/monkey-cage/wp/2014/07/17/what-the-new-bank-of-brics-is-all-about/ (accessed 4 July 2017).

34 Peggy Antrobus, 'DAWN, the Third World Feminist Network: Upturning Hierarchies', in Rawwida Baksh and Wendy Harcourt (eds), *The Oxford Handbook of Transnational Feminist Movements* (New York: Oxford University Press, 2015), pp. 159–87.

35 http://www.sewa.org/ (accessed 4 July 2017).

36 The Homeworkers' Protection Act in Thailand provides for protection of wages, occupational health and safety, and the responsibility of employers towards homeworkers. This legislation impacts about two million workers in Thailand. See Homeworkers' Protection Act, B.E. 2553 (2010).

37 Amartya Sen, *Identity and Violence: The Illusion of Destiny* (New Delhi: Penguin, 2007).

38 Amartya Sen, *The Idea of Justice* (Cambridge, MA: Harvard University Press, 2009).

39 Longino, 'Feminist Standpoint Theory and the Problems of Knowledge'.

40 See Connolly, 'Democracy and Territory'.

41 Elson and Jain, *Harvesting Feminist Knowledge for Public Policy*.

42 Jain, 'Women's Participation in the History of Ideas'; Devaki Jain, 'Feminism and Feminist Expression: A Dialogue', in Kamala Ganesh and Usha Thakkar (eds), *Culture and the Making of Identity in Contemporary India* (New Delhi: Sage, 2005), p. 184 (see chapter 5, this volume); see also Jain, *Indian Women*.

43 George Akerlof, Oliver J. Blanchard, David Romer and Joseph E. Stiglitz (eds), *What Have We Learned? Macroeconomic Policy after the Crisis* (Cambridge, MA: MIT Press, 2014).

44 Mama, 'Talking about Feminism in Africa'.

CHAPTER 14

Looking Back at the South Commission

The South Commission was one of my most significant experiences, enlarging both my mind and my politics. I was fortunate to be engaged with an officially convened group of some of the world's most famous feminist policy economists as well as bankers and retired heads of state, grappling with an idea—the idea of reclaiming intellectual leadership for the former colonies in both the political as well as economic spheres. While one section of the commission's members, including its leader, the former president of Tanzania Julius Nyerere, were committed to finding new roads, new economic principles and perhaps even daring ideas to challenge the economic hegemony of the North, the group also had bureaucrats from the South and North who could not overthrow their intellectual memory. Hence, both the mobilisation in terms of bringing ideological consistency as well as the proposals that came out of the commission failed in the objective of liberating development theory and practice from the hegemony of the North. In this chapter, I show the potential of the commission as well as the loss represented by its failure. The essay is based on a lecture I delivered at Ambedkar University, New Delhi, on 11 February 2015.

As has been written in many other books and papers,[1] the vision of a global South emerged due to two earlier developments.[2] These were the emergence of NAM and the affirmation of the North as a united political economy by the Brandt Commission (1977–80) and the Brundtland Commission (1983–87). The two commissions in turn were influenced by other developments and processes. In 1980, the Brandt Report,[3] prepared by an independent commission chaired by the former German chancellor Willy Brandt, tried to provide an understanding of the drastic differences in the economic development of the northern and southern hemispheres of the world. The Brundtland Commission, formally known as the World Commission on Environment and Development, was set up by the UN to rally countries to work together and pursue sustainable development. The commission was chaired by Gro Harlem, the former prime minister of Norway.

Led as they were by retired heads of state of powerful nations of the North, the ideas and proposals put forward by these commissions gained currency across the world, especially among international financial institutions. The leaders of NAM, along with its then chairperson, Robert Gabriel Mugabe (in 1986), resolved to put together a commission whose members would be drawn from the former colonies, to define a vision and a roadmap for the member countries to rehabilitate themselves, drawing from their own strengths. Julius Nyerere, the leader of the liberation struggle in Tanzania and its first president, was requested to take up leadership of this commission. Nyerere, known as Mwalimu (the Swahili term for 'teacher'), was a socialist and a freedom fighter who had the political fire in his belly to challenge global hegemony. Liberation from colonisation could not bear fruit, he argued, unless an end was put to the North's economic exploitation and intellectual domination. He reminded us of Gandhi's argument that political freedom is not fruitful without economic freedom.[4]

The NAM group,[5] a political configuration, gave the South Commission its political identity and fire. Its platform was built around anti-imperialism and liberation from colonisation. While the term 'non-aligned' suggests neutrality towards the two powerful blocs, East and West, or socialist and capitalist, to put it starkly, the club's purpose, domain and actions went beyond the literal interpretation of the phrase. The keyword was 'movement'. Anti-imperialism and liberation from superpowers and their political domination was the basis of NAM. The club became a movement for claiming sovereignty for the newly liberated nations as well as asserting their independence to design their future based on their own histories, cultures and economic landscapes. What the South Commission hoped to do was to give an economic identity to the South, an economic ideology to the former colonies. It is my argument that we failed in this effort.

It is worth recalling that this was the era of rebuilding the colonies as free nations, and leaders were forging innovative ways to engage in that reconstruction. Nyerere tried experiments in Tanzania and instituted a programme called *ujamaa*,[6] which was inspired by the concept of the kibbutz in Israel.[7] In both these cases, the idea of building communities, even collectives, was the goal. Even in India, at the dawn of independence, the left had recommended collective farms, not co-operatives. Nyerere's explanation for initiating ujamaa—which eventually failed, as did the kibbutz—was that the nations in Africa were so fractured by tribal identities and warring chiefs that they could never become modern states. The colonisers, he argued, had capitalised on these tribal wars. Hence, he thought that replacing tribal villages by collectives might work towards creating a modern nation-state.

The findings and recommendations of the commission culminated in the report *The Challenge to the South*;[8] the challenge was whether an economic South could be built and what were the necessary conditions, processes and goals. But looking back, it seems to me, it would have been better if the report had been titled 'The Economic South'. In other words, if we had defined a virtual economic South, described our economies and their strengths, and then built over that, it would have been more productive than seeing whether we could challenge the North.

THE MANDATE

The idea of setting up the South Commission got the nod during the eighth NAM summit in Zimbabwe in September 1986, and it became operational in August 1987, with headquarters in Geneva. A crucial aspect of the South Commission was the personality and politics of its chairman, Nyerere. He was a socialist, and the first president of Tanzania. He founded the Tanganyika African National Union, the principal political party which had led the freedom movement in Tanzania. His personality is a crucial part of this story. He was deeply engaged with his culture and was a devout Christian. He was full of folklore and narrated inspirational parables and anecdotes in Swahili.

His constant refrain was, let us try, let us build our strength through South–South co-operation. At a meeting of the three heads of state from West Africa—Daniel Arap Moi (Kenya), Ali H. Mwinyi

(Tanzania) and Yoweri K. Museveni (Uganda)—in Nairobi,[9] he put a copy of the just-published report of the commission, *The Challenge to the South*, on the table (I was sitting by his side). He said, 'Brothers this is the book, this is your Bible,' and kept tapping the book in front of them, exhorting them to read it. 'Take your country on this journey. It will be our second liberation.' Or when we went to China in November 1989, prior to the publication of the report, and had an audience with the Chinese prime minister Li Peng (Manmohan Singh, who was the secretary general of the commission, could not join us for this), Mwalimu called me before the meeting and said, 'Tell the Premier, that if India and China combine they can defeat the North.' The miracle is that I did!

We travelled to about seven to eight countries, and had long sessions with heads of state and with members of civil society everywhere. Wherever we went, Nyerere was revered as a gentle but clear-headed leader of the ex-colonies. In Africa, he was often seen as the Gandhi of the continent because of his humility and generosity of spirit. When we were in South Africa in 1998–99, we heard so many stories of how Tanzania was unique in offering asylum to those who were struggling against apartheid in South Africa or were being hunted. His dream was always for the continent and not only for Tanzania.

In Cuba particularly, Fidel Castro was reverential towards Mwalimu, and the commission was given the royal treatment. We were invited to stay for nearly eight days and travelled all over the country. Castro would join us most of the time. At the end of the visit, Mwalimu said, 'Friends, what are we waiting for, we have here the design for the South, we have here the redefinition of economic progress, we have here the Model we were looking for,' much to the dismay of many of the commissioners who were uncomfortable with the concepts of socialism and communism.

Nyerere was always supportive, in fact very excited by ideas that captured the strength and potential of our countries. For example, during an expert group meeting on the potential of South–South co-operation, I presented a paper titled 'Women, Waste and Planet Safety: Proposal for the North–South Alliance'. I categorised countries on the basis of waste generation, waste recycling and so on. The point was to show that the culture in our countries encouraged reuse of items that would otherwise be seen as waste. I also tried to show that large-scale waste generation was associated with a consumption-oriented society.

In the end, the commission's report turned out to be an anaemic development report, untethered to any political economy framework. It was sanitised, as most of the commissioners were drawn from some form of bureaucracy or the other—bankers, senior international civil servants—and were largely above 60 years of age. There was only one scientist, the Nobel Laureate Abdus Salam, a wonderful thinker who provided strong support to the affirmation of models of manufacturing in the developing countries. He put forward scientific evidence to show that small-scale manufacturing is more effective than large-scale manufacturing, as it accommodates innovation without too much loss of overheads. He founded the Third World Academy of Sciences in 1983 as an affirmation of Third World scientific knowledge, innovation and progress.[10]

There were four professional economists, but most came from bureaucratic structures such as the UN or governments, and only one was an academic—Celso Furtado. There were only three women commissioners, including me and two more. So those engaged with society and the political spaces in the South were a small minority. Therefore, no great exchange of new ideas and knowledge took place; rather, the proposals that were put forward were of the sort typically issued by governments. And the final report was spearheaded by an economist, assisted by two other economists, none of whom had any experience of political or social movements.

THE STRUCTURAL ADJUSTMENT ERA

The era of structural adjustment—liberalisation, globalisation and privatisation, euphemistically called 'reforms'—began in the 1980s. Structural adjustment programmes (SAPs) were pushed down the throats of the former colonies as conditions for receiving aid from the World Bank and the IMF. Structural adjustment programmes had evolved as a result of the impact of three global crises, namely, the oil crisis, the debt crisis, and the global recession in the late 1970s and the early 1980s in developing countries. These countries faced unprecedented pressure in their external accounts after these three consecutive global crises. Though SAPs were created to deal with the increasing economic instability, they came with many conditions and looked to the market instead of the state for solutions. These programmes encouraged privatisation and the abandonment of the socialist approach, where the state played a greater role in economic management.

Typically, by the time countries sought adjustment loans, they had suffered from high deficits, rapid inflation and capital flight. The price paid by developing countries to gain access to foreign exchange in this situation was to agree to carry out significant policy reforms under SAPs. The SAPs were the beginning of the 'bonding' between private capital or the banks and political leaders/the state. As Thandika Mkandawire, former director of the Council for the Development of Social Science Research in Africa,[11] had argued as far back as the 1980s, SAPs gradually shrank democratic spaces in African countries, sowing the seeds of fascism.

During the course of the commission's work, we not only visited several countries but also had long interview sessions with heads of state, met with groups of intellectuals and academics, and undertook some field visits. In certain countries like Cuba, we spent almost a week visiting hospitals or studying the achievements of the country, for example, in the fields of medical technology and machinery. Another place where we stayed for more than seven days was China. We went to see the dams, the city of Shanghai, and various other projects.

One of the more moving moments was a long interview with the president of Mozambique, Joaquim Chissano, who described to us the way the Portuguese had ripped apart Mozambique's infrastructure before they left. Apparently when they left, there was only one person in the whole of Mozambique who had passed high school. Also, the terrible impact of the civil war which was raging in Mozambique was visible all over the country. Child soldiers in large numbers were recruited for the child army by the counter-revolutionaries—RENAMO,[12] who sometimes chopped off their hands and sometimes their ears.[13]

FAULTLINES

The first faultline lay in the composition of the commission. The objective of the South Commission was fine, the context was appropriate, but the human element of the commission was flawed.[14] Members had been selected to represent not only 'geography' but also different sources of knowledge. However, the outcome was that the members were not only predominantly male but also elderly—leaders and bureaucrats—who had little involvement with civil society organisations. Out of the 29 commissioners,[15] 11 had retired from political or bureaucratic positions. Fortunately, we had a few economists such as Gamani Corea from Sri Lanka (known for having set up the United Nations Conference on Trade and Development), Celso Furtado, an economist from Brazil, Solita Collas-Monsod from the Philippines, and myself. But people like Shridath Ramphal, secretary general of the Commonwealth, were more British than the British themselves. He was brought in because he was also a member of the Brundtland Commission and was as conventional and as stereotypical as any bureaucrat could get. Retired bankers (for example, from Mozambique) and retired UN civil servants (for example, from the former Yugoslavia) dominated the commission. Finally, it was believed, even by Mwalimu, that it was governments that had the power to change the system. This was an endemic flaw.

The largely conventional members of the commission found it difficult to accept radical ideas. I had proposed a methodology for the construction of an economic South, which at the time of proposal received immense support but was overruled later by others. I had proposed five themes to characterise ourselves (the South) and then build a theory on that base. These themes were: the worker in the South or the Southern worker; industry in the South; the markets of the South; the children of the South (especially their health); and the last theme was local development management institutions.

I had spelt these out in detail. Here, I elaborate on the first theme—the worker in the South or the Southern worker—as an illustration of the logic of my proposal. The task required profiling the worker and documenting his or her predominant characteristics and needs. It involved questioning workers about their gender and age (identified/unidentified); whether they worked at home or at a factory, and whether they fell in the organised or unorganised category; and the patterns and structure of employment wages. This could be followed by getting to know the demand side of the issue. An examination of policies, both in terms of production as well as labour legislation, which affected the workers, and whether these were appropriate given the existing conditions, was also required. We could then analyse what this investigation revealed about concepts in economic statistics, strategies of employment promotion and poverty alleviation, and labour laws/international standards and definitions.

From this study, we could derive a Southern perspective for the future. We could prepare this by collating existing knowledge and exchanges which took place during travels, seminars and meetings with worker/workers' organisations. Thus, South–South exchanges and co-operation could be built through the lived experience of workers from the developing nations. The outcome could lead to the initiation of programmes/projects addressed to Southern workers, building up theories for economic progress, and public policies that would arise from that framework. It is my argument that we lost this opportunity, because we did not define an economic South but kept looking at the North and thinking only of ways to retaliate or contain it.

Another example of the conservatism of the members was the response of the commissioners to a suggestion that we should consult and give voice to people's movements in the South in order to understand the aspirations of people. One of the members, in fact the secretary general, said he did not understand the concept of people's movements! So there was neither any way of capturing the pulse of the nations of the global South nor of mobilising their support for our ideas.

When the first draft of the report was being discussed, together with two other women colleagues, I mentioned that there should be a chapter on the gender dimension. The Arabs said there was no word for 'gender' in their language, and this was something they could not understand! Since other male members also scoffed at the idea, there was a strong view that this was not necessary. However, the three of us persisted, sought help from our sisters, for example, in Egypt and Morocco, to arrive at a translation of the concept, and finally the word 'gender' was accepted; but the resultant chapter was abysmal.

The second faultline related to the funding of the commission and the location of its headquarters. One of the reasons it was based in Geneva, as opposed to one of the nations of the South, was that the connectivity between Europe and the nations of the South, both in terms of transport as well as telephone, was considered better as compared to the connectivity between the countries of the South. Further, the developed countries, especially the European nations, were bearing the expenditure of the commission along with some of the better-off countries of the South, such as Malaysia and India. Both these factors, however, undermined the commission's involvement with the poorer and less advanced nations of the South.

While we were thinking of the South as a space for expressing solidarity against the common 'adversary', namely the countries of the North, Kuwait was invaded by Iraq in August 1990. One of our most brilliant members, Abdlatif Al-Hamad, an economist and a generous donor, was a Kuwaiti and the chairperson of the Arab Fund for Economic and Social Development. He was devastated by the developments, which had shattered the myth of a politically linked South. The rest of the world was completely preoccupied with this invasion and its political and economic consequences. So the launch of the report, *The Challenge to the South*, in 1990, got no notice at all in the press.

This was in complete contrast to the attention and publicity received by reports emanating from the North, that is, the Brundtland and the Brandt Reports, and was a blow from which I do not think we ever recovered.

RECONFIGURING THE SOUTH

The South Commission had a tenure of three years, which ended in 1990. It recommended the setting up of the South Centre,[16] which was finally established in 1995 in Geneva. Nyerere's dream was that the centre should function like the OECD, and provide information as well as build solidarity among countries of the South on economic positions. However, the South Centre, in my view, is also concentrating on governments and on traditional international, intergovernmental issues and events. The agency has neither become a focal point for intellectuals and people's movements of the South, nor has it provided a voice to the people of the South. So one may ask, is there any space for reconfiguring the South?

The *HDR* of 2013, titled *The Rise of the South*,[17] has recommended setting up a new South Commission to deal with the new phenomenon described as 'the striking transformation of a large number of developing countries into dynamic major economies with growing political influence', which 'is having a significant impact on human development progress'.[18] Laying stress on South–South co-operation, the report further states:

> New institutions and partnerships can help countries share knowledge, experiences and technology. This can be accompanied by new and stronger institutions to promote trade and investment and accelerate experience sharing across the South. One step would be to establish a new South Commission to bring a fresh vision of how the diversity of the South can be a force for solidarity.

The BRICS grouping in the last few years has been fostered as a space for united action. The BRICS bank has been applauded, and hopes to gain some autonomy in managing the international flow of finance and its regulation. I will admit that I see it as a plus, as even the South Commission had recommended a South Bank in its report *The Challenge to the South*.

On what principles of political economy are these initiatives being proposed? The South has been appreciated because of the economic progress it has made—GDP rates have been rising in many developing countries. However, the exclusion and inequalities associated with this economic growth are not on the agenda. We are back to the globalisation, liberalisation and privatisation mantra. A new imperialism has been birthed by the better-off economies of the South. For example, at the meeting of the India–Africa Forum Summit held in Addis Ababa in May 2011, where our former prime minister Manmohan Singh led a delegation of our 'captains of industry', the president of Ethiopia said, 'Welcome brothers, we have thousands of hectares of land, develop them etc.' An Indian entrepreneur, part of the delegation, bought thousands of hectares of land to grow biofuel. The Ethiopian pastoral lands and hills are known for pastoral farming and the wool produced there. As a result of this transaction, there was a massive displacement of pastoral farmers, jeopardising their livelihoods.

Another illustration is from Liberia, which was wracked by civil war for many years, and is now making a remarkable attempt to develop its economy. Its current president Ellen Johnson Sirleaf was elected by a majority vote of women petty vendors—women who sold anything and everything from Lux soap to food, cooked and uncooked, women engaged in business in the streets of the capital, Monrovia. The coffers of the Central Bank of Liberia were empty, as the chairman of its board told me when I visited in 1998, but, as he said, 'The cash is all in the streets.' It was the mobilisation of these women micro-entrepreneurs and their political vote that brought Sirleaf into power, indicating that small businesses run by women in developing countries like those in Africa and Asia are the backbone of these economies, providing livelihood, production and exchange. In Liberia, they may have transformed the political setup, but the question is will the new initiatives to strengthen the country's economy continue to see them as an engine of growth? Will the government build social and economic infrastructure to support them? Or will the rush to tap the mineral wealth of Liberia turn the state's attention away from these women and into the kind of unequal and 'world-led' economy that we are witnessing in other mineral-rich countries?[19] This is the key question. The news so far indicates that Sirleaf has gone the neoliberal way and has forgotten the women on the streets.

There are many more examples of Indian and Chinese companies looking for minerals, land and other scarce resources in less financially advanced regions of the South to the detriment of the larger populations residing in those regions. So is there a way? Or are there other types of initiatives that can rebuild the ex-colonies? Just as I suggested to the South Commission decades ago, we need to develop economic reasoning which is derived from our economic strengths on the ground, and in my opinion it has to start from the worker, the work and the wage. There are now theories on wage-led growth in contrast to capital-led growth.[20]

GALLOPING ECONOMIC INEQUALITY

Growing inequality is pungent and disabling across all nations. The review of global reports on rising economic inequality at the World Social Forum held in Davos in 2014 shows that fast-growing countries could face another financial crisis, and one more global meltdown was likely if they continued with the current economic philosophy of capital and free flow of finance-led growth.[21] The UNDP report, *Humanity Divided: Confronting Inequality in Developing Countries*, states reasons for the rising inequality in the developing world: 'Economic progress in these countries has not alleviated disparities, but rather exacerbated them. Increases in inequality over the last two decades were mainly on account of trade and financial globalization processes that weakened the bargaining position of relatively immobile labour vis-à-vis fully mobile capital.'[22] According to the *Trade and Development Report, 2010*,

> Wages would have to be perceived, not just as a cost of production, but as a major source of aggregate demand, such that rising wage bills can actually propel economic recovery in slumps, and generate conditions for stable growth. The inability of economic growth to create sufficient decent work to meet the requirements of the labour force is a major part of the problem.[23]

The ILO's report dealing with wage-led growth states: 'It is time to reconsider the validity of pro-capital distributional policies, and to examine the possibility of an alternative path, one based on pro-labour distributional policies, accompanied by legislative changes and structural policies.[24]

So, I wish to argue that we can use the handle of galloping economic inequality to turn the tide—reconstruct an economic ideology for the South, by defining our characteristics, redoing measures of success by drawing on our base of economic activity and building on that. I call this alternative the 'bubbling-up theory of growth'[25]—a theory which is grounded in reality and in the characteristics of the colonised South, in contrast to the trickle-down approach.[26]

NOTES

1 Prashad, *The Darker Nations*; Vijay Prashad, *The Poorer Nations* (New Delhi: LeftWord, 2013).
2 The author would like to acknowledge Neha Choudhary and Smriti Sharma's assistance in writing this piece.
3 Centre for Global Negotiations, 'About the Brandt Commission', http://www.brandt21forum.info/About_BrandtCommission.htm (accessed 5 July 2017).
4 Devaki Jain, 'Bubbling-Up v Trickling-Down', Gateway House, 28 April 2011, http://www.gatewayhouse.in/bubbling-versus-trickling-down/ (accessed 5 July 2017).
5 The Non-Alignment Movement was founded in Belgrade in 1961. See Ministry of External Affairs, Government of India, 'History and Evolution of Non-Aligned Movement', 22 August 2012, http://mea.gov.in/in-focus-article.htm?20349/History+and+Evolution+of+NonAligned+Movement (accessed 5 July 2017).
6 'Ujamaa' was the concept that formed the basis of Julius Nyerere's social and economic development policies in Tanzania after it gained independence from Britain in 1961. It means 'socialism' in Swahili.
7 The Israeli kibbutz was a collective that was traditionally based on agriculture. These utopian communities were based on a combination of socialism and Zionism.
8 South Commission, *The Challenge to the South*.
9 The East African presidents met in Nairobi in November 1991 and set up a committee of foreign affairs ministers, with the mandate of exploring the modalities for promoting further co-operation in the region.
10 The Third World Academy of Sciences is an institution for the advancement of science in developing countries. See http://twas.org/ (accessed 6 July 2017).
11 See Council for the Development of Social Science Research in South Africa, http://www.codesria.org/ (accessed 6 July 2017).

12 The Mozambican National Resistance (RENAMO) was a liberation movement established in 1975, following Mozambique's independence, as an anti-communist political organisation which later turned into a political party led by Afonso Dhlakama. It fought against the Mozambique Liberation Front in the Mozambican Civil War and against the Zimbabwe African National Union movement led by Robert Mugabe from 1975 to 1992.

13 Later on, I was appointed as a member of the Eminent Persons' Group that was set up by the UN, with Graca Machel as its chair, to study the impact of armed conflict on children. This was a confrontation with war cruelties not very different from what is being perpetrated by the Boko Haram today.

14 M. B. Mohamad and J. K. Nyerere, 'Objectives and Terms of Reference of the South Commission', Kuala Lumpur, 1–3 March 1988.

15 The commissioners were: Julius K. Nyerere, Chairman (Tanzania); Manmohan Singh, Secretary-General (India); Ismail Sabri Abdalla (Egypt); Abdlatif Al-Hamad (Kuwait); Paulo Evaristo Arns (Brazil); Solito Collas-Monsod (Philippines); Eneas Da Conceiçao Comiche (Mozambique); Gamani Corea (Sri Lanka); Aboubakar Diaby-Ouattara (Ivory Coast); Aldo Ferrer (Argentina); Celso Furtado (Brazil); Enrique Iglesias (Uruguay); Devaki Jain (India); Simba Makoni (Zimbabwe); Michael Norman Manley (Jamaica); Jorge Navarrete (Mexico); Pius Okigbo (Nigeria); Augustin Papic (Yugoslavia); Carlos Andres Perez (Venezuela); Jiadong Qian (China); Shridath Ramphal (Guyana); Carlos Rafael Rodriguez (Cuba); Abdus Salam (Pakistan); Marie-Angélique Savané (Senegal); Tan Sri Ghazali Shafie (Malaysia); Tupua Tamasese Tupuola Efi (Western Samoa); Nitisastro Widjojo (Indonesia); Layachi Yaker (Algeria); Amir Jamal (Tanzania).

16 For details see the South Centre, http://www.southcentre.int (accessed 7 July 2017).

17 UNDP, *Human Development Report 2013: The Rise of the South—Human Progress in a Diverse World* (New York: UNDP, 2013).

18 Ibid.

19 Devaki Jain, 'The Women behind Sirleaf', *Indian Express*, 14 September 2013, http://archive.indianexpress.com/news/the-women-behind-sirleaf/1168952/ (accessed 7 July 2017).

20 Stephanie Seguino and Caren A. Grown, 'Feminist-Kaleckian Macroeconomic Policy for Developing Countries', Economics Working Paper Archive, no. 446, Levy Economics Institute, New York, 2006.

21 See Devaki Jain, 'Exploring Economic Inequality from Piketty through Arvind Adiga to Gandhi', lecture delivered at Azim Premji University, Bengaluru, 13 November 2014.

22 UNDP, *Humanity Divided*, p. 1.

23 United Nations Conference on Trade and Development, *Trade and Development Report, 2010: Employment, Globalization and Development* (New York: UN, 2010).

24 Marc Lavoie and Engelbert Stockhammer, 'Wage-Led Growth: Concept, Theories and Policies', Conditions of Work and Employment Series, no. 41, ILO, Geneva, 2012.

25 Devaki Jain, 'The First Challengers', MakingItMagazine.Net, 5 February 2013, http://www.makingitmagazine.net/?p=6349 (accessed 7 July 2017). A version of this essay is reproduced as chapter 12, this volume.

26 L. C. Jain, Civil Disobedience (New Delhi: Book Review Literary Trust, 2011).

BIBLIOGRAPHY

Abelin, Mari, Sarah McPhee and Eva Poluha. 'Integrating Women as a Means of Rural Development: A Case Study of the Swedish CADU Project, 1976–1974', SIDA Group, Stockholm, September 1982.

Acharya, Poromesh. 'Education: Panchayat and Decentralisation—Myths and Reality', *Economic and Political Weekly*, vol. 37, no. 8 (23 February 2002), pp. 788–96.

Acker, Joan, and Karen Ericksen Paige. 'The Gendered Nature of Social Structure and Culture', paper presented at the International Sociological Congress, New Delhi, 1986.

Aggarwal, Anil. 'Try Asking the Women First', *Indian Express*, 20 July 1982.

Akerlof, George, Oliver J. Blanchard, David Romer and Joseph E. Stiglitz (eds). *What Have We Learned? Macroeconomic Policy after the Crisis* (Cambridge, MA: MIT Press, 2014).

Amoah, Elizabeth. 'Women, Witches and Social Change in Ghana', in Diana Eck and Devaki Jain (eds), *Speaking of Faith: Cross-Cultural Perspectives on Women, Religion and Social Change* (New Delhi: Kali for Women, 1986).

Antrobus, Peggy. 'DAWN, the Third World Feminist Network: Upturning Hierarchies', in Rawwida Baksh and Wendy Harcourt (eds), *The Oxford Handbook of Transnational Feminist Movements* (New York: Oxford University Press, 2015), pp. 159–87.

Anveshi. 'Reworking Gender Relations, Redefining Politics: Nellore Village Women against Arrack', *Economic and Political Weekly*, vol. 28, nos 3–4 (January 1993), pp. 87–90. Based on a report by Anveshi, Hyderabad, 1991.

Ardener, Edwin. 'The Problem of Dominance', in Dube et al., *Visibility and Power*.

Baden, Sally, and Anne Marie Goetz. 'Who Needs [Sex] When You Can Have [Gender]? Conflicting Discourses on Gender at Beijing', in Cecile Jackson and Ruth Pearson (eds), *Feminist Visions of Development: Gender Analysis and Policy* (New York: Routledge, 1998).

Banerjee, Nirmala. *A Case Study Reviewing Indian Women's Experience of Development in a Historical Perspective—Using Demographic, Economic, Cultural and Political Variables* (Calcutta: Centre for the Study of Social Sciences, 1986).

Banerjee, Nirmala, and Devaki Jain. 'Indian Women's Experience of Development', ICSSR, New Delhi, 1990.

Basu, Amrita. 'Introduction', in Amrita Basu (ed.), *The Challenge of Local Feminisms: Women's Movements in Global Perspectives* (Boulder, CO: Westview Press, 1995).

Batliwala, Srilatha. *Empowerment of Women in South Asia: Concepts and Practices* (New Delhi: Food and Agriculture Organization, 1993).

Becker, Elizabeth. 'Study Finds a Growing Gap between Managerial Salaries for Men and Women', *New York Times*, 24 January 2002.

Bhagwat, Vidyut. 'Maharashtrian Bhakti: Women's Voices of Protest from 13th to 18th Century', paper presented at the panel on 'Indigenous Feminism: Concepts, Experiments, Limitations', conference on 'Cultural Transformations in Post-colonial India', Asiatic Society of Mumbai, 1 October 1997.

Bhagwati, Jagdish. 'Globalization Has a Human Face', lecture at the India Habitat Centre, New Delhi, 18 October 1999.

Bhan, Gautam. *India Gender Profile: Report Commissioned for Sida*, no. 62, BRIDGE, Institute of Development Studies, Brighton, August 2001.

Bharucha, Rustom. 'Between Truth and Reconciliation: Experiments in Theatre and Public Culture', *Economic and Political Weekly*, vol. 36, no. 39 (2001), pp. 3763–73.

Bhasin, Kamla, and Nigat Said Khan. *Some Questions on Feminism and Its Relevance in South Asia* (New Delhi: Kali for Women, 1986).

Bose, Ashish. 'A Demographic Profile', in Devaki Jain (ed.), *Indian Women* (New Delhi: Publications Division, Ministry of Information and Broadcasting, Government of India, 1975).

Boserup, Ester. *My Professional Life and Publications 1929–1998* (Copenhagen: Museum Tusculanum Press, 1999).

———. *Women's Role in Economic Development* (New York: St Martin's Press, 1970).

Carr, Marilyn, and Marty Chen. *Globalization and the Informal Economy: How Global Trade and Investment Impact on the Working Poor* (Geneva: ILO, 2002).

Centre for Global Negotiations. 'About the Brandt Commission', http://www.brandt21forum.info/About_BrandtCommission.htm (accessed 5 July 2017).

Chatterjee, Partha. *Nationalist Thought and the Colonial World: A Derivative Discourse?* (Tokyo: Zed Books, 1986).

Chattopadhyay, Kamaladevi. *Inner Recesses Outer Spaces* (New Delhi: Niyogi Books, 2014).

Chung Hyun Kyung. 'Theology in the Context of Religious Pluralism and the Search for a New Spirituality from an Asian Feminist Perspective', Bangalore, August 1992.

Connolly, William. 'Democracy and Territory', in M. Ringrose and A. J. Lerner (eds), *Reimagining the Nation* (Buckingham: Open University Press, 1993).

Cooper, Barbara M. 'The Politics of Difference and Women's Association in Niger: "Prostitutes", the Public and Politics', *Signs*, vol. 20, no. 4 (Summer 1995).

DAWN (Development Alternatives with Women for a New Era). 'Challenging the Given: DAWN's Perspectives on Social Development', presented at the World Summit on Social Development, New York, August–September 1994.

Desai, Narayan. *The Fire and the Rose* (Ahmedabad: Navajivan Publishing House, 1995).

Desai, Raj M., and James Raymond Vreeland. 'What the New Bank of BRICS Is All About', *Washington Post*, 17 July 2014, http://www.washingtonpost.com/blogs/monkey-cage/wp/2014/07/17/what-the-new-bank-of-brics-is-all-about/ (accessed 4 July 2017).

Drèze, Jean, and Amartya Sen. *India: Economic Development and Social Opportunity* (New Delhi: Oxford University Press, 1995).

D'Souza, Dilip. *The Narmada Dammed: An Inquiry into the Politics of Development* (New Delhi: Penguin, 2002).

Dube, Leela, and Rajni Palriwala (eds). *Structures and Strategies: Women, Work, and Family in Asia* (New Delhi: SAGE, 1990).

Dube, Leela, Eleanor Leacock and Shirley Ardener (eds). *Visibility and Power: Essays on Women in Society and Development* (New Delhi: Oxford University Press, 1989).

Eck, Diana, and Devaki Jain. *Speaking of Faith: Cross-Cultural Perspectives on Women, Religion and Social Change* (New Delhi: Kali for Women, 1986).

Economist. 'The BRICS Bank: An Acronym with Capital', 19 July 2014, http://www.economist.com/news/finance-and-economics/21607851-setting-up-rivals-imf-and-world-bank-easier-running-them-acronym (accessed 4 July 2017).

Elson, Diane. 'For an Emancipatory Socio-Economics', paper presented at the UN Research Institute for Social Development seminar, 'The Need to Rethink Development Economics', Cape Town, September 2001.

Elzinga, Aant. 'Evaluating the Evaluation Game: On the Methodology of Project Evaluation, with Special Reference to Development Cooperation', SAREC Report no. 1, Stockholm, 1981.

Emmerij, Louis. 'Development Thinking, Globalization and Cultural Diversity', paper prepared for the North–South Roundtable, 'Imperative of Tolerance and Justice in a Globalised World', Cairo, 27–28 November 2002.

Emmerij, Louis, Richard Jolly and Thomas Weiss. *Ahead of the Curve? UN Ideas and Global Challenges*, 1st edn (Bloomington: Indiana University Press, 2001).

Facio, Alda. 'What Will You Do? Women's Human Rights: Excerpts, Statement by the Center for Women's Global Leadership, 13 September 1995', *Women's Studies Quarterly*, vol. 24, nos 1–2 (1996), pp. 66–68.

Feminist Review Collective. *Feminist Politics: Colonial/Postcolonial Worlds*, no. 49 (Spring 1995), pp. 1–137.

Fine, Ben. 'Globalisation and Development: The Imperative of Political Economy', paper presented at the conference 'Towards a New Political Economy of Development: Globalisation and Governance', Sheffield, July 2002.

Folbre, Nancy. *Who Pays for the Kids? Gender and the Structures of Constraint* (New York: Routledge, 1994).

Food and Agriculture Organization. 'FAO Plan of Action for Women in Development', FAO Conference, 28th Session, 20 October–2 November 1995.

Forum against Oppression of Women. *National Conference on 'Perspectives for the Autonomous Women's Movements in India', Bombay, 23–26 December 1985: A Report* (Bombay: Forum against Oppression of Women, 1985).

Fukuda-Parr, Sakiki, James Heinz and Stephanie Seguino. 'Critical Perspectives on Financial and Economic Crises: Heterodox Macroeconomics Meets Feminist Economics', *Feminist Economics*, vol. 19, no. 13 (2013), pp. 4–31.

Gandhi, M. K. 'Economic Constitution of India', *Young India*, 15 November 1928.

Gandhi, Ramchandra. *I Am Thou: Meditations on the Truth of India* (Pune: Indian Philosophical Quarterly Publications, 1984).

Gandhi, Sonia. 'Women as Agents of Change', Commonwealth Lecture, London, 17 March 2011.

Geetha, V. 'Periyar, Women and an Ethic of Citizenship', paper presented at the National Seminar on 'Early Years of Indian Independence: Women's Perspectives', IAWS, Baroda, August 1997.

Gerardi, Kristopher S., Andreas Lehnert, Shane M. Sherland and Paul S. Willen, 'Making Sense of the Subprime Crisis', *Brookings Papers on Economic Activity*, vol. 39, no. 2 (Fall 2008), pp. 69–159.

Goldschmidt-Clermont, Luisella. 'Unpaid Work in the Household: A Review of Economic Evaluation Methods', ILO, Geneva, 1981.

Gopalan, C. 'Population: The Qualitative Dimension', inaugural speech for the Indian Association for the Study of Population, 26 December 1982.

Government of India. *Towards Equality: Report of the Committee on Status of Women in India* (New Delhi: Department of Social Welfare, Ministry of Education and Social Welfare, 1974).

Government of Karnataka. *Human Development in Karnataka 1999* (Bangalore: Planning Department, Government of Karnataka, 1999).

Guru, Gopal. 'How Egalitarian Are the Social Sciences in India?', *Economic and Political Weekly*, vol. 37, no. 51 (14 December 2002), pp. 5003–09.

Hameed, Syeda. *Report of the Steering Committee on Handlooms and Handicrafts Constituted for the Twelfth Five-Year Plan (2012–17)* (New Delhi: Planning Commission, 2012).

Henderson, Hazel. *Paradigms in Progress: Life beyond Economics* (Indianapolis: Knowledge Systems, Inc., 1991).

Hettne, Björn. 'Development Theory and the Third World', Swedish Agency for Research Cooperation with Developing Countries (SAREC) Report, Stockholm, 1982.

Hewlett, Sylvia Ann. 'Is a Woman in Brazil Better Off than a Woman in the U.S.?', *Time*, 24 October 2011, http://ideas.time.com/2011/10/24/is-a-woman-in-brazil-better-off-than-a-woman-in-the-u-s/ (accessed 4 July 2017).

Hoskyns, Catherine, and Michael Newman (eds). *Democratizing the European Union: Issues for the Twenty-First Century* (Manchester: Manchester University Press, 2000).

ICD List. 'ICD-10 Diagnosis Code Z59.5: Extreme Poverty', http://icdlist.com/
icd-10/Z59.5 (accessed 11 September 2017).

ILO (International Labour Organization). *Gender, Poverty and Employment: Turning
Capabilities into Entitlements* (Geneva: ILO, 1995).

———. *Wage-Led Growth: An Equitable Strategy for Economic Recovery*, Marc Lavoie
and Engelbert Stockhammer (eds) (Basingstoke: Palgrave Macmillan, 2013).

———. *World Employment Report 1998–99: Employability in the Global Economy—
How Training Matters* (Geneva: ILO, 1998).

Institute of Social and Economic Change. 'Monitoring and Evaluation of World
Bank Sericulture Project', mimeo, Bangalore.

International Centre for Research on Women, *Domestic Violence in India: A Summary
Report of Three Studies* (Washington, D.C.: ICRW, September 1999).

ISST (Institute of Social Studies Trust). 'A Case Study in the Social and Cultural
Implications of Tasar Production for Tribal Communities', New Delhi, August
1982.

———. 'An Assessment of Women's Roles: The Karnataka Sericulture Development
Project', Task Force on Sericulture, Government of Karnataka, 1982 (mimeo,
ISST, Bangalore).

———. 'Impact on Women Workers: Maharashtra Employment Guarantee
Scheme', mimeo, ILO, Geneva, December 1979.

———. 'Integrating Women's Interests into a State Five Year Plan', report submitted to the Ministry of Social Welfare, Government of India, September 1984.

Jad, Islah. 'Claiming Feminism, Claiming Nationalism: Women's Activism in the
Occupied Territories', in Amrita Basu (ed.), *The Challenge of Local Feminisms:
Women's Movements in Global Perspectives* (Boulder, CO: Westview Press,
1995), pp. 240–46.

Jain, Devaki. 'Advances in Feminist Theory: An Indian Perspective', paper presented at the World Sociology Conference, New Delhi, August 1986.

———. 'Alternative Development for Women: Five Page Summary', Women's
Studies Summer Program, Mediterranean Women's Studies Institute
(KEGME), Athens, 1986.

———. 'Are We Knowledge Proof? Development as Waste', Lovraj Kumar
Memorial Lecture, New Delhi, 26 September 2003 (reprinted in *Wastelands
News*, vol. 19, no. 1 [August–October 2003], pp. 19–30).

———. 'Are Women a Separate Issue?', *Populi*, vol. 5, no. 1 (1978), pp. 7–15.

———. 'Asian Women: In Search of an Identity', paper presented at the conference
on 'Role and Rights of Women in Asia', Asian Students Association, Manila,
28 August–4 September 1982.

———. 'A View from the South: A Story of Intersections', in Arvonne S. Fraser and
Irene Tinker (eds), *Developing Power: How Women Transformed International
Development* (New York: Feminist Press, 2004), pp. 128–37.

———. 'Bubbling-Up v Trickling-Down', Gateway House, 28 April 2011, http://
www.gatewayhouse.in/bubbling-versus-trickling-down/ (accessed 5 July
2017).

Jain, Devaki. 'Can Feminism Be a Global Ideology?', *Quest Quarterly* (Winter, 1978).

———. 'Changing Status of Women in East Europe: Report of the Conference on the Status of Women in East Europe', *Economic and Political Weekly*, vol. 17, no. 8 (February 1982), pp. 275–77.

———. 'Close Encounters of Another Kind: Building Regional Economic Cooperation on Women's Advice and Leadership', Asian Development Bank, Manila, 2 March 1998.

———. 'Conference Journeys: What Have We Not Done? Where Have We Gone Wrong?', presentation at the Conference of Non-governmental Organizations, New York, June 2000.

———. 'Development Theory and Practice: Insights Emerging from Women's Experiences', *Economic and Political Weekly*, vol. 25, no. 27 (1990), pp. 1454–55.

———. 'Dialogues with Feminists from the North: A Conversation', mimeo, Athens, June 1985.

———. 'Enabling Poverty and Inequality Reduction in South Asia', paper presented at the UN Population Fund Consultation on Population, Reproductive Health, Gender and Poverty Reduction, New York, 30 September–2 October 2002.

———. 'Enabling Reduction of Poverty and Inequality in South Asia', in *Population and Poverty: Achieving Equity, Equality and Sustainability* (New York: United Nations Population Fund, 2003).

———. 'Exploring Economic Inequality from Piketty through Arvind Adiga to Gandhi', lecture delivered at Azim Premji University, Bengaluru, 13 November 2014.

———. 'Feminism and Feminist Expression: A Dialogue', in Kamala Ganesh and Usha Thakkar (eds), *Culture and the Making of Identity in Contemporary India* (New Delhi: SAGE, 2005).

———. 'For Women to Lead—Ideas and Experiences from Asia: A Study on the Legal and Political Impediments to Gender Equality in Governance', paper presented at 'A Vision for the 21st Century', Asia Ministerial Conference on Governance for Sustainable Growth, Lahore, 1997.

———. *For Women to Lead—Ideas and Experience from Asia* (New York: UNDP, 1997).

———. 'Gandhian Contributions towards a Feminist Ethic', in Diana Eck and Devaki Jain (eds), *Speaking of Faith: Cross-Cultural Perspectives on Women, Religion and Social Change* (New Delhi: Kali for Women, 1986), pp. 255–70.

———. 'Gender Inequity as Racism', *Hindu*, 23 September 2000.

———. 'Globalism and Localism: Negotiating Feminist Space', paper presented at the seminar 'Rethinking Gender, Democracy and Development: Is Decentralisation a Tool for Local Effective Political Voice?', Ferrara University and Modena University, Italy, 20–22 May 2002.

———. 'Growth, Poverty and Inequality: The Linkages and Relevance of Macroeconomic Policies', UNDP Gender Equality, Economic Growth and

Poverty Reduction Expert Group Meeting, Essex University, UK, 21–22 June 2007.

Jain, Devaki (ed.). *Indian Women* (New Delhi: Publications Division, Government of India, 1975).

———. 'Indian Women Today and Tomorrow', Padmaja Naidu Memorial Lecture, Teen Murti House, New Delhi, November 1982.

———. 'Leadership Gap: A Challenge to Feminists', Presidential Address, IAWS Conference, Mysore, 1993.

———. *Minds, Bodies and Exemplars: Reflections at Beijing and Beyond* (New Delhi: British Council Division, 1996).

———. 'Need of the Hour: Political Response to Violence against Women— Perspective from India', SADC Conference on the Prevention of Violence against Women, Durban, 5 March 1998.

———. 'Night Patrollers of Manipur', in Devaki Jain, Nalini Singh and Malini Chand, *Women's Quest for Power: Five Case Studies* (New Delhi: Vikas, 1980).

———. 'Note for Anti-Arrack Meeting', India International Centre, New Delhi, 18 April 1997.

———. 'Panchayat Raj: Women Changing Governance', Gender in Development Monograph Series #5, UNDP, New York, September 1996.

———. 'Power through the Looking Glass of Feminism', paper presented at the symposium on 'The Gender of Power', Leiden University, 1990.

———. 'PRI Impact on Private Structure (Domestic Sphere): How Important Is the Private–Public Dichotomy—The Case of the EWRS', Seminar on 'Women in Panchayat Raj', New Delhi, 27–28 April 2000.

———. 'Questioning Economic Success through the Lens of Hunger', in Devaki Jain and Diane Elson (eds), *Harvesting Feminist Knowledge for Public Policy: Rebuilding Progress* (New Delhi: SAGE, 2011).

———. 'Spaces and Hopes', *Hindu*, 3 April 2005.

———. 'The Empire Strikes Back: A Report on the Asian Social Forum', *Economic and Political Weekly*, vol. 38, no. 2 (11 January 2003).

———. 'The First Challengers', MakingItMagazine.Net, 5 February 2013, http://www.makingitmagazine.net/?p=6349 (accessed 7 July 2017). A version of this essay is reproduced as chapter 12, this volume.

———. 'The Household Trap: Report on a Field Survey of Female Activity Patterns', in Devaki Jain and and Nirmala Banerjee (eds), *Tyranny of the Household: Investigative Essays on Women's Work*, Workshop on Women in Poverty (New Delhi: Shakti Books, 1985), pp. 215–46.

———. 'The Natural Power of Women', in *Sarla Behn Smriti Granth* (New Delhi: Himalaya Seva Sangha, 1984). New Delhi.

———. 'The Poverty Thing', presented at a special event organised by UNDP, New York, 20 May 1997.

———. 'The Role of People's Movement in Economic and Social Transformation', paper presented at 'The Role of NGOs in the 21st Century: Inspire, Empower, Act', Seoul International Conference of NGOs, Seoul, 10–16 October 1999.

Jain, Devaki. 'The Self-Employed Women's Association', in *From Dissociation to Rehabilitation: Report on an Experiment to Promote Self-Employment in an Urban Area* (Bombay: Allied, 1975).

———. 'The Social Image', *Seminar*, no. 53 (December 1963), pp. 20–23.

———. *The Vocabulary of Women's Politics* (New Delhi: Friedrich Ebert Stiftung, 2001).

———. 'The Women behind Sirleaf', *Indian Express*, 14 September 2013, http://archive.indianexpress.com/news/the-women-behind-sirleaf/1168952/ (accessed 7 July 2017).

———. 'Through the Looking Glass of Poverty', paper presented at New Hall, Cambridge, 19 October 2001.

———. 'Using the Turbulence to the Advantage of the Less Privileged', paper presented at 'Turning the Global Economic Crisis into Opportunity: Women's Ideas', Commission on the Status of Women, UNDP, 53rd Session, New York, March 2009.

———. 'Valuing Women: Signals from the Ground', paper presented at the conference on 'Cultural Diversity and Universal Norms', University of Maryland, 1 June 2001.

———. 'Valuing Work: Time as a Measure', *Economic and Political Weekly*, vol. 31, no. 43 (26 October 1996), pp. WS46–WS57.

———. 'Women and Development: A Two-Sector Model', *Social Action* (New Delhi: Council for Social Development).

———. 'Women and Poverty Eradication', *Mainstream*, vol. 16, no. 9 (29 October 1977), pp. 21–23.

———. *Women, Development, and the UN: A Sixty-Year Quest for Equality and Justice* (New York: Indiana University Press, 2005).

———. 'Women in Extreme Poverty', Expert Group Meeting, Vienna, 1992.

———. 'Women in the Sixth Plan', *Yojana*, vol. 35, no. 19 (16–31 October 1981).

———. 'Women: New Vision of Leadership', Opening Plenary, Global Forum of Women, Dublin, 9–12 July 1992.

———. 'Women's Economic Reasoning and Development Economics: A Discussion on Some Intersections', SCA Joint Project Workshop, Sixth Conference of the Science Council of Asia, New Delhi, 17 April 2006.

———. 'Women's Opinion on National Issues: Need of the Hour', *Indian Express*, 11 January 1990.

———. 'Women's Participation in the History of Ideas: The Importance of Reconstructing Knowledge', National Institute for Advanced Studies, Indian Institute of Science, Bangalore, 6 February 2004.

Jain, Devaki, and C. P. Sujaya (eds). *Indian Women Revisited* (New Delhi: Publications Division, Government of India, 2014).

Jain, Devaki, and Deepshikha Batheja. 'Using Inequality to Engineer Growth', *LiveMint*, 13 June 2014, http://www.livemint.com/Opinion/HC2XT2gQSdtck73VsP6e7H/Using-inequality-to-engineer-growth.html (accessed 3 July 2017).

Jain, Devaki, and Diane Elson. *Harvesting Feminist Knowledge for Public Policy* (New Delhi: SAGE, 2012).

Jain, Devaki, and Malini Chand. 'Patterns of Female Work: Implications for Statistical Design, Economic Classification and Social Priorities', paper prepared for the National Conference on Women's Studies, Bombay, April 1981 (mimeo, ISST, New Delhi).

Jain, Devaki, and Mukul Mukherjee. 'Women and Their Households: The Relevance of Men and Macro Economic Policies—An Indian Perspective', paper prepared by ISST for ILO, 1984.

Jain, Devaki, and Nirmala Banerjee (eds). *Tyranny of the Household: Investigative Essays on Women's Work*, Workshop on Women in Poverty (New Delhi: Shakti Books, 1985).

Jain, Devaki, and Samia Ahmad, 'Towards Just Development: Identifying Meaningful Indicators', Working Paper, UNDP, South Africa, 1999.

Jain, Devaki, and Seromena Asem. 'A Feminist Mart: Women's Empowerment', *Deccan Herald*, 26 October 2007, http://archive.deccanherald.com/DeccanHerald.com/Content/Oct262007/editpage2007102532303.asp (accessed 26 June 2017).

Jain, Devaki, and Shubha Chacko. 'Unfolding Women's Engagement with Development and the UN: Pointers for the Future', *Forum for Development Studies*, vol. 35, no. 1 (June 2008), pp. 5–36.

Jain, Devaki, Nalini Singh and Abha Bhaiya. 'Role of Rural Women in Community Life: A Case Study from India', Report of the Expert Group Meeting, *Economic Bulletin for Asia and the Pacific*, vol. 29, no. 2 (December 1978).

Jain, Devaki, Nalini Singh and Malini Chand. *Women's Quest for Power: Five Case Studies* (New Delhi: Vikas, 1980).

Jain, L. C. *Civil Disobedience* (New Delhi: Book Review Literary Trust, 2011).

Jayawardena, Kumari. *Feminism and Nationalism in the Third World in the 19th and Early 20th Centuries*, History of the Women's Movement Lecture Series, part II (The Hague: Institute of Social Studies, 1982).

———. *The Rise of the Labor Movement in Ceylon* (North Carolina: Duke University Press, 1972).

Jhabvala, Renana. 'SEWA and Home-Based Workers in India: Their Struggle and Emerging Role', paper presented at the technical workshop on 'Indigenizing Human Rights Education in Indian Universities', Karnataka Women's Information and Resource Centre, Bangalore, December 2001.

Jolkboron, Riva. 'A Case Study of the Women's Bureau of Sri Lanka', SIDA Group, Stockholm, September 1982.

Joshi, Pushpa. *Gandhi on Women* (Ahmedabad: Navajivan Trust, and New Delhi: Centre for Women's Development Studies, 1988).

Kabeer, Naila. *Reversed Realities: Gender Hierarchies in Development Thought* (London: Verso, 1994).

Kagame, Paul, Uhurru Kenyata and Yoweri Museveni. 'The Dream of an African Century', *LiveMint*, 8 August 2014, http://www.livemint.com/Opinion/

fsvyGkHNIt0MSFmm4koVgL/The-dream-of-an-African-century.html (accessed 12 September 2017).

Kandiyoti, Deniz. 'Bargaining with Patriarchy', *Gender and Society*, vol. 2, no. 3 (1988), pp. 274–90.

Keck, Margaret E., and Kathryn Sikkink. *Activists beyond Borders: Advocacy Networks in International Politics* (Ithaca, NY: Cornell University Press, 1998).

Kishwar, Madhu. 'An Alternative Women's Reservation Bill', *Indian Express*, 18 March 2003.

Kothari, Ashish, and Rahul N. Ram. *Environmental Impacts of the Sardar Sarovar Project* (Pune: Kalpavriksh, December 1994).

Krishna, Raj. 'The Inequity of the International Economic Order: Some Explanations and Policy Implications', mimeo, Manila, November 1982.

Krishnaraj, Maithreyi. *State of the Indian Farmer: A Millennium Study*, vol. 25: *Women in Agriculture* (New Delhi: Department of Agriculture and Cooperation, Ministry of Agriculture, Government of India, 2004).

———. 'Taking Stock', paper presented at 'Women's Studies and Higher Education: A Symposium', Centre for Women's Development Studies, New Delhi, 1991.

Krishnaswamy, K. S., and Shashi Rajagopal. 'Women in Employment: A Micro Study in Karnataka' (based on the ISST Bangalore Report), in Devaki Jain and Nirmala Banerjee (eds), *Tyranny of the Household: Investigative Essays on Women's Work*, Workshop on Women in Poverty (New Delhi: Shakti Books, 1985).

Lal, Lakshmi. 'You Have Given Birth to a Hero', *Times of India*, 25 May 1986.

Lavoie, Marc, and Engelbert Stockhammer. 'Wage-Led Growth: Concept, Theories and Policies', Conditions of Work and Employment Series, no. 41, ILO, Geneva, 2012.

Lederer, Edith M. 'UN Summit Pledges to Help Children', Associated Press, New York, 12 May 2002.

Longino, Helen E. 'Feminist Standpoint Theory and the Problems of Knowledge', *Signs*, vol. 19, no. 1 (Autumn 1993), pp. 201–12.

MacKinnon, Catharine A. 'Feminism, Marxism, Method, and the State: An Agenda for Theory', in Nannerl O. Keohane, Michelle Z. Rosaldo and Barbara C. Gelpi (eds), *Feminist Theory: A Critique of Ideology* (Chicago: University of Chicago Press, 1981).

Mahbub ul Haq Human Development Centre. *Human Development in South Asia 2001: Globalisation and Human Development* (Oxford: Oxford University Press, 2002).

Mair, Lucille Mathurin. 'International Women's Decade: A Balance Sheet', Third J. P. Naik Memorial Lecture, Centre for Women's Development Studies, New Delhi, 15 December 1984.

Mama, Amina. 'Talking about Feminism in Africa', Interview by Elaine Salo, *African Feminisms*, vol. 1, no. 50 (2001), pp. 58–63, http://www.wworld.org/programs/regions/africa/amina_mama.htm (accessed 8 June 2017).

Mangahas, Mahar, and Teresa Jayme-Ho. 'Income and Labour Force Participation Rates of Women in the Philippines', Discussion Paper, School of Economics, University of Philippines, 1976.

Mathew, Dinoo Anna. 'Panchayats Alone Are Not to Blame', *Economic and Political Weekly*, vol. 37, no. 18 (4–10 May 2002), pp. 1767–68.

Mathew, George (ed.). *Status of Panchayati Raj in the States of India, 1994* (New Delhi: Concept Publishing, 1995).

Mazumdar, Vina. *The Role of Rural Women in Development*, Report of an International Study Seminar, Institute of Development Studies, University of Sussex, 5 January–10 February 1977 (Bombay: Allied, 1978).

McPhee, Sarah. 'The Checklist Project: Project Evaluation Techniques and Women's Contribution', SIDA Group, Stockholm, November 1982.

Mernissi, Fatima. 'Femininity as Subversion: Reflections on the Muslim Concept of Nushuz', in Diana Eck and Devaki Jain (eds), *Speaking of Faith: Cross-Cultural Perspectives on Women, Religion and Social Change* (New Delhi: Kali for Women, 1986).

———. *Women in Moslem Paradise* (New Delhi: Kali for Women, 1986).

Ministry of External Affairs. 'History and Evolution of Non-Aligned Movement', Government of India, 22 August 2012, http://mea.gov.in/in-focus-article.htm?20349/History+and+Evolution+of+NonAligned+Movement (accessed 5 July 2017).

Morrisson, C., and J. P. Jutting. 'Women's Discrimination in Developing Countries: A New Data Set for Better Policies', *World Development*, vol. 33, no. 7 (July 2005), pp. 1065–81.

Morse, Bradford, and Thomas R. Berger. *Sardar Sarovar: Report of the Independent Review* (Ottawa: Resource Futures International, 1992).

Moulik, T. K., and P. Purushotham. 'The Predicament in Silk Industry', Indian Institute of Management, Ahmedabad.

Narmada Bachao Andolan. 'We Will Struggle Comrades: The Struggle of the People of Narmada Valley', July 1994.

National Commission for Enterprises in the Unorganised Sector (NCEUS). *Report on Conditions of Work and Promotion of Livelihood in the Unorganized Sector* (New Delhi: Government of India, August 2007).

Nuzhat, Parveen, and N. H. Patil. 'Women in Informal Sector: A Case Study of Construction Industry', *International Research Journal*, vol. 1, no. 11 (August 2010).

Oxfam. 'Working for the Few: Political Capture and Economic Inequality', Oxfam Briefing Paper 178, 20 January 2014.

Palmer, John. 'Book Review: Capital in the Twenty-First Century by Thomas Piketty', *Red Pepper*, April 2014, http://www.redpepper.org.uk/book-review-capital-in-the-twenty-first-century-by-thomas-piketty/ (accessed 3 July 2017).

Parikh, Kirit S. (ed.). *India Development Report 1999–2000* (New Delhi: Oxford University Press, 1999).

Parthasarathy, G. 'Rural Poverty and Female Heads of Household: Need for Quantitative Analysis', paper presented at the Technical Seminar on 'Women's Work and Employment', ISST, New Delhi, April 1982.

Pereira, Charmaine. 'National Council of Women's Societies and the State, 1985–1993: The Use of Discourses of Womanhood by the NCWS', in Attahiru Jega (ed.), *Identity Transformation and Identity Politics under Structural Adjustment in Nigeria* (Uppsala: Nordiska Afrikainstitutet, and Kano: Centre for Research and Documentation, 2000).

Pietilä, Hilkka. 'Women's Movement and Internationalisation', ECPR Workshop, Mannheim, 26–31 March 1999, https://ecpr.eu/Filestore/PaperProposal/81ecca4f-4dc8-4050-990c-c861489849f2.pdf (accessed 11 September 2017).

Piketty, Thomas. *Capital in the Twenty-First Century* (Cambridge, MA: Harvard University Press, 2014).

Planning Commission. *Fifth Five-Year Plan, 1974–79* (New Delhi: Government of India).

———. *National Human Development Report 2001* (New Delhi: Government of India, March 2002).

Prashad, V. *The Darker Nations: A People's History of the Third World* (New York: The New Press, 2007).

———. *The Poorer Nations* (New Delhi: LeftWord, 2013).

Prugl, Elisabeth, and Mary K. Meyer (eds). *Gender Politics in Global Governance* (Oxford: Rowman and Littlefield, 1999).

Ramachandran, Vimala. 'Gendered Inequality and Education', Advocacy Brief, UNESCO Bangkok Asia-Pacific Programme of Education for All, 2010, http://unesdoc.unesco.org/images/0018/001898/189825e.pdf (accessed 3 July 2017).

———. 'Right to Education Act: A Comment', *Economic and Political Weekly*, vol. 40, no. 28 (July 2009), pp. 155–57.

Reddy, Y. V. 'Global Economic Developments and India', 17th Prem Bhatia Memorial Lecture, 2012, http://www.prembhatiatrust.com/lecture17.htm (accessed 12 September 2017).

Robinson, Joan. 'Teaching Economics', in Joan Robinson, *Collected Economic Papers*, vol. 3 (Oxford: Basil Blackwell, 1965), pp. 1–6.

Rothschild, Emma. 'An Infinity of Girls: The Political Rights of Children in Historical Perspective', mimeo, Centre for History and Economics, Cambridge University, 2000.

Roy, Aruna. 'Time to Move Ahead of RTI', *New Indian Express*, 10 November 2013, http://www.newindianexpress.com/states/odisha/2013/nov/10/Time-to-move-ahead-of-RTI-Aruna-Roy-535878.html (accessed 3 July 2017).

Roy, Arundhati. 'Democracy: Who's She When She's at Home?', *Outlook* (Mumbai), 6 May 2002.

———. 'The New American Century', *Nation*, 9 February 2004, https://www.thenation.com/article/new-american-century/ (accessed 28 May 2017).

Saradamoni, K. *Finding the Household: Conceptual and Methodological Issues* (New Delhi: SAGE, 1992).

Seguino, Stephanie, and Caren A. Grown. 'Feminist-Kaleckian Macroeconomic Policy for Developing Countries', Economics Working Paper Archive, no. 446, Levy Economics Institute, New York, 2006.

Sen, Amartya. *Development as Freedom* (Oxford: Oxford University Press, 1999).

———. 'Food Battles', Coromandel Lecture, India International Centre, 6 December 1982.

———. 'Food Battles: Conflicts in the Access to Food', *Food and Nutrition*, vol. 10, no. 1 (1984), pp. 81–89.

———. 'Exclusion and Inclusion', paper presented at the conference on 'Including the Excluded', South Asians for Human Rights, New Delhi, 11–12 November 2001.

———. 'How to Judge Globalism', *American Prospect*, Winter (2002).

———. *Identity and Violence: The Illusion of Destiny* (New Delhi: Penguin, 2007).

———. 'Many Faces of Gender Inequality', inaugural lecture at the New Radcliffe Institute, Harvard University, 24 April 2001.

———. 'Missing Women', *British Medical Journal*, vol. 304 (1992), pp. 586–87.

———. 'More Than 100 Million Women Are Missing', *New York Review of Books*, 20 December 1990, http://www.nybooks.com/articles/1990/12/20/more-than-100-million-women-are-missing/ (accessed 2 September 2017).

———. 'Population Policy: Authoritarianism vs. Cooperation', John D. and Catherine T. MacArthur Foundation, International Lecture Series on Population Issues, New Delhi, 17 August 1995.

———. 'The Ends and Means of Sustainability', Keynote Address, International Conference on 'Transition to Sustainability in the 21st Century', Inter Academy Panel on International Issues, Tokyo, May 2000.

———. *The Idea of Justice* (Cambridge, MA: Harvard University Press, 2009).

Sen, Gita, and Caren Grown. *Development, Crises and Alternative Visions: Third World Women's Perspectives* (London: Earthscan, 1988).

Sethi, J. D. 'India's Biological Decay', *Indian Express Magazine*, 5 December 1982.

SEWA (Self-Employed Women's Association). *SEWA Marches On* (Ahmedabad: SEWA, 1981).

South Commission. *The Challenge to the South: The Report of the South Commission* (New York: Oxford University Press, 1990).

South-South News. 'Algiers Ministerial Conference of the Non-Aligned Movement (NAM) Reviews Existing, New and Emerging Challenges to the Developing World', 16 June 2014.

Sreenivasan, M. A. *Of the Raj, Maharajas and Me* (New Delhi: Ravi Dayal Publications, 1991).

Srivastava, K., N. Dey and N. Mishra. 'Taking Democracy Forward: The Right to Information Movement in Rajasthan', paper presented at the technical workshop on 'Indigenizing Human Rights Education in Indian Universities',

Karnataka Women's Information and Resource Centre, Bangalore, December 2001.

Standing, Guy, Jeemol Unni, Renana Jhabvala and Uma Rani. *Social Income and Insecurity: A Study in Gujarat* (New Delhi: Routledge, 2010).

Stern, Nicholas. *A Strategy for Development* (Washington, D.C.: World Bank, 2001).

Stiglitz, Joseph. 'Globalism's Discontent', *American Prospect*, Winter (2002), pp. A16–A21.

————. 'The Great GDP Swindle', *Guardian*, 13 September 2009, https://www.theguardian.com/commentisfree/2009/sep/13/economics-economic-growth-and-recession-global-economy (accessed 12 September 2017).

Subbarao, Duvvuri. 'Ethics and the World of Finance', Keynote Address at the conference organised by Sri Sathya Sai University, Prasanthi Nilayam, Andhra Pradesh, 28 August 2009, https://www.rbi.org.in/scripts/BS_SpeechesView.aspx?id=434 (accessed 12 September 2017).

Sudha, S., and S. Irudaya Rajan. 'Intensifying Masculinity of Infancy Sex Ratio in India: Preliminary Evidence from the 1981 and 1991 Censuses', T. N. Krishnan Memorial Seminar on 'Development Experience of Southern States in a Comparative Perspective', Centre for Development Studies, Thiruvananthapuram, 9 September 1997.

Sullivan, Donna J. 'The Public/Private Distinction in International Human Rights Law', in *Women's Rights, Human Rights: International Feminist Perspectives* (New York: Routledge, 1995).

————. 'Women's Human Rights and the 1993 World Conference on Human Rights', *American Journal of International Law*, vol. 88 (1994), pp. 152–67.

Swaminathan, M. S. 'Women in Rural Development', J. P. Naik Memorial Lecture, Centre for Women's Development Studies, New Delhi, September 1982.

Sylvester, Christine. 'African and Western Feminisms: World-Traveling the Tendencies and Possibilities', *Signs*, vol. 20, no. 4 (Summer 1995), pp. 941–69.

————. 'Homeless in International Relations? "Women's" Place in Canonical Texts and in Feminist Reimaginings', in Anne Phillips (ed.), *Feminism and Politics* (Oxford: Oxford University Press, 1998), pp. 44–66.

Topley, Marjorie. 'Marriage Resistance in Rural Kwangtung', in Margery Wolf and Roxane Witke (eds), *Women in Chinese Society* (Stanford: Stanford University Press, 1975), pp. 86–88.

Toye, John. *Dilemmas of Development* (Oxford: Blackwell, 1993).

Ul Haq, Mahbub. 'Human Development in a Changing World', Occasional Paper 1, Topical Background Research for HDR 1992, UNDP, http://hdr.undp.org/sites/default/files/mahbub_ul_haq.pdf (accessed 21 June 2017).

————. 'Overview: The Revolution for Gender Equality', in UNDP, *Human Development Report 1995* (New York: Oxford University Press, 1995).

UN (United Nations). *2004 World Survey on the Role of Women in Development: Women and International Migration*, Department of Economic and Social Affairs, Division for the Advancement of Women (New York: UN, 2005).

UN (United Nations). *2009 World Survey on the Role of Women in Development: Women's Control over Economic Resources and Access to Financial Resources, including Microfinance*, Department of Economic and Social Affairs, Division for the Advancement of Women (New York: UN, 2009).

———. 'Action for Equality, Development and Peace', Fourth World Conference on Women, Beijing, 4–15 September 1995.

———. *Inequality Matters: Report on the World Social Situation 2013* (New York: UN Department of Economic and Social Affairs, 2013).

———. 'Report of the Fourth World Conference on Women, Beijing, 4–15 September 1995, including the Agenda, the Beijing Declaration and the Platform for Action (Extract)', in *The United Nations and the Advancement of Women, 1945–1996* (Department of Public Information, UN, 1996), pp. 649–735.

———. 'Resource Paper on Women in Developing Countries and Monetary and Fiscal Matters in the Context of International Development Strategy', Expert Group Meeting, Vienna, September 1982.

———. 'The Nairobi Forward Looking Strategies', Third World Conference on Women, Nairobi, 1985.

———. *The World's Women 2000: Trends and Statistics* (New York: United Nations Statistics Division, 2000).

———. *The World's Women 2010: Trends and Statistics* (New York: United Nations Statistics Division, 2010).

United Nations Conference on Trade and Development. *Trade and Development Report, 2010: Employment, Globalization and Development* (New York: UN, 2010).

UNDP (United Nations Development Programme). *Human Development Report 1995* (New York: Oxford University Press, 1995).

———. *Human Development Report 1997* (New York: Oxford University Press, 1997).

———. *Human Development Report 1998* (New York: Oxford University Press, 1998).

———. *Human Development Report 1999* (New York: Oxford University Press, 1999).

———. *Human Development Report 2002: Deepening Democracy in a Fragmented World* (New York: Oxford University Press, 2002).

———. *Human Development Report 2013: The Rise of the South—Human Progress in a Diverse World* (New York: UNDP, 2013).

———. *Humanity Divided: Confronting Inequality in Developing Countries* (New York: UNDP Bureau for Development Policy, November 2013).

———. *Post-2015 Development Agenda*, http://www.undp.org/content/brussels/en/home/mdgoverview/mdg_goals/post-2015-development-agenda.html (accessed 3 July 2017).

UN Economic and Social Council. 'Assessment of the Implementation of the System-wide Medium-Term Plan for the Advancement of Women 1996–2001', Resolution 1996/34, 25 July 1996.

UNESCO (UN Educational, Scientific and Cultural Organization). *World Culture Report 2000: Cultural Diversity, Conflict and Pluralism* (UNESCO, 2000).

UN General Assembly. *1999 World Survey on the Role of Women in Development: Globalization, Gender and Work*, Report of the Secretary General, 18 August 1999.

UNPF (United Nations Population Fund). *Population, Food Production and Nutrition in India* (New Delhi: UNPF, October 1999).

UN Women and ILO. 'Decent Work and Women's Economic Empowerment: Good Policy and Practice', Policy Brief, 2012, http://www.ilo.org/wcmsp5/groups/public/—ed_emp/—emp_ent/—ifp_seed/documents/genericdocument/wcms_184878.pdf (accessed 2 July 2017).

van der Gaag, Nikki. 'Women: Still Something to Shout About', *New Internationalist Magazine*, no. 270 (August 1995).

Waring, Marilyn. *If Women Counted: A New Feminist Economics* (San Francisco: Harper & Row).

Wieringa, Saskia (ed.). *Subversive Women: Women's Movements in Africa, Asia, Latin America and the Caribbean* (New Delhi: Kali for Women, 1995).

Woodward, Alison. 'Building Velvet Triangles: Gender in EU Policy Making', Paper in Revision from the European Consortium for Political Research, 28th Joint Session, Copenhagen, April 2000.

Woolf, Virginia. *A Room of One's Own* (Toronto: Granada, 1977 [1929]).

Working Group of Feminist Economists. *Engendering Public Policy: A Report on the Work of the Working Group of Feminist Economist during the preparation of Eleventh Five Year Plan 2007–12* (New Delhi: Planning Commission, Government of India, May 2010).

World Bank. *Inequality in Focus*, http://www.worldbank.org/en/topic/isp/publication/inequality-in-focus (accessed 3 July 2017).

———. *World Development Report 1995: Workers in an Integrating World* (New York: Oxford University Press, 1995).

———. *World Development Report 1999/2000: Entering the 21st Century* (New York: Oxford University Press, 1999).

World Commission on Dams. *Dams and Development: A New Framework for Decision-Making* (London: Earthscan Publications, 2001).

World Economic Forum. 'The Reshaping of the World: Consequences for Society, Politics and Business', World Economic Forum Annual Meeting 2014, Davos-Klosters, Switzerland, 22–25 January 2014.

INDEX

ABOUT THE AUTHOR

Devaki Jain, Honorary Fellow St Anne's College, Oxford University, is Founder and former Director of the Institute of Social Studies Trust, New Delhi, India. She was previously a lecturer at the University of Delhi, a founding member of Development Alternatives with Women for a New Era (DAWN), member of the South Commission (chaired by Julius Nyerere), and of the UN eminent persons group concerned with child soldiers. She has an honorary doctorate from the University of Westville in Durban, Republic of South Africa, and has held fellowships at Harvard and Sussex Universities. She has been a member of State Planning boards and many of the Government of India's special committees related to gender and its inclusion.